Applied Management Science for Decision Making

First Edition

Philip Vaccaro

Learning Solutions

New York   Boston   San Francisco
London   Toronto   Sydney   Tokyo   Singapore   Madrid
Mexico City   Munich   Paris   Cape Town   Hong Kong   Montreal

Pearson Learning Solutions, 501 Boylston Street, Suite 900, Boston, MA 02116
A Pearson Education Company
www.pearsoned.com

Printed in the United States of America

2 3 4 5 6 7 8 9 10 V036 16 15 14 13 12 11

000200010270656568

CY/JG

ISBN 10: 0-558-93204-5
ISBN 13: 978-0-558-93204-6

Copyright Acknowledgments

Contents

Preface

A Note to the Student

In the thirty years that I have been teaching operations research, statistics, and forecast management courses, I have always remained determined never to teach those courses as they were taught to me. One salient reason was that most of the textbooks were long, rambling, tedious, and pretentious. There were little or no understandable examples that conveyed the essence of a concept or technique, or could be easily applied toward solution of homework and examination problems. Another reason was that many of the textbooks seemed to be written for the benefit of the adopting professor. Qualitative and quantitative concepts totally unknown to the student would frequently and mysteriously appear, elaborate equations and models were introduced with insufficient notes or computations, and absolutely no effort was made to justify their usefulness to the student.

In contrast, I have written short, concise chapters with straightforward, yet realistic examples that demonstrate in detail, the fundamentals of production and operations management. I have also tried to write a book that can be readily understood by students possessing the most basic background in algebra, accounting, management, and statistics. Finally, I have tried to stress critical concepts and techniques that have high visibility in general management and underscore a logical approach to problem solving that will serve the student in any endeavor.

A Note to the Instructor

I wrote this book with a view toward making the instructor's task less stressful and more personally fulfilling. The book addresses all topics normally considered part of an introductory production/operations management course, with the notable exception of product design, purchasing, and reliability/maintenance. From my experience at several universities, the above topic areas are usually covered in separate courses, many of which are advanced electives. It is quite possible, therefore, for an instructor to cover over ninety percent of a traditional introductory P/OM course in one semester, and since all chapters focus on a single topic or several closely related topics, they are self-contained and can be covered in virtually any sequence.

I also designed this book as a supplement to any standard P/OM textbook. It is my hope that with its avoidance of complex mathematical notation and formulas, step-by-step solution approaches, carefully selected and student-tested charts, and lesson-plan format, the book will provide instructors with more time to discuss selected areas in depth, impart more of their valuable industrial experiences to their students, introduce computer software solution approaches, and assign extended homework and case studies. The book may also prove useful as a self-directed refresher for those students planning to enroll in advanced P/OM courses.

Introduction

Chapter 1

Operations Management and Strategy

Chapter 1 focuses on the reasons why P/OM is taught in all business schools, its importance to the U.S. Economy, and its applications within various professions and sciences.

Chapter 1 also introduces the considerations involved in formulating a firm's mission statement and strategy, and the supporting role that P/OM plays in implementing the firm's mission and strategy over the short, intermediate, and long term.

Virtually every American business school requires its graduate and/or undergraduate students to take an introductory course in the concepts and principles related to the "conversion process": the transformation of material, investment, and labor into finished goods and services. This course is usually taught from a management point of view and addresses such topics as product/process design, capacity planning, plant layout, scheduling, quality control, demand forecasting, job design, performance standards setting, and inventory management.

Usually this course is taught under a variety of titles to include: Production Management, Operations Management, Production/Operations Management, and Introduction to Industrial Engineering. The course objectives are usually two-fold: First, to offer the business student a broad exposure to the concepts, tools, and techniques of manufacturing within the context of several different types of manufacturing processes. Second, to demonstrate to the student the interrelationships and dynamics between the functional areas of Management, Marketing, Finance, Accounting, and the manufacturing process.

The purpose of this book is to certainly accomplish the above objectives, but also, more importantly, to show the student how the principles and concepts of manufacturing can be transferred to any business setting, whether it be profit or non-profit, manufacturing or service, with just a little imagination and creativity, so as to increase a manager's effectiveness and efficiency, with the firm as beneficiary.

The formal development of the discipline of P/OM can be traced back to the Industrial Revolution in England during the late 1700s. Virtually all contributions to the discipline (then called Production Management) from 1776 to 1939, focused on improvement of factory operations. With the advent of World War II in 1939, the discipline was tasked with the additional responsibility of improving military operations. Professionals in England and the United States, working within the "operations" sections of military organizations developed mathematical models and techniques for solving military problems. Their work was called "operations research," and those professionals (originally commanders) who implemented those models and techniques came to be known as "operations managers." The term "operations management" evolved to now describe a discipline tasked to solve operational problems wherever they may be. It should also be noted that the terms "operations research" and a later term "management science" are used interchangeably.

In today's fiercely competitive global economy, both operations research and operations management play a pivotal role in insuring each firm's survival and success.

Historical Developments

1733–1807	*The Industrial Revolution*—Modern production management begins in England. Technological advances create profound changes in the methods and scale of manufacturing.
1776	*Adam Smith*—Develops the concept of specialization of labor wherein the production process is broken down into discrete components so that specially designed machines or narrowly-trained workers could perform each step of the manufacturing process at lowest cost with least material waste and maximum productivity.
1785	*James Watt*—His invention of the steam engine in 1769 realizes its 1st industrial applications, replacing human and animal power.
1798	*Eli Whitney*—Establishes the 1st factory utilizing interchangeable parts made on machines.
1832	*Charles Babbage*—Recommended the use of wage incentive plans, research and development to improve products and processes, economic analysis for selecting the location of facilities, and the matching of jobs to the appropriate worker skill level for cost reduction and quality control purposes.
1900	*Frederick Taylor*—The father of scientific management: a belief that there were laws governing production systems, just as there were laws for natural systems. Once identified through experimentation and observation, these laws could be used to find the best way to perform any job and the best way to make a product (*time + motion study*). Taylor also called for separation of responsibilities between floor workers and managers. Managers would specialize in developing processes, jobs, work methods, selection and training, planning, and coordinating. He also developed production documents that greatly improved information flow in factories.
1901	*Henry Gantt*—Develops the 1st manufacturing planning and control techniques and systems, scheduling techniques for workers, machines, and jobs.
1913	*Henry Ford and Charles Sorensen*—Develop the concept of the automobile assembly line where workers stood still and material moved. Each worker on the line had only a small amount of work to perform before the automobile chassis moved to the next station. Labor input decreases 90%, making autos affordable to the average person.
1915	*Ford W. Harris*—Develops inventory control models which calculate how much and when to purchase or produce a part or finished product, so as to meet customer demand with minimum stockage costs.

1921	*Agner Erlang*—Constructs models of waiting lines for the purpose of studying their behavior and reducing costs of customer service and customer waiting time.
1924	*Walter Shewhart*—Combined statistics with the need for quality control and provides the foundation for statistical sampling in quality control.
1935	*H.F. Dodge and H.G. Romig*—Develop sampling plans—the determination of sample size, sampling frequency, and methodology.
1940	*Operations Research*—U.S. and British governments create interdisciplinary teams of scientists to perform research on military operations such as logistics, tactics, strategies, and weapons vulnerability. This work is designated *operations research*. The resulting mathematical models are so successful that they are applied to solving operational problems in business and government after World War II.
1947	*George Dantzig*—U.S. Air Force civilian mathematician develops *linear programming*: an algebraic technique designed to help managers make the most effective use of an organization's resources in the creation of products or services, with a view toward profit maximization or cost-time-distance minimization.
1950	*A. Charnes and W.W. Cooper*—Develop the mechanics for integrating stochastic variables (variables that change in random fashion) into business decision-making models.
1955	*IBM Corporation*—Develops digital computers with rapid computational capabilities. Makes the growth of operations research/management science models and techniques possible.
1957	*Dupont Corporation*—Builds a new chemical plant in one-third less time via *PERT/CPM*—a network model for planning, scheduling, and controlling long-term, one-of-a-kind projects.
1960	*Lawrence Cummings and Lawrence Porter*—Organizational behavior theory integrated into traditional production job design and production layout design.
1970	*Oliver Wight and Joseph Orlicky*—Develop MRP (materials requirement planning)—an information system software that "explodes" or disaggregates a finished product or major assembly into its various parts and materials by type and quantity. It then aggregates (sums) the gross requirements for all products or assemblies containing those parts and materials, checks them against current inventory stock levels, and then automatically orders them at specific times necessary to insure their arrivals just before actual production of each product begins. This software program virtually eliminates the need to hold inventories within the firm since inventory is only shipped to the firm when needed to support production.
1970	*Wickham Skinner*—Harvard professor who called for the integration of quantitative methods, decision-making methods, and mathematical models into the firm's overall strategy, goals, and systems because only those tools can solve tomorrow's complex management problems.
1970s	*Computers in Manufacturing*—Manufacturing becomes the second major functional area of business (after accounting) to utilize the computer. Applications include machine movement control, equipment and material temperature monitoring, and continuous adjustment of rollers, valves, heaters, tool settings, and fluid flow rates.
1980	*W. Edward Deming and J.M. Juran*—American production experts who went to Japan after World War II to teach quality and management practices, which in turn, led to the development of the *Japanese production system*. This system, based

on old American ideas that were synthesized and improved by the Japanese, stressed that everyone is responsible for quality rather than using inspectors; making the product correct the first time to avoid rework; relying on workers—not experts—to make suggestions; and eliminating any activity or material that costs money but does not add value to the product.

1990   *Flexible Manufacturing Systems (FMS)*—Computers are used to control and coordinate the movement of materials among machines, and to continuously change tool settings for the machines.

Computer-Aided Design (CAD)—Software programs are developed that allow the user to draw or easily modify product designs on a computer screen and automatically encode them as machine instructions for computer-controlled machines. This saves considerable time and cost of hand-programming the machines, and it reduces the chance of errors.

2000   *Computer-Integrated Manufacturing (CIM)*—Database systems and all manufacturing equipment and subsystems are integrated into a single system. In theory, the CIM would control and coordinate every phase of production from initial customer order, to custom-product design, inventory purchase orders, tooling requirements, production schedules, tracking, quality control monitoring, assembly of information on productivity, profitability, and tool wear, to shipment and billing.

The 10 Critical Decisions of Operations Management

Decision Area	*Issues*
Service and Product Design	What good or service should we offer?
	How should we design these products?
Quality Management	Who is responsible for quality?
	How do we define quality?
Process and Capacity Design	What process and what capacity will these products require?
	What equipment and technology is necessary for these processes?
Location	Where should we put the facility?
	On what criteria should we base the location decision?
Layout Design	How should we arrange the facility?
	How large must the facility be to meet our plan?
Human Resources and Job Design	How do we provide a reasonable work environment?
	How much can we expect our employees to produce?
Supply Chain Management	Should we make or buy this component?
	Who are our suppliers, and who can integrate into our e-commerce program?

Decision Area	Issues
Inventory, Material Requirements Planning and Just-in-Time	How much inventory of each item should we have? When do we reorder?
Intermediate and Short-Term Scheduling	Are we better off keeping people on the payroll during slowdowns? Which job do we perform next?
Maintenance	Who is responsible for maintenance? When do we perform maintenance?

All good managers perform the basic functions of the management process. The **management process** consists of *planning, organizing, staffing, leading,* and *controlling.* Operations managers apply this management process to the decisions they make in the OM function.

The Value of Operations Management

1. Managers of accounting, finance, marketing, human resources, and information systems must closely support the generation and distribution of their firm's goods and services. The more they know about the system that generates the firm's products and services, the better able they are to perform their responsibilities.

2. Managers of other functions are also managers of their own operations. The challenges they face are the same.

3. More than half of all workers in the United States are directly involved in the operations functions of their organizations whether they be in the manufacturing or service sector.

4. Over seventy-five percent (75%) of a typical organization's material and equipment costs are incurred by the operations function. Small cost savings here, translate into huge increases in profit.

5. Operations management, finance, and marketing are the three major functions within any organization, and there is considerable interaction among them. It is important therefore, to understand how the operations management component functions.

6. Operations management can improve the quality of one's personal life as well. Decisions on whether or not to take quantity discounts at the grocery store, buy or lease a car, ways to make household chores less tiring and quicker, or whether or not to purchase insurance involve large amounts of time, money, and risk, all of which lend themselves quite well to analytical techniques and models learned in operations management.

7. As societies become more affluent, most of their resources are devoted to the generation of services rather than the manufacture of goods. In the United States, seventy-five percent (75%) of the workforce is employed in the service sector. Although productivity improvements are difficult to achieve in the service sector, operations management is the primary vehicle for making those improvements. Moreover, it is only through increases in productivity that the standard of living can improve, the nation prospers, and individual firms survive.

8. The traditional application of operations management in the manufacturing sector is important because:

- 25% of the U.S. workforce is steadily engaged in manufacturing.

- a strong industrial base is absolutely essential in order to maintain this country's dominant military, economic, and political posture in world affairs.

- 58% of non-manufacturing workers in the U.S. earn wages below the national average.

- the creation of one manufacturing job in turn creates six other jobs, whereas the creation of one service sector job in turn creates only one additional job.

- Half of the revenues earned by the Standard and Poor 500 corporations originate from overseas sales of manufactured goods. Seven million Americans are involved.

- Every one billion dollars in the U.S. trade deficit results in the loss of 20,000 American jobs.

- United States manufacturing comprised a larger percentage of the U.S. gross national product (GNP) in 1999 than it did in 1955! It is over fifty percent (50%).

Mission Statement and Goals

Before any company produces its first product or generates its first service, it must identify its mission. The mission states the purpose of the organization, the reason for its existence, i.e., "What business are we in?".

The mission statement provides a general direction for the organization and is the basis for its goals, i.e., annual profitability or sales growth of "x" percent per year for the next decade, or a world-wide presence in the manufacture and service of product "x".

Mission statement development is critical to even the largest firm's survival and success because no firm has sufficient resources to do "everything" and to be "all things to all people".

A mission statement usually requires several months to one year of intense thought and analysis, and may even transcend mention of the firm's current product offerings. A clearly defined mission statement enables the firm's top executives to formulate sound strategies.

Mission Statement Examples

- "To manufacture and service a growing and profitable global household appliance business that exceeds customers' expectations."

- "To provide society with superior products, innovations, and solutions that improve the quality of health and well-being of our customers, and to provide investors with a superior rate of return."

- "To provide consulting services for new businesses."

- "To remodel existing commercial buildings, while providing employees with meaningful work, advancement opportunities, and no layoffs."

- "To design, manufacture, and service passenger vehicles that offer safety and peace of mind."

Corporate Strategy

Once the firm's mission statement and goals have been crafted, its overall or corporate strategy must be developed. Strategies are general plans that provide focus for achieving the firm's mission. They are long-term by nature.

Corporate strategy formulation should consider both *internal* and *external* factors affecting the organization. Key internal factors are:

- employees' skills, abilities, dedication, and experience.
- cash flow, funding sources, and debt.
- existing and future technology.
- existing plants, capacities, age, and replacement costs.
- understanding of customer needs and assessment of loyalty.
- existing products and services.
- supplier reliability, quality, and flexibility.
- existing patents, labor relations, company image, and distribution channels.
- the degree of harmony between the firm's marketing, finance, and operations functions.

Key external factors are:

- competitors' strengths and weaknesses, prospective industry entrants, substitution products, ease of market entry, and the basis of competition, i.e., price, quality, features.
- markets' size, location, segments, demographics, firm shares, stability, and growth prospects.
- product innovation rates, current and future process design and technology.
- present and future state of economy, inflation, interest rates, tax law, and tariffs.
- present and future state of environmental laws, anti-trust laws, product liability laws, labor laws, government regulations, and trade restrictions.
- present and future commitment of suppliers and distributors.
- government and general population's attitude toward business in general, political stability or instability, and wars.
- the stage or stages of the *product life cycle* in which the firm's various products and services are currently positioned.

Each external and internal factor must be analyzed and evaluated in terms of how it may contribute or conflict with the corporate mission and goals. The outcome of this process is a corporate strategy which specifies which products and services to offer, which industries and market segments to enter, and which competitive advantages the firm will exploit. Competitive advantages are also called *critical success factors*. The selection of critical success factors (CSFs) stems from the realization that customers consider many factors when buying a product or service, such as price, quality, utility, convenience, innovation, styling, prompt delivery, and service. Yet, it is almost impossible for a company to be superior to its competitors in every factor, i.e., lowest price, best quality, best service. So companies try to excel in one or two of these factors and perform adequately in the other factors. This eliminates the risk of dissipating scarce resources on one hand, and failing to differentiate their products on the other hand. Both consequences tend to characterize unsuccessful organizations.

Functional Strategies

Corporate strategy dictates the individual strategies of the firm's three functional units: marketing, finance, and operations. In particular, *operations functional strategy* should delineate the tasks that the operations function must do well (in conjunction with those tasks delineated for marketing and finance) in order to support and achieve the corporate strategy.

The *operations functional strategy* should identify tasks related to the planning, design, and operation of the production conversion system. Interestingly enough, almost any operations task can be used to support a company's strategy, but most firms can compete very effectively by emphasizing one or two. For example, a retailer who competes on the critical success factor of large product selection should have detailed operations functional sub-strategies for inventory storage capacity and inventory management control systems. Additionally, the operations functional strategy should be consistent with the marketing and finance functional strategies. It would be disastrous, for example, if operations focused on long production runs of a few products in order to reduce per-unit costs, while marketing focused on promoting custom-made products and quick delivery.

The ten operations management decisions developed in this chapter provide an excellent checklist for identifying the particular tasks that *operations functional strategy* must perform in supporting and achieving the firm's overall strategy.

The Operations Functional Strategy Checklist

1. Quality (customer quality expectations; quality systems design; quality measures and standards)
2. Product (customized or standardized)
3. Supply Chain (sole or multiple vendors; type of distribution system)
4. Labor (specialized skills or multiple skills)
5. Maintenance ("as needed" or preventive)
6. Layout (project, work cells, or assembly line)
7. Inventory (ordering policy, stockage levels, type of system)
8. Process (scale of operation; choice of technology; in-house production or outsourcing)
9. Scheduling (stable or variable)
10. Location (near supplier or customer)

Strategy Implementation and Performance Measurement

As previously discussed, *operations functional strategy* should identify those tasks that the operations unit must perform in order for the organization to realize its strategies and thereby achieve its goals. To insure their implementation, it is critical that the operations strategy include tasks that can be evaluated in terms of their *effectiveness* (timely and complete attainment) and their *efficiency* (non-wasteful use of assigned resources of labor, equipment, material, and cash).

There are three types of operations-task performance measures:

I. **Productivity:** the amount of output produced divided by the amount of input used.

II. **Cost:** the identification, classification, and allocation of costs to organizational units, products, and processes for the purpose of determining their levels of profitability.

III. **Goal-Based:** measures of performance dealing with quality defects, on-time delivery, employee turnover, number of employee accidents, average new product leadtime, and machine availability. Such measurements can dramatically reduce costs, insure long-term competitiveness, and less obviously, actually generate increased revenues!

It is important to evaluate the operations tasks under all three types of performance measures because cost minimization and efficiency alone ignore many critical success factors that affect sales and revenue such as quality, product variety, and on-time delivery.

Figure 1–1 portrays the relationship between mission, corporate strategy, and functional strategies. The implication is that mission and external and internal factors combine to shape corporate strategy, which in turn shapes functional strategies. It is important that marketing, finance, and operations provide input to corporate mission and strategy formulation. Otherwise, there is significant risk that corporate mission and strategy will not match current and future functional capabilities, thereby jeopardizing their success.

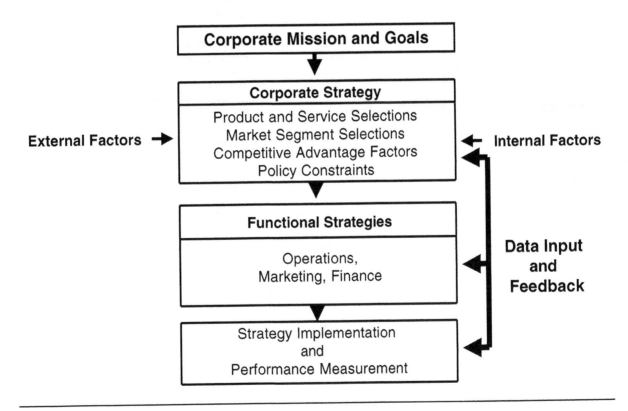

Figure 1–1

The Dynamics of Strategy

Strategies change over time for two reasons. First, because of changes within the organization (the internal factors). For example, changes in technology, product, or process affect a firm's strengths and weaknesses, and therefore, its strategy.

Figure 1–2 shows possible change in both corporate strategy and operations management functional strategy during a product's *life cycle*:

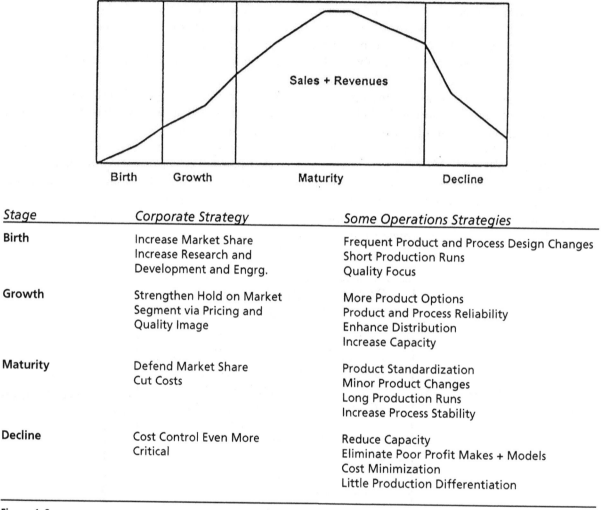

Stage	Corporate Strategy	Some Operations Strategies
Birth	Increase Market Share Increase Research and Development and Engrg.	Frequent Product and Process Design Changes Short Production Runs Quality Focus
Growth	Strengthen Hold on Market Segment via Pricing and Quality Image	More Product Options Product and Process Reliability Enhance Distribution Increase Capacity
Maturity	Defend Market Share Cut Costs	Product Standardization Minor Product Changes Long Production Runs Increase Process Stability
Decline	Cost Control Even More Critical	Reduce Capacity Eliminate Poor Profit Makes + Models Cost Minimization Little Production Differentiation

Figure 1–2

Strategies change over time secondly, because of changes in the environment (the external factors).

The Business Unit Strategy

Large firms are usually divided into separate divisions, subsidiaries, or product groups that operate as relatively autonomous business units, controlling their own marketing, finance, and production (operations) functions. Therefore, each should have its own business strategy because of differences in their competitive strengths and weaknesses and market conditions.

Differences Between Goods and Services

In identifying the tasks that the *operations functional strategy* must perform in supporting and achieving the corporate strategy, it is important to recognize the significant differences between goods and services, as summarized below:

Task	Goods	Services
Quality	precisely-measured standards	subjective standards (customer perception)
Facility Location	near raw materials or labor force	near customer
Layout	enhances production efficiency	enhances product (i.e., fine restaurant)
Labor	focused on technical skills; labor standards fixed	focused on customer interaction skills; standards depend on customer needs
Production Process and Capacity Design	customer not involved	customer may be directly involved (i.e., haircut); capacity must match demand
Scheduling	focus on leveling production rates	focus on meeting customer's schedule
Inventory	raw material, work-in-process, and finished goods may be inventoried	services cannot be inventoried
Supply Chain	relationships critical to finished good	relationships may not be critical
Maintenance	preventive maintenance located at the production site	repair maintenance located at the customer's site
Design	product is usually tangible	product is not tangible, a range of attributes, i.e., a smile, attentiveness

P

A

R

T

2

Decision-Making
Techniques
in P/OM

Chapter 2

Game Theory

Available on Student CD

Chapter

3

Decision Theory

Chapter 3 discusses simple and complex decision models: model-building considerations and game plan formulation.

Decision theory was developed by the Austrian mathematicians Oscar Morgenstern and John von Neumann during the late 1920s. It was first used by the Germans during the invasion of Russia in 1940, and later by the Americans in planning strategies for the battle of Leyte Gulf in the Philippines in late 1944. *Decision theory* became very popular among marketing managers after World War II, when battles over market share replaced those involving land and ocean. It also proved suitable for a wide range of management decisions involving capacity and facility location planning, as well as new product, equipment, and technology selection.

There are two major classes of decision models:

1. *Simple Decision-Making Models*: (also known as static or single-stage decision models). These models generate a single decision in present time. Past or future decisions have no relevance to the selected decision.

2. *Complex Decision-Making Models*: (also known as dynamic, multi-stage, sequential, or "decision-tree" models). These models generate a chain of decisions over a relatively long period of time (months, years, or decades). Here, past decisions influence present decisions, and present decisions influence future decisions. The individual decisions within the "chain" are not necessarily optimal per se. However, the identified "chain" is the best possible one.

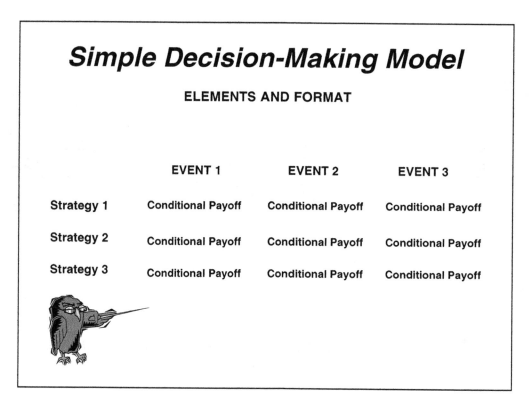

Simple Decision-Making Model

ELEMENTS AND FORMAT

	EVENT 1	EVENT 2	EVENT 3
Strategy 1	Conditional Payoff	Conditional Payoff	Conditional Payoff
Strategy 2	Conditional Payoff	Conditional Payoff	Conditional Payoff
Strategy 3	Conditional Payoff	Conditional Payoff	Conditional Payoff

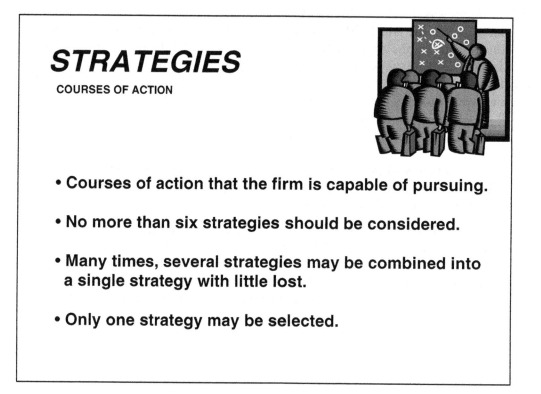

STRATEGIES

COURSES OF ACTION

- Courses of action that the firm is capable of pursuing.

- No more than six strategies should be considered.

- Many times, several strategies may be combined into a single strategy with little lost.

- Only one strategy may be selected.

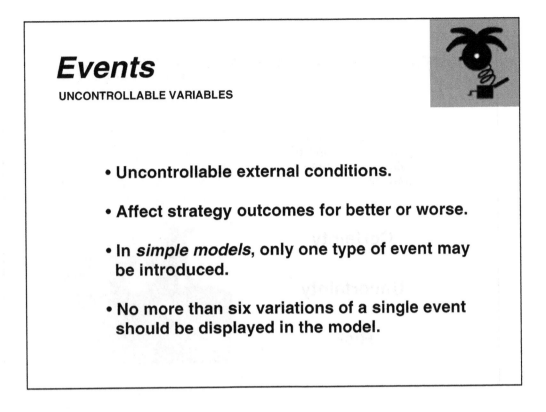

Events

UNCONTROLLABLE VARIABLES

- **Uncontrollable external conditions.**

- **Affect strategy outcomes for better or worse.**

- **In *simple models*, only one type of event may be introduced.**

- **No more than six variations of a single event should be displayed in the model.**

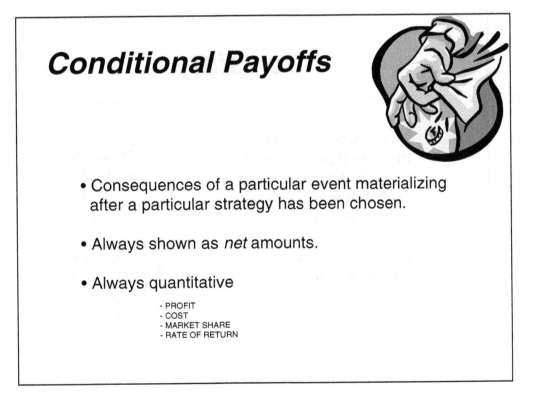

Conditional Payoffs

- Consequences of a particular event materializing after a particular strategy has been chosen.

- Always shown as *net* amounts.

- Always quantitative
    - PROFIT
    - COST
    - MARKET SHARE
    - RATE OF RETURN

The Three States of Nature

Decision making takes place within one of the following states of nature:

Certainty

Uncertainty

Risk

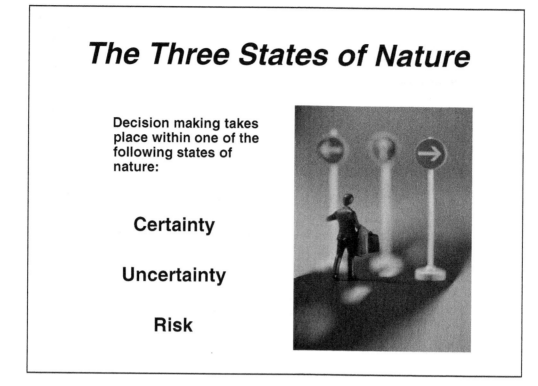

Certainty

- An environment where the firm makes a decision with total assurance of which event will take place (P = 100%)

- The firm then selects a strategy that maximizes or minimizes the conditional payoff.

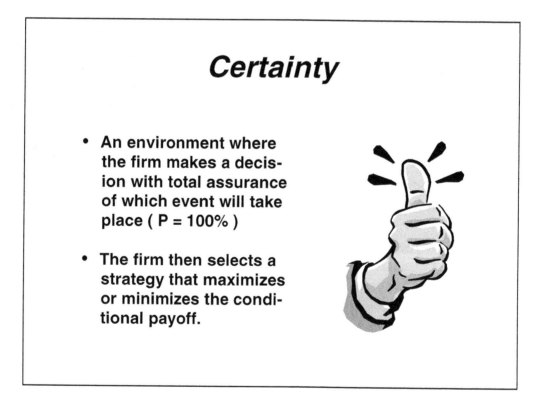

Uncertainty

- An environment where the firm makes a decision with absolutely no idea of which event will take place.

- At best, the firm may assume that all events have an equal chance of occurring.

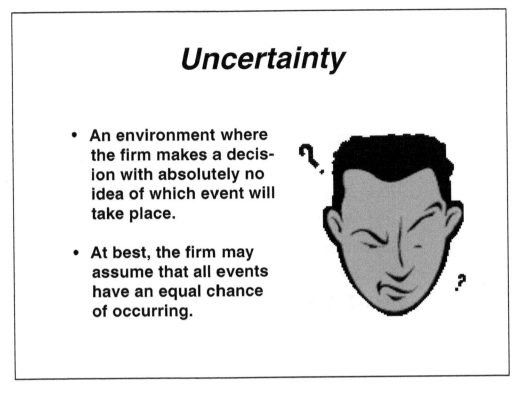

Risk

- An environment where the firm makes a decision with the knowledge of the relative probabilities of each event.

- When events are more or less likely to occur than others, the firm can make better quality decisions.

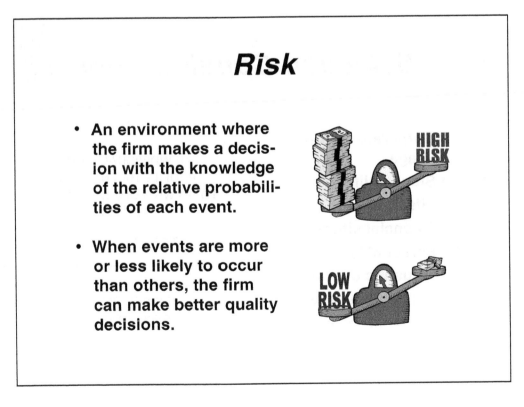

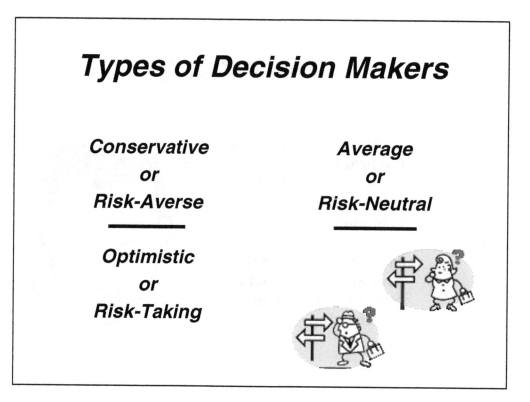

Types of Decision Makers

Conservative
or
Risk-Averse
———

Optimistic
or
Risk-Taking

Average
or
Risk-Neutral

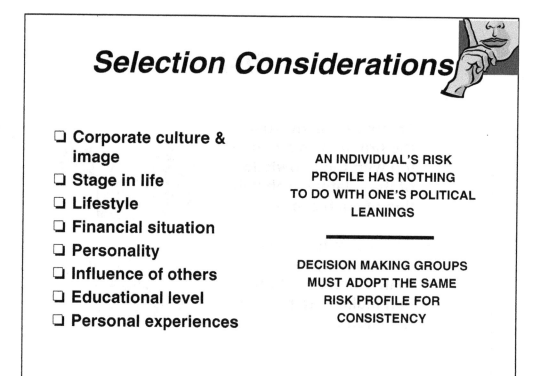

Selection Considerations

- ❏ Corporate culture & image
- ❏ Stage in life
- ❏ Lifestyle
- ❏ Financial situation
- ❏ Personality
- ❏ Influence of others
- ❏ Educational level
- ❏ Personal experiences

AN INDIVIDUAL'S RISK PROFILE HAS NOTHING TO DO WITH ONE'S POLITICAL LEANINGS

———

DECISION MAKING GROUPS MUST ADOPT THE SAME RISK PROFILE FOR CONSISTENCY

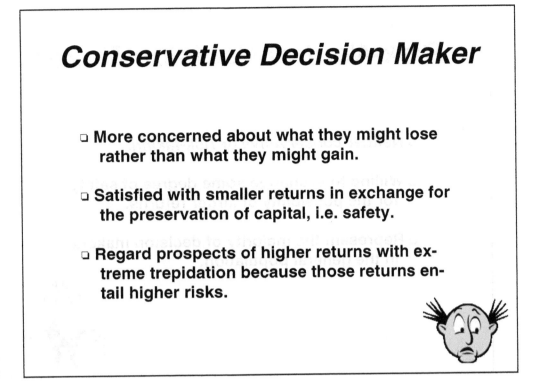

Conservative Decision Maker

❑ More concerned about what they might lose rather than what they might gain.

❑ Satisfied with smaller returns in exchange for the preservation of capital, i.e. safety.

❑ Regard prospects of higher returns with ex-treme trepidation because those returns en-tail higher risks.

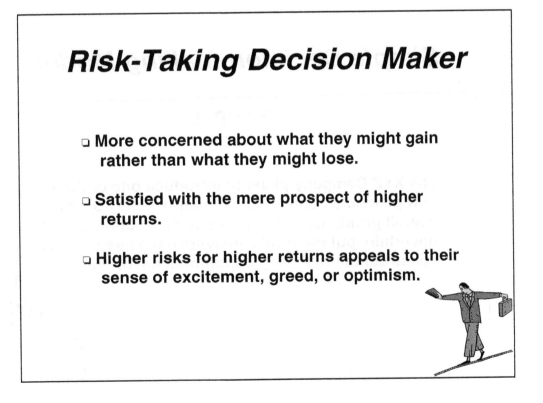

Risk-Taking Decision Maker

❑ More concerned about what they might gain rather than what they might lose.

❑ Satisfied with the mere prospect of higher returns.

❑ Higher risks for higher returns appeals to their sense of excitement, greed, or optimism.

Part 2 / Decision-Making Techniques in P/OM

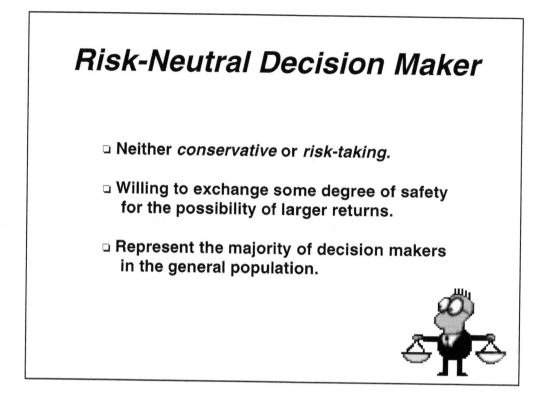

Risk-Neutral Decision Maker

- Neither *conservative* or *risk-taking.*

- Willing to exchange some degree of safety for the possibility of larger returns.

- Represent the majority of decision makers in the general population.

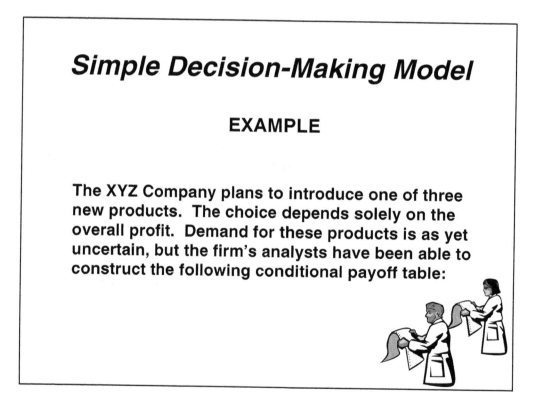

Simple Decision-Making Model

EXAMPLE

The XYZ Company plans to introduce one of three new products. The choice depends solely on the overall profit. Demand for these products is as yet uncertain, but the firm's analysts have been able to construct the following conditional payoff table:

Simple Decision-Making Model

EXAMPLE

DEMAND STRATEGY	LOW E1	MEDIUM E2	HIGH E3
S1: Product A	$20,000.	$150,000.	$400,000.
S2: Product B	($20,000.) *	$250,000.	$540,000.
S3: Product C	($200,000.) *	$300,000.	$700,000.

* DENOTES A LOSS

Decision Making Criteria

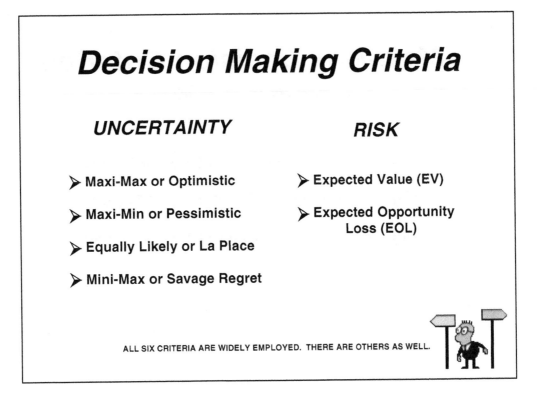

UNCERTAINTY

➤ Maxi-Max or Optimistic

➤ Maxi-Min or Pessimistic

➤ Equally Likely or La Place

➤ Mini-Max or Savage Regret

RISK

➤ Expected Value (EV)

➤ Expected Opportunity
   Loss (EOL)

ALL SIX CRITERIA ARE WIDELY EMPLOYED. THERE ARE OTHERS AS WELL.

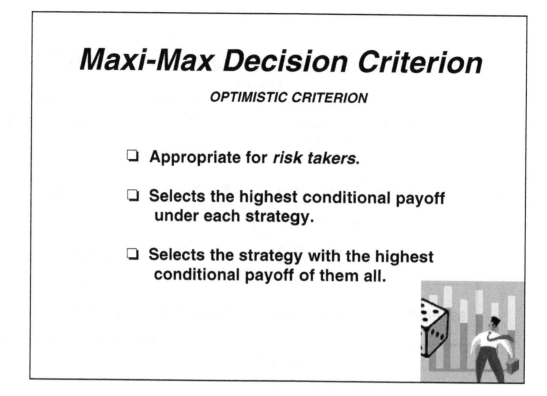

Maxi-Max Decision Criterion

OPTIMISTIC CRITERION

- ❑ Appropriate for *risk takers*.

- ❑ Selects the highest conditional payoff under each strategy.

- ❑ Selects the strategy with the highest conditional payoff of them all.

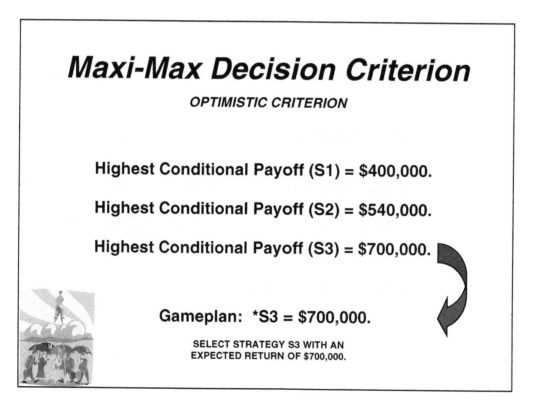

Maxi-Max Decision Criterion

OPTIMISTIC CRITERION

Highest Conditional Payoff (S1) = $400,000.

Highest Conditional Payoff (S2) = $540,000.

Highest Conditional Payoff (S3) = $700,000.

Gameplan: *S3 = $700,000.

SELECT STRATEGY S3 WITH AN
EXPECTED RETURN OF $700,000.

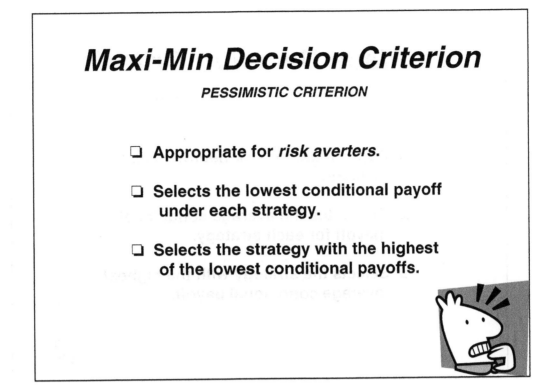

Maxi-Min Decision Criterion

PESSIMISTIC CRITERION

- ❏ Appropriate for *risk averters*.

- ❏ Selects the lowest conditional payoff under each strategy.

- ❏ Selects the strategy with the highest of the lowest conditional payoffs.

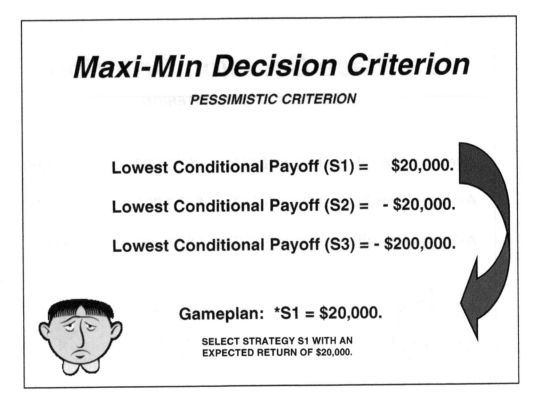

Maxi-Min Decision Criterion

PESSIMISTIC CRITERION

Lowest Conditional Payoff (S1) = $20,000.

Lowest Conditional Payoff (S2) = - $20,000.

Lowest Conditional Payoff (S3) = - $200,000.

Gameplan: *S1 = $20,000.

SELECT STRATEGY S1 WITH AN
EXPECTED RETURN OF $20,000.

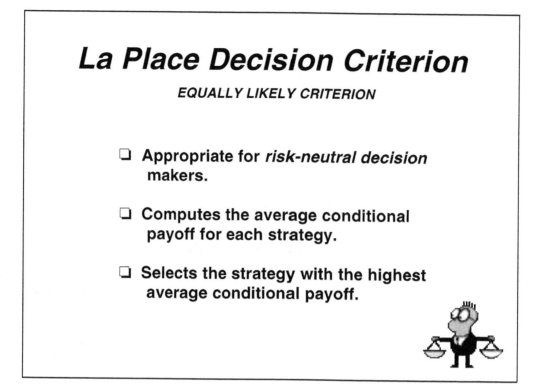

La Place Decision Criterion

EQUALLY LIKELY CRITERION

- ❏ Appropriate for *risk-neutral decision makers*.

- ❏ Computes the average conditional payoff for each strategy.

- ❏ Selects the strategy with the highest average conditional payoff.

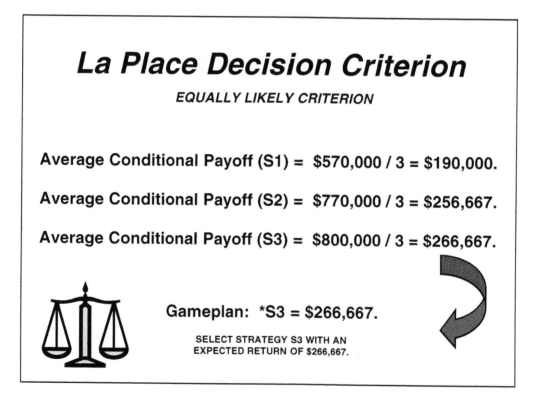

La Place Decision Criterion

EQUALLY LIKELY CRITERION

Average Conditional Payoff (S1) = $570,000 / 3 = $190,000.

Average Conditional Payoff (S2) = $770,000 / 3 = $256,667.

Average Conditional Payoff (S3) = $800,000 / 3 = $266,667.

Gameplan: *S3 = $266,667.

SELECT STRATEGY S3 WITH AN
EXPECTED RETURN OF $266,667.

Expected Value Criterion

EXPECTED MONETARY VALUE CRITERION

- Used whenever probabilities can be assigned to the events

- Appropriate for all decision makers who now become *risk-neutral*

- Involves calculation of the long-range, weighted-average return under each strategy

- Selects the strategy with the highest or lowest expected value*

WHEN CONDITIONAL PAYOFFS ARE PROFITS, HIGHEST EV STRATEGY IS SELECTED.
WHEN CONDITIONAL PAYOFFS ARE COSTS, LOWEST EV STRATEGY IS SELECTED.

Simple Decision-Making Model

CONDITIONAL PAYOFF MATRIX

DEMAND / STRATEGY	LOW (E1) .10	MEDIUM (E2) .60	HIGH (E3) .30
S1: Product A	$20,000.	$150,000.	$400,000.
S2: Product B	($20,000.) *	$250,000.	$540,000.
S3: Product C	($200,000.) *	$300,000.	$700,000.

* DENOTES A LOSS

Expected Value Criterion

EXPECTED MONETARY VALUE CRITERION

EV (S1) = .10 ($20,000.) + .60 ($150,000.) + .30 ($400,000.) = $212,000.

EV (S2) = .10 (-$20,000.) + .60 ($250,000.) + .30 ($540,000.) = $310,000.

EV (S3) = .10 (-$200,000.) + .60($300,000.) + .30 ($700,000.) = $370,000.

Gameplan: *S3 = $370,000.

SELECT STRATEGY S3 WITH AN EXPECTED RETURN OF $370,000.

Expected Value Criterion

SOLUTION POSTSCRIPT

- **Strategy *S3* - Product *C* was selected because its long-range, weighted-average return was highest ($370,000.)**

- **Literally, this means that if Product *C* were selected each year, given the identical events and conditional payoffs, we could expect an average return of $370,000. per year indefinitely.**

- ***Bayes Theorem*, however, allows us to make a one-time decision - like this - using the expected value criterion.**

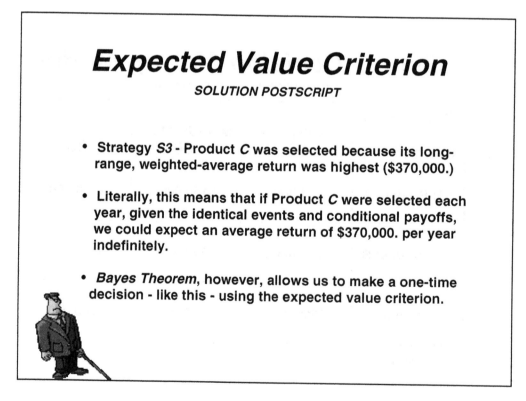

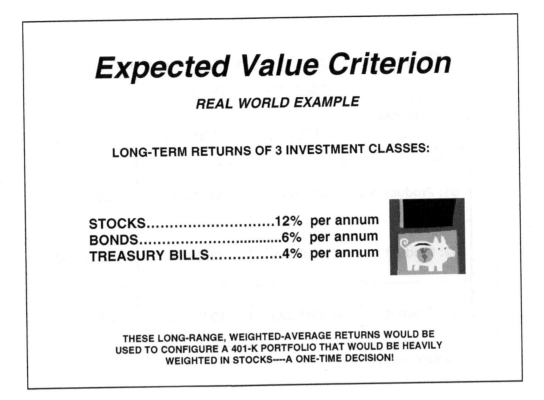

Expected Value Criterion

REAL WORLD EXAMPLE

LONG-TERM RETURNS OF 3 INVESTMENT CLASSES:

STOCKS.............................12% per annum
BONDS.................................6% per annum
TREASURY BILLS................4% per annum

THESE LONG-RANGE, WEIGHTED-AVERAGE RETURNS WOULD BE
USED TO CONFIGURE A 401-K PORTFOLIO THAT WOULD BE HEAVILY
WEIGHTED IN STOCKS----A ONE-TIME DECISION!

The Mini-Max or Savage Regret Decision Criterion

The Mini-Max or Savage Regret decision criterion would be appropriate for decisionmakers who tend to second-guess their decisions and/or regret not having made the best choice for the event that ultimately occurs. This criterion will select a strategy that will be closer to the best possible conditional payoffs than any other strategy.

Execution

Step #1: Convert the conditional payoff (CP) matrix to an opportunity loss (OL) matrix, on a *column-by-column* basis.

Step #2: Identify the highest (worst) opportunity loss under each strategy listed in the matrix.

Step #3: Select the strategy with the lowest (best) opportunity loss.

Example

The original conditional payoff matrix is:

Simple Decision-Making Model

CONDITIONAL PAYOFF MATRIX

DEMAND / STRATEGY	LOW (E1)	MEDIUM (E2)	HIGH (E3)
S1: Product A	$20,000. _least regret_	$150,000.	$400,000.
S2: Product B	($20,000.) *	$250,000.	$540,000.
S3: Product C	($200,000.) *	$300,000. _least regret_	$700,000. _least regret_

* DENOTES A LOSS

If event E1 ultimately occurred, the best strategy would have been S1 with a return (CP) of $20,000. The regret factor or opportunity loss factor for this strategy would be zero (0) since it was the correct selection under the circumstances for maximizing profit.

If strategy S2 had been selected, the return would have been $40,000. less, that is, a failure to make $20,000. plus a loss of $20,000. as well. The regret factor therefore is $40,000.

If strategy S3 had been selected, the return would have been $220,000. less, that is, a failure to make $20,000. plus a loss of $200,000. as well. The regret factor therefore is $220,000.

If event E2 ultimately occurred, the best strategy would have been S3 with a return (CP) of $300,000. The regret factor or opportunity loss factor for this strategy would be zero (0) since it was the correct selection under the circumstances for maximizing profit.

If strategy S1 had been selected, the return would have been $150,000. less. The regret factor therefore is $150,000.

If strategy S2 had been selected, the return would have been $50,000. less. The regret factor therefore is $50,000.

The 3rd column of the above matrix would have been converted in a similar fashion, yielding the opportunity loss matrix shown below:

Simple Decision-Making Model
OPPORTUNITY LOSS MATRIX

DEMAND / STRATEGY	LOW (E1)	MEDIUM (E2)	HIGH (E3)
S1: Product A	0	150,000	300,000
S2: Product B	40,000	50,000	160,000
S3: Product C	220,000	0	0

Analysis

The worst regret factor (OL) for strategy S1 = $300,000.

The worst regret factor (OL) for strategy S2 = $160,000.

The worst regret factor (OL) for strategy S3 = $220,000.

Conclusion

The game plan would call for selecting strategy S2 because, regardless of which demand event ultimately materializes, strategy S2 will never be more than $160,000. away from the best possible return (CP).

*S2 = $160,000.

The Expected Opportunity Loss Criterion (EOL)

The expected opportunity loss criterion or EOL would be appropriate for all decision-makers (especially risk-neutral decision-makers) whenever probabilities can be assigned to the uncontrollable events (i.e., E1, E2, E3, etc.). The EOL criterion identifies that particular strategy that will be closest to the best possible returns over the long run.

The EOL and EV criteria select the *identical* strategy because whatever strategy yields the highest returns over the long term also is the closest one to the best possible returns over the long term as well.

The EOL criterion is not as widely-used as the EV criterion because it involves more computations and also, the lesser-understood concept of opportunity loss.

Execution

Step #1:   Convert the conditional payoff (CP) matrix to an opportunity loss (OL) matrix, on a *column-by-column* basis.

Step #2:   Compute the EOL for each strategy.

Step #3:   Select the strategy with the lowest EOL.

Example

Simple Decision-Making Model
CONDITIONAL PAYOFF MATRIX

DEMAND ⟍ STRATEGY	LOW (E1) .10	MEDIUM (E2) .60	HIGH (E3) .30
S1: Product A	$20,000.	$150,000.	$400,000.
S2: Product B	($20,000.) *	$250,000.	$540,000.
S3: Product C	($200,000.) *	$300,000.	$700,000.

* DENOTES A LOSS

Simple Decision-Making Model

OPPORTUNITY LOSS MATRIX

DEMAND / STRATEGY	LOW (E1) .10	MEDIUM (E2) .60	HIGH (E3) .30
S1: Product A	0	150,000	300,000
S2: Product B	40,000	50,000	160,000
S3: Product C	220,000	0	0

Given that the   P (E1-Low Demand) = 10%

P (E2-Medium Demand) = 60%

P (E3-High Demand) = 30%

EOL (S1) = .10 ($0.) + .60 ($150,000.) + .30 ($300,000.) = $180,000.

EOL (S2) = .10 ($40,000.) + .60 ($50,000.) + .30 ($160,000.) = $82,000.

EOL (S3) = .10 ($220,000.) + .60 ($0.) + .30 ($0.) = $22,000.

Conclusion

The game plan would call for selecting strategy S3 whether this decision had to be made repeatedly under identical conditions over the long term, or only once.

It is the strategy that will never be more than $22,000. away from the best possible return over the long run.

*S3 = $22,000.

Additional Comments

- conditional payoffs are computed by accounting, finance, and marketing/sales professionals. The production/operations function accepts those conditional payoffs as valid and integrates them into the decision model.

- it makes little or no difference whether the decisionmakers are individuals or groups. In most companies, it is not usual for all decisionmakers to share the same risk propensities, as a result of the corporate culture.

- only those "events" which have a one percent (1%) or greater probability of occurrence should be included in the decision model.

- the sum of the probabilities for all "events" should equal one-hundred percent (100% or 1.00).

- it is possible for more than one strategy to be selected under any performance criterion.

- decisionmakers should be consistent. That is, they should employ the same performance criterion in all their decision-making processes.

- more often than not, a different strategy will be selected under each performance criterion.

- if the difference in returns between two or more strategies is small, then those strategies should be considered equally acceptable by the decisionmaker. The difference could be attributable to normal bias inherent in estimating payoffs.

Complex Decision-Making Models

Whenever several decisions need to be made over an extended period of time, or whenever the decision process involves more than one major type of event, or whenever the decision process involves two or more states of nature, the *complex decision-making model* must be employed. These models are popularly referred to as "decision trees" and have a distinct format consisting of the following elements:

1. **Decision Node** (□) a point in time or "platform" where a decision must be made. They are usually numbered as "1" for the first decision, "2" for the second decision, and so on.

2. **Decision Arrows (Arcs)** (→) the strategies or courses of action open to the decision maker at that particular point in time. They are usually labeled "S1" for the first strategy, "S2" for the second strategy, and so on.

3. **Event Node** (○) a warning of two or more events to follow after a strategy has been selected. Usually labeled as small case letters, "a," "b," "c," and so on.

4. **Event Arcs (----)** the actual events themselves. They are usually labeled "E1," "E2," "E3," and so on. They are followed by their respective conditional payoffs.

5. **Slashes** (‖) symbolize the rejection of a particular strategy, or its elimination from further consideration.

6. **Thickened Arc** (——) symbolizes the selection of a particular strategy.

The example that was used to discuss the *simple decision-making model* will also be used to discuss the *complex decision-making model*.

Simple Decision-Making Model

EXAMPLE

DEMAND STRATEGY	LOW E1	MEDIUM E2	HIGH E3
S1: Product A	$20,000.	$150,000.	$400,000.
S2: Product B	($20,000.) *	$250,000.	$540,000.
S3: Product C	($200,000.) *	$300,000.	$700,000.

* DENOTES A LOSS

Decision Tree Elements

TEXT EXAMPLE

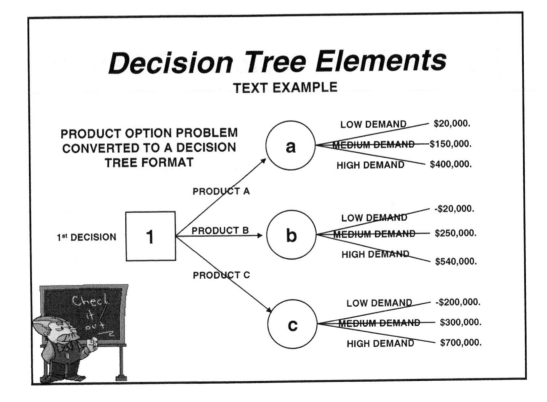

PRODUCT OPTION PROBLEM CONVERTED TO A DECISION TREE FORMAT

1st DECISION — 1

PRODUCT A — a
LOW DEMAND — $20,000.
MEDIUM DEMAND — $150,000.
HIGH DEMAND — $400,000.

PRODUCT B — b
LOW DEMAND — -$20,000.
MEDIUM DEMAND — $250,000.
HIGH DEMAND — $540,000.

PRODUCT C — c
LOW DEMAND — -$200,000.
MEDIUM DEMAND — $300,000.
HIGH DEMAND — $700,000.

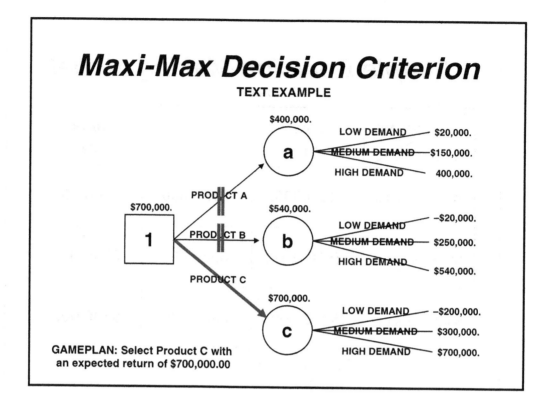

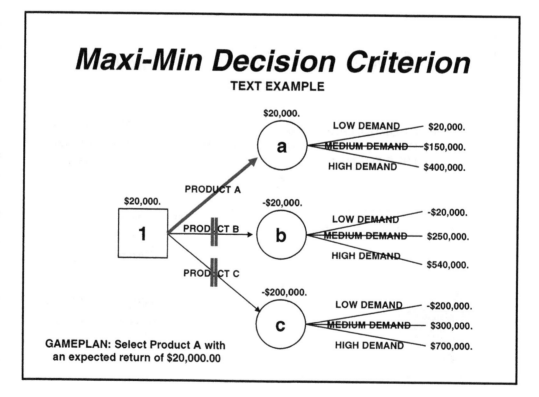

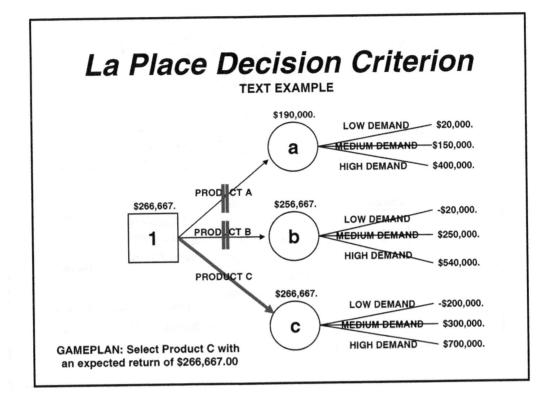

La Place Decision Criterion

TEXT EXAMPLE

$190,000.

a
LOW DEMAND — $20,000.
MEDIUM DEMAND — $150,000.
HIGH DEMAND — $400,000.

$266,667.

1

PRODUCT A

$256,667.

PRODUCT B

b
LOW DEMAND — -$20,000.
MEDIUM DEMAND — $250,000.
HIGH DEMAND — $540,000.

PRODUCT C

$266,667.

c
LOW DEMAND — -$200,000.
MEDIUM DEMAND — $300,000.
HIGH DEMAND — $700,000.

GAMEPLAN: Select Product C with
an expected return of $266,667.00

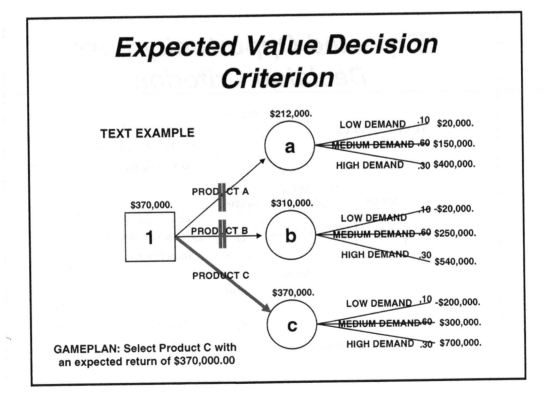

Expected Value Decision Criterion

TEXT EXAMPLE

$212,000.

a
LOW DEMAND .10 $20,000.
MEDIUM DEMAND .60 $150,000.
HIGH DEMAND .30 $400,000.

$370,000.

1

PRODUCT A

$310,000.

PRODUCT B

b
LOW DEMAND .10 -$20,000.
MEDIUM DEMAND .60 $250,000.
HIGH DEMAND .30 $540,000.

PRODUCT C

$370,000.

c
LOW DEMAND .10 -$200,000.
MEDIUM DEMAND .60 $300,000.
HIGH DEMAND .30 $700,000.

GAMEPLAN: Select Product C with
an expected return of $370,000.00

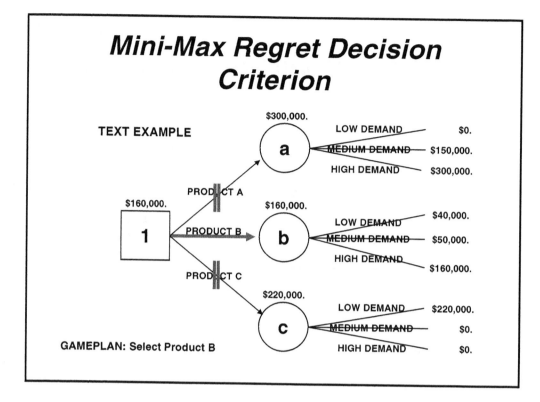

Mini-Max Regret Decision Criterion

TEXT EXAMPLE

$300,000.

a

LOW DEMAND — $0.
MEDIUM DEMAND — $150,000.
HIGH DEMAND — $300,000.

$160,000.

1

PRODUCT A

PRODUCT B

PRODUCT C

$160,000.

b

LOW DEMAND — $40,000.
MEDIUM DEMAND — $50,000.
HIGH DEMAND — $160,000.

$220,000.

c

LOW DEMAND — $220,000.
MEDIUM DEMAND — $0.
HIGH DEMAND — $0.

GAMEPLAN: Select Product B

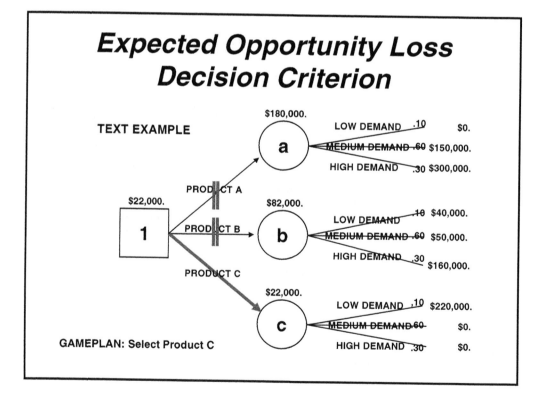

Expected Opportunity Loss Decision Criterion

TEXT EXAMPLE

$180,000.

a

LOW DEMAND .10 $0.
MEDIUM DEMAND .60 $150,000.
HIGH DEMAND .30 $300,000.

$22,000.

1

PRODUCT A

PRODUCT B

PRODUCT C

$82,000.

b

LOW DEMAND .10 $40,000.
MEDIUM DEMAND .60 $50,000.
HIGH DEMAND .30 $160,000.

$22,000.

c

LOW DEMAND .10 $220,000.
MEDIUM DEMAND .60 $0.
HIGH DEMAND .30 $0.

GAMEPLAN: Select Product C

SOLVED PROBLEM

Decision Tree for a New Venture

You are deciding between two business ventures: A and B.

If you choose venture A , there is a 50/50 chance of going broke or earning $45,000. in profits.
If venture A fails , you face two options: incur a debt of $3,000. or file for personal bankruptcy in which case there is chance that all your debts will be cancelled, and a 60% chance that you will have to pay back $4,000.
If you choose venture B , there is a 75% chance of earning $35,000. If venture B fails, you still have the option of either settling for $500. in cash from the liquidation of assets or selling your interests in venture B in exchange for a stock option in a growing firm that could be worth $60,000. (with a 20% probability) or zero dollars within one year.

What should you do?

Business Venture "Tree"

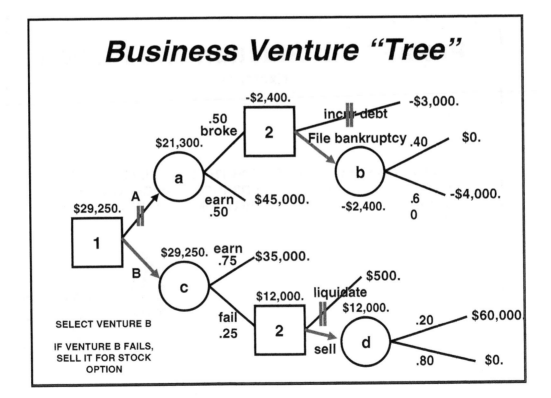

Product Introduction and Pricing
Example

A firm must decide whether to introduce an economy line, a deluxe line, or choose not to introduce a new line at all.

If the firm introduces an economy line, the competition may either introduce its own economy line, a deluxe line, or nothing, with probabilities of 50%, 40%, and 10% respectively.

If the firm introduces a deluxe line, the competition may either introduce its own economy line, deluxe line, or nothing, with probabilities of 40%, 55%, and 5% respectively.

If both the firm and the competition introduce an economy line, the firm must then decide whether to price it at $5.00 (S4) or $6.00 (S5).

If the firm introduces an economy line and the competition introduces a deluxe line, the firm must then decide whether to price it at $5.00 (S4) or $6.00 (S5).

If no competition develops, then the firm must still decide whether to price it at either $5.00 (S4) or $6.00 (S5).

Product Introduction and Pricing
Example

THIS PROBLEM CONTINUES FOR THE DELUXE LINE INTRO-DUCTION, FOLLOWED BY A PRICING DECISION, WHICH IN TURN, WILL INVITE THE COMPETITION'S PRICING RESPON-SES.

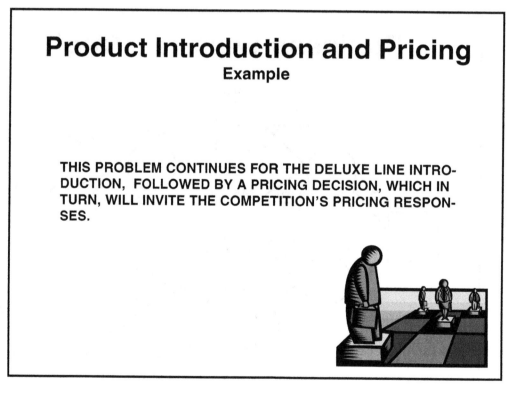

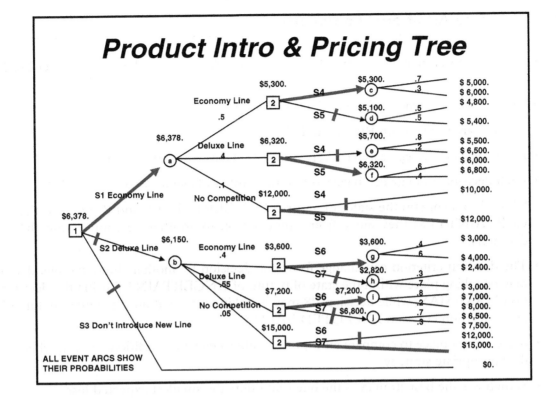

Product Intro & Pricing Tree

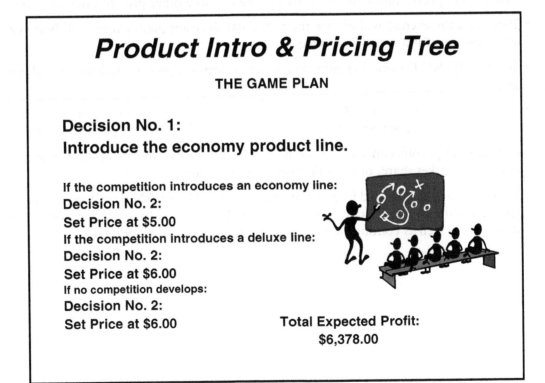

Product Intro & Pricing Tree

THE GAME PLAN

Decision No. 1:
Introduce the economy product line.

If the competition introduces an economy line:
Decision No. 2:
Set Price at $5.00
If the competition introduces a deluxe line:
Decision No. 2:
Set Price at $6.00
If no competition develops:
Decision No. 2:
Set Price at $6.00

Total Expected Profit:
$6,378.00

Decision Tree Additional Comments

- "Trees" can employ any of the decision criteria discussed under Simple Decision Making models.

- "Trees" are constructed from LEFT to RIGHT.

- "Trees" are solved from RIGHT to LEFT.

- Each decision strategy can have very different events associated with it.

- Each decision strategy can have a different number of events associated with it.

- "Trees" can contain the states of nature of UNCERTAINTY and RISK (and theoretically CERTAINTY) as they move from one decision to another decision within the chain of decisions.

- The decision criterion can change from one decision to another. For example, decision #7 may be taking place within the state of nature of UNCERTAINTY using the decision criterion MAXI-MAX, while decision #8 may be taking place within the state of nature of RISK using decision criterion EXPECTED VALUE.

- It is commonplace to compare an expected value against a conditional payoff when selecting the appropriate strategy.

- Sometimes the best strategy is the one that offers the smallest expected loss.

- Some event probabilities are explicitly provided, while other probabilities must be inferred.

- Fate (i.e., the events) will dictate the particular decision platform we will find ourselves on when facing a future strategy choice.

- It is usually NOT a simple matter to convert a decision process, written or oral, into a decision tree.

- A decision maker must develop the ability to anticipate future strategy options and their consequences (conditional payoffs) over an extended period of time, perhaps decades.

- Conditional payoffs can take the form of dollars + cents, returns on investments, gains (or losses) in market share, or any other quantifiable value.

- Every decision tree should be accompanied by a GAME PLAN shown usually to the bottom left. It should especially state which strategy will be chosen for each decision in the chain of decisions as well as contingency actions connected with those strategies.

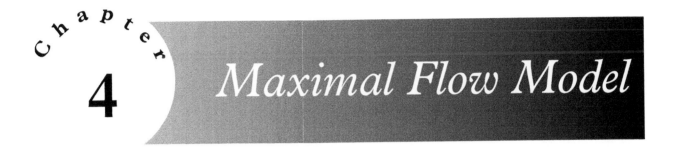

Maximal Flow Model

Chapter 4

Available on Student CD

Chapter 5

Simulation

Chapter 5 introduces simulation models (mathematical duplications of real-world systems) wherein proposed decisions are evaluated in advance.

Simulation is one of the three most widely used quantitative techniques in the world today. The others are basic statistics and linear programming. In business, simulation involves the construction of mathematical models that can duplicate the behavior of real-world systems and operations. Proposed decisions or courses of action can then be "run" through the simulation, or evaluated as to their impacts, for better or worse, on the system/operation. The proposed decision that fares best in the simulation is usually selected for actual implementation.

What makes simulation so unique is that it is the "model of last resort." When all other quantitative models prove inadequate because their underlying mathematical assumptions are violated, or whenever the complexity of the operations problem overwhelms them, simulation stands alone. It is completely free of mathematical assumptions or limitations, and it is completely flexible.

Most simulations, by virtue of their complexity, must be run on a computer or clusters of computers. The intent of this chapter, however, is to develop an appreciation for the role that simulation can play in solving many complicated business-related problems, and to present the basic building blocks that all simulations are comprised of.

An Elementary Simulation Example

Suppose that a store wanted to estimate a salesperson's average daily commissions. Assume that a salesperson receives a $10.00 commission for each television set sold, and that only one model of television set is offered. Assume also, that only six (6) levels of sales are possible on a given business day: 0, 1, 2, 3, 4, 5 units. The store wants to run the simulation over ten (10) business days.

If we chose to develop this simulation on paper (as opposed to writing a computer program), we would construct a spreadsheet similar to the one below:

No. TVs Sold	Sales Probability	Cumulative Probability	Random Number Interval
0	0.15	0.15	01–15
1	0.20	0.35	16–35
2	0.30	0.65	36–65
3	0.20	0.85	66–85
4	0.10	0.95	86–95
5	0.05	1.00	96–00

Column 1: Shows 6 events connected with TV demand. TV demand is a *relevant variable* which is any variable that helps to explain the behavior of a system/operation. Analysts attempt to identify a sufficient number of these variables and their dynamic interrelationships, so as to duplicate the system/operation real-world behavior. In this problem, only one relevant variable is required to explain sales commission behavior: daily TV demand.

Column 2: Shows the probability of each daily sales demand. It is developed from historical sales records or management's best estimate. All event probabilities must sum to "1.00" (100%). Note how TV demand appears to follow a normal distribution. Most real-world phenomena in fact follow the normal distribution as well. However, a relevant variable may follow *any* probability distribution, whether it be normal, poisson, hypergeometric, exponential, or uniform.

Column 3: A cumulative probability distribution is built on the preceding column's probability distribution:

$$P \text{ (0 sales)} = .15$$

$$P \text{ (0 or 1 sale)} = .15 + .20 = .35$$

$$P \text{ (0 or 1 or 2 sales)} = .15 + .20 + .30 = .65$$

. . . etc.

Column 4: This is the "RN" or Random Number Interval column. Here, an arbitrary block of 100 numbers is broken down into smaller blocks of numbers (or "intervals") on a proportional basis for each demand "event." For example, P (0 sales) = 15%. The first 15 numbers in the block of 100 will be allocated to this demand event: 01 to 15. The cumulative probability value in the preceding column sets the upper boundary of "15" for this interval.

The "fuel" that drives the simulation forward in time, and also enables it to duplicate reality is the *random number string:* a series of true random numbers selected from a random number table in any mathematics or statistics textbook, generated by any computer utility program, or even drawn as numbered marbles from a fishbowl.

The key premise upon which simulation is built, is that all real-world phenomena behave on a random basis, yet they are more or less likely to occur than others. Combining random behavior and probability results in the duplication of reality.

In our problem, the demand events with the highest probabilities for occurrence also have the longest random number intervals. If we generate random numbers to in turn generate "simulated" sales for each day, those demand events with the longest RN intervals have the greatest chances of "capturing" the daily random numbers, which will, in turn, represent them as sales each day. This all sounds rather complicated, but can be better seen by example:

Day	1st	2nd	3rd	4th	5th	6th	7th	8th	9th	10th
Random Number	51	08	62	01	29	69	63	42	94	52
Simulated Sales	2	0	2	0	1	3	2	2	4	2

Running the Simulation

Starting with a random number string : 51086201296963429452 and breaking it into 2-digit numbers of: 51 08 62 01 29 69 63 42 94 52, simulated sales for the 1st day will be determined by random number "51" which falls within the RN interval "36-65" which in turn, is associated with the demand event "2 TVs."

Simulated sales for the 2nd day will be determined by random number "08" which falls within the RN interval "01-15" which, in turn, is associated with the demand event "0 TVs."

Simulated sales for the 3rd day will be determined by random number "62" which falls within the RN interval "36-65" which, in turn, is associated with the demand event "2 TVs" . . . and so on, until we have simulated daily sales for all ten business days.

Total simulated sales over the ten-day period are: 2+0+2+0+1+3+2+2+4+2 = 18 TVs.

18 TVs/10 days = 1.8 TVs sold on average per day.

1.8 TVs × \$10.00 commission per TV sold = \$18.00 average daily sales commissions.

A More Complex (and More Typical) Simulation Example

- it shows the interaction of two (2) relevant variables (barge arrival rate and crew unloading rate) in assessing the performance of the current-sized crew.

- two simulations are run. The first simulation assesses the performance of the existing crew. The second simulation assesses the performance of a doubled crew. The question to be answered: Which crew staffing level is most effective, and by how much?

- the simulation begins on "day 1" and continues for fifteen days.

- each relevant variable has its own "spreadsheet" showing events, probabilities, cumulative probabilities, and random number intervals.

- each relevant variable has its own random number string, although it is perfectly acceptable for relevant variables to share a common random number string.

- a "time-incremented" simulation is being conducted, that is, the simulation is deliberately moved forward in time on a day-to-day basis, and on each day, it "looks to see" how many barges (if any) arrive and how many unloadings (if any) are accomplished. An "event-incremented" simulation, on the other hand, would be one where no activity occurs until some event first materialized, i.e., repairs cannot begin on a machine until the machine breaks down.

- this type of simulation could easily become a cost analysis as well, by including labor hour costs, non-unloading barge opportunity costs, and pier overhead costs.

A Typical Business Simulation

Fully loaded barges arrive at night in New Orleans following their long trips down the Mississippi River from industrial midwestern cities. The number of barges docking on any given night ranges from 0 to 5. The probability of 0, 1, 2, 3, 4, and 5 arrivals is displayed in the table. In the same table, we establish cumulative probabilities and corresponding random number intervals for each possible value.

OVERNIGHT BARGE ARRIVAL RATES AND RANDOM NUMBER INTERVALS.

Number of Arrivals	Probability	Cumulative Probability	Random Number Interval
0	.13	.13	01 through 13
1	.17	.30	14 through 30
2	.15	.45	31 through 45
3	.25	.70	46 through 70
4	.20	.90	71 through 90
5	.10	1.00	91 through 00
	1.00		

A study by the dock superintendent reveals that because of the nature of their cargo, the number of barges unloaded also tends to vary from day to day. The superintendent provides information from which we can create a probability distribution for the variable *daily unloading rate*. As we just did for the arrival variable, we can set up an interval of random numbers for the unloading rates.

Barges are unloaded on a first-in, first-out basis. Any barges that are not unloaded the day of arrival must wait until the following day. Tying up a barge in dock is an expensive proposition, and the superintendent cannot ignore the angry phone calls from barge line owners reminding him that "time is money!"

UNLOADING RATES AND RANDOM NUMBER INTERVALS.

Daily Unloading Rates	Probability	Cumulative Probability	Random Number Interval
1	.05	.05	01 through 05
2	.15	.20	06 through 20
3	.50	.70	21 through 70
4	.20	.90	71 through 90
5	.10	1.00	91 through 00
	1.00		

He decides that, before going to the Port of New Orleans's controller to request additional unloading crews, a simulation study of arrivals, unloadings, and delays should be conducted. A 100-day simulation would be ideal, but for purposes of illustration, the superintendent begins with a shorter 15-day analysis.

To generate Daily Arrivals, use the random number string:

52, 06, 50, 88, 53, 30, 10, 47, 99, 37, 66, 91, 35, 32, 00

To generate Daily Unloading Rates, use the random number string:

37, 63, 28, 02, 74, 35, 24, 03, 29, 60, 74, 85, 90, 73, 59

The following table shows the day-to-day port simulation.

QUEUING SIMULATION OF PORT OF NEW ORLEANS BARGE UNLOADINGS.

(1) Day	(2) Number Delayed from Previous Day	(3) Random Number	(4) Number of Nightly Arrivals	(5) Total to Be Unloaded	(6) Random Number	(7) Number Unloaded
1	(–)[1]	52	3	3	37	3
2	0	06	0	0	63	(0)[2]
3	0	50	3	3	28	3
4	0	88	4	4	02	1
5	3	53	3	6	74	4
6	2	30	1	3	35	3
7	0	10	0	0	24	(0)[3]
8	0	47	3	3	03	1
9	2	99	5	7	29	3
10	4	37	2	6	60	3
11	3	66	3	6	74	4
12	2	91	5	7	85	4
13	3	35	2	5	90	4
14	1	32	2	3	73	(3)[4]
15	0	00	5	5	59	3
	20		41			39
	Total delays		Total arrivals			Total

unloadings

1. We can begin with no delays from the previous day. In a long simulation, even if we started with five overnight delays, that initial condition would be averaged out.

2. Three barges *could* have been unloaded on day 2. But because there were no arrivals and no backlog existed, zero unloadings took place.

3. The same situation as noted in footnote 2 takes place.

4. This time four barges could have been unloaded, but since only three were in queue, the number unloaded is recorded as 3.

The superintendent will likely be interested in at least three useful and important pieces of information:

$$\frac{\text{Average number of barges}}{\text{delayed to the next day}} = \frac{20 \text{ delays}}{15 \text{ days}}$$

$$= 1.33 \text{ barges delayed per day}$$

$$\text{Average number of nightly arrivals} = \frac{41 \text{ arrivals}}{15 \text{ days}}$$

$$= 2.73 \text{ arrivals per night}$$

$$\text{Average number of barges unloaded each day} = \frac{39 \text{ unloadings}}{15 \text{ days}}$$

$$= 2.60 \text{ unloadings per day}$$

When the above data are analyzed in the context of delay costs, idle labor costs, and the cost of hiring extra unloading crew, it will be possible for the dock superintendent and port controller to make a better staffing decision. They may even elect to resimulate the process assuming different unloading rates that would correspond to increased crew sizes. Although simulation is a tool that cannot guarantee an optimal solution to problems such as this, it can be helpful in recreating a process and identifying good decision alternatives.

An increase in the size of the barge-unloading crew at the Port of New Orleans has resulted in a new probability distribution for daily unloading rates:

Daily Unloading Rate	Probability
1	.03
2	.12
3	.40
4	.28
5	.12
6	.05

Resimulate 15 days of barge unloadings and compute the average number of barges delayed, average number of nightly arrivals, and average number of barges unloaded each day.

To generate DAILY ARRIVALS, use the random number string:

37, 77, 13, 10, 02, 18, 31, 19, 32, 85, 31, 94, 81, 43, 31

To generate DAILY UNLOADING RATES, use the random number string:

69, 84, 12, 94, 51, 36, 17, 02, 15, 29, 16, 52, 56, 43, 26

How do these simulated results compare with the utilization of a smaller size barge-unloading crew?

Number of Arrivals	Probability	Cumulative Probability	Random Number Interval
0	0.13	0.13	01–13
1	0.17	0.30	14–30
2	0.15	0.45	31–45
3	0.25	0.70	46–70
4	0.20	0.90	71–90
5	0.10	1.00	91–00

Daily Unloading Rate	Probability	Cumulative Probability	Random Number Interval
1	0.03	0.03	01–03
2	0.12	0.15	04–15
3	0.40	0.55	16–55
4	0.28	0.83	56–83
5	0.12	0.95	84–95
6	0.05	1.00	96–00

Day	Number Delayed	Ran Num	Daily Arrivals	Total to be Unloaded	Ran Num	Number Unloaded
1	—	37	2	2	69	2
2	0	77	4	4	84	4
3	0	13	0	0	12	0
4	0	10	0	0	94	0
5	0	02	0	0	51	0
6	0	18	1	1	36	1
7	0	31	2	2	17	2
8	0	19	1	1	02	1
9	0	32	2	2	15	2
10	0	85	4	4	29	3
11	1	31	2	3	16	3
12	0	94	5	5	52	3
13	2	81	4	6	56	4
14	2	43	2	4	43	3
15	1	31	2	3	26	3
	$\Sigma = 6$ total delays		$\Sigma = 31$ total arrivals			$\Sigma = 31$ total unloads

$$\text{Average number of barges delayed per day} = \frac{6}{15} = 0.4$$

$$\text{Average arrivals per day} = \frac{31}{15} = 2.07$$

$$\text{Average unloaded per day} = \frac{31}{15} = 2.07$$

The short time-span simulated (15 days) introduces volatility in both the daily arrival rate (from 2.73 arrivals per day in the original example to only 2.07 in this modified simulation). This, coupled with speedier unloading rate, produces a much lower average delay rate (from 1.33 per day down to only 0.4 per day).

Barge Simulation Postscript

- *Repeating Random Number Strings* should be used for generating arrival and unloading rates under both crew staffing options *if* you want to isolate and observe the impact of each option on the system. Accordingly, any differences found in unloading rates become directly attributable to crew size alone, since all other elements are held constant in the system.

- *Non-repeating Random Number Strings* should be used for generating arrival and unloading rates under both crew staffing options *if* you want to test for consistent results of the impact of each option on the system. To yield valid conclusions however, you must ensure that the simulation is run over a sufficiently long period of evenings, in order to allow the numbers to "settle down" to long-term averages (expected values).

- It should be obvious that even if we ran this simulation over dozens or hundreds of evenings, the crew of 12 longshoremen would still be more productive than a crew of 6. However, when costs are added to the problem, the outcome could be very different. For example, if barge traffic were only moderate over the long term, the labor costs and other fixed costs of supporting a crew of 12 may be unjustified. Some possible costs to be considered are:
  - opportunity costs (of barge delays)
  - labor costs (crew wages and fringe benefits)
  - workmens' compensation insurance (which would rise with crew size)
  - management and administrative costs
  - training and recruiting costs
  - facility under- and over-utilization costs
  - overtime pay, subcontracting, part-time pay

- In addition, the number of barge arrivals and their individual probabilities of occurrence could be affected by:
  - the season of the year (i.e., ice could reduce expected daily arrivals)
  - weather conditions each evening (i.e., rain, wind, humidity, fog) can affect unloading rates
  - competitors vying for the same barge business each evening
  - minimum and maximum staffing levels required by union contract negotiations and insurance regulations

All of these factors can be integrated into the simulation model to enhance its realism and accuracy.

- Sources of data for the arrival and unloading rates can be obtained from similar docks on rivers with similar barge traffic and weather conditions, etc.; industrial engineering studies on longshoremen done anywhere; insurance company accident statistics; local and regional wage data from chambers of commerce and government.

Generator Breakdown Simulation

TIME BETWEEN RECORDED MACHINE FAILURES (hours)	PROBABILITY	CUMULATIVE PROBABILITY	RANDOM NUMBER INTERVAL
½	.05	.05	01 - 05
1	.06	.11	06 - 11
1 ½	.16	.27	12 - 27
2	.33	.60	28 - 60
2 ½	.21	.81	61 - 81
3	.19	1.00	82 - 00
Σ	1.00		

Generator Breakdown Simulation

REPAIR TIME REQUIRED (HOURS) [a]	PROBABILITY	CUMULATIVE PROBABILITY	RANDOM NUMBER INTERVAL
1	.28	.28	01 - 28
2	.52	.80	29 - 80
3	.20	1.00	81 - 00
Total	1.00		

a – MAINTENANCE TIME IS ROUNDED TO HOURLY TIME BLOCKS

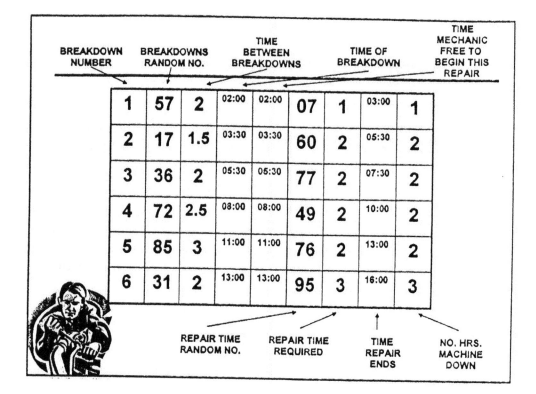

BREAKDOWN NUMBER	BREAKDOWNS RANDOM NO.		TIME BETWEEN BREAKDOWNS		TIME OF BREAKDOWN		TIME MECHANIC FREE TO BEGIN THIS REPAIR	
1	57	2	02:00 / 02:00		07	1	03:00	1
2	17	1.5	03:30 / 03:30		60	2	05:30	2
3	36	2	05:30 / 05:30		77	2	07:30	2
4	72	2.5	08:00 / 08:00		49	2	10:00	2
5	85	3	11:00 / 11:00		76	2	13:00	2
6	31	2	13:00 / 13:00		95	3	16:00	3

REPAIR TIME RANDOM NO.   REPAIR TIME REQUIRED   TIME REPAIR ENDS   NO. HRS. MACHINE DOWN

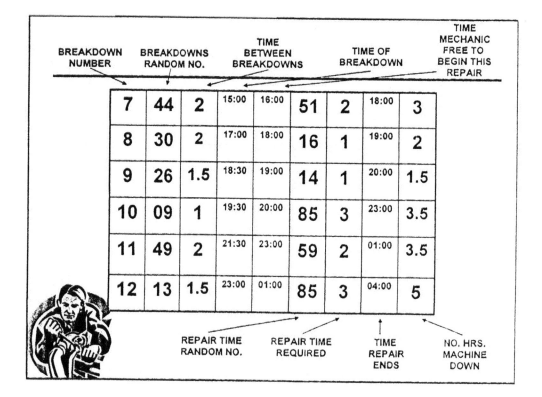

BREAKDOWN NUMBER	BREAKDOWNS RANDOM NO.		TIME BETWEEN BREAKDOWNS		TIME OF BREAKDOWN		TIME MECHANIC FREE TO BEGIN THIS REPAIR	
7	44	2	15:00 / 16:00		51	2	18:00	3
8	30	2	17:00 / 18:00		16	1	19:00	2
9	26	1.5	18:30 / 19:00		14	1	20:00	1.5
10	09	1	19:30 / 20:00		85	3	23:00	3.5
11	49	2	21:30 / 23:00		59	2	01:00	3.5
12	13	1.5	23:00 / 01:00		85	3	04:00	5

REPAIR TIME RANDOM NO.   REPAIR TIME REQUIRED   TIME REPAIR ENDS   NO. HRS. MACHINE DOWN

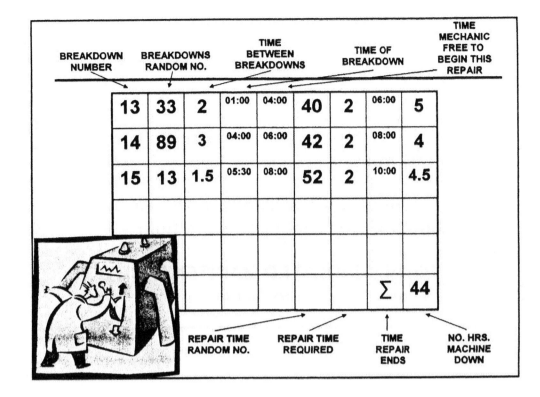

BREAKDOWN NUMBER	BREAKDOWNS RANDOM NO.	TIME BETWEEN BREAKDOWNS			TIME OF BREAKDOWN			TIME MECHANIC FREE TO BEGIN THIS REPAIR
13	33	2	01:00	04:00	40	2	06:00	5
14	89	3	04:00	06:00	42	2	08:00	4
15	13	1.5	05:30	08:00	52	2	10:00	4.5
							Σ	44

REPAIR TIME RANDOM NO. REPAIR TIME REQUIRED TIME REPAIR ENDS NO. HRS. MACHINE DOWN

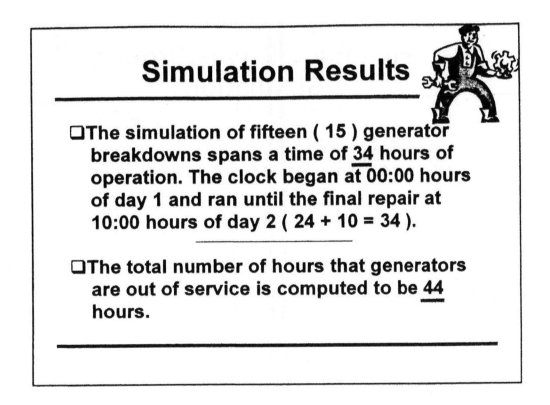

Simulation Results

☐ The simulation of fifteen (15) generator breakdowns spans a time of <u>34</u> hours of operation. The clock began at 00:00 hours of day 1 and ran until the final repair at 10:00 hours of day 2 (24 + 10 = 34).

☐ The total number of hours that generators are out of service is computed to be <u>44</u> hours.

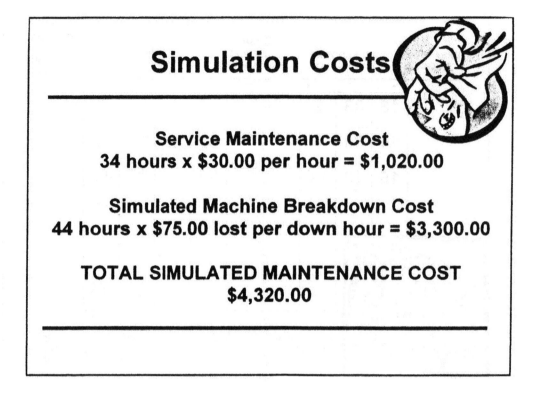

Simulation Costs

Service Maintenance Cost
34 hours x $30.00 per hour = $1,020.00

Simulated Machine Breakdown Cost
44 hours x $75.00 lost per down hour = $3,300.00

TOTAL SIMULATED MAINTENANCE COST
$4,320.00

Fast Food Drive-Through Simulation

ARRIVAL	RN for TIME between ARRIVALS	TIME BETWEEN ARRIVALS	TIME	RN for SERVICE TIME	SERVICE TIME	Waiting Time	CUSTOMER LEAVES
1st	14	1 min.	11:01	88	3 min.	0	11:04
2nd	74	3 min.	11:04	32	2 min.	0	11:06
3rd	27	2 min.	11:06	36	2 min.	0	11:08
4th	03	1 min.	11:07	24	1 min.	1	11:09

(ASSUME THE DRIVE-THROUGH OPENS AT 11:00 AM)

The Seven Steps Involved in Using Simulation

1. identify and clearly define the problem. This is often the most difficult and most important step.

2. identify and define the relevant variables.

3. construct the actual simulation model.

4. determine the alternative courses of action that are to be tested.

5. operate ("run") the simulation model under the alternative courses of action selected.

6. analyze the operational results.

7. reach a decision. Implement it if in a line position; recommend it if in a staff position.

Advantages of Simulation

A. Straightforwardness and flexibility make these models more understandable to managers.

B. Operations problems may be so complex that their mathematical solution is impractical.

C. There might not even be a mathematical model in existence for solving the problem.

D. Simulation models tend to draw the manager into the model creation thereby giving the manager a stake in the usage of the results.

E. Simulation models allow the testing of alternatives with great facility.

F. Elimination of the need to actually try alternatives on the real-world system or problem with potentially damaging results.

G. Time Compression: the ability to study the impact of alternatives on the system/problem over many "years" in just a few seconds of computer run time.

H. The probability distributions of the relevant variables do not have to follow any rigid set of model assumptions.

Disadvantages of Simulation

A. Model development may be expensive and time consuming for a complex problem where the relevant variables are difficult to clearly identify and their interrelationships with one another difficult to measure.

B. A model that yields reliable outcomes may not even be attainable unless a sufficient number of relevant variables were first identified.

C. While most quantitative models yield an optimal solution, simulation only allows a comparison of the alternative courses of action conceived by the user. Many of those alternate courses of action may even be mediocre, with the simulation model selecting the "best" of them.

D. A complex problem or system recreation for solving a problem will require a considerable amount of managerial input. Such demand on the manager's time may be considered unacceptable.

E. When a simulation model has solved the immediate problem, it may very well serve no further useful purpose. Even related problems might require a very different simulation model for solution.

Chapter 6

Queuing Theory

Chapter 6 focuses on the use of queuing theory (the study of waiting lines) in balancing service provision costs and customer (people, products, vehicles, or machines) waiting costs.

A "queue" is the British and operations research term for a waiting line, and queuing theory is the study of waiting lines. The mathematical foundation of queuing theory was developed by Agner K. Erlang, a Danish mathematician who was searching for a solution to the telephone network congestion problems of the city of Copenhagen in 1917.

In recent years, the application of queuing theory in the service sector has proliferated as customers increasingly equate quality service with rapid service. In general, companies can reduce customer waiting time and provide faster service by adding more servers, i.e., more checkout clerks at a supermarket, or more tellers at a bank. However, this tactic has a cost, and therein lies the basis of queuing theory—the tradeoff between the cost of improved service and the cost of making customers wait, as illustrated below:

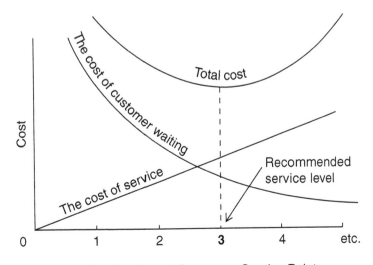

The Number of Servers or Service Points

As the level of service increases, the cost of service increases and the cost of customer waiting decreases. The sum of both costs is reflected in the total cost curve. The level of service that should be maintained is the level where the total cost curve is at a minimum.

A second, more detailed example of the cost tradeoff utilizing cost input from accounting, customer traffic input from marketing, and calculations from selected queuing formulas can assume the form of a spreadsheet indicating the recommended level of clerical staffing at a supermarket.

Problem: How many check out clerks should there be at a local supermarket?

Number of Customers	If Number of check out clerks is:			
	"1" 300	"2" 300	"3" 300	"4" 300
Average waiting time/ customer	$\frac{1}{6}$ hour (10 minutes)	$\frac{1}{10}$ hour (6 minutes)	$\frac{1}{15}$ hour (4 minutes)	$\frac{1}{20}$ hour (3 minutes)
Total customer waiting time	50 hours	30 hours	20 hours	15 hours
Cost per waiting hour	$5	$5	$5	$5
Total waiting costs	$250	$150	$100	$75
Check out clerk hourly salary	$4	$4	$4	$4
Total pay of clerks for 8 hour shift	$32	$64	$96	$128
Total expected cost	$282	$214	$196	$203

computed from queuing formulas when the average customer arrival rate and average customer service rate are known.

Optimal number of check out clerks on duty = 3
(at this staffing level, the total costs of customer waiting time and customer service are minimized).

As the previous example shows, waiting line characteristics input from operations, cost input from accounting/finance, and customer traffic inputs from marketing can eventually be combined to develop a spreadsheet indicating the optimal balance between service provision and customer waiting costs.

Service Provision Costs

- depreciation and maintenance costs associated with service points such as toll-booths, check-out counters, bank teller windows.

- cost of direct labor required to staff service points.

- cost of labor fringe benefits.

Customer Waiting Costs

- employee non-productive time as a result of waiting for materials deliveries, processing machines, or tools.

- the value of a customer's own time at home or at work.

- lost customer patronage (revenues) due to fewer or no return trips to the service facility.

- negative comments made to relatives and friends by customers, resulting in additional lost patronage (revenues).

However, the accumulation of the basic data for the queuing formulas and adherence to their rigid assumptions, are the most daunting tasks facing a manager and staff, and particularly those in the operations function.

The queuing system consists of three major elements:

1. *System arrivals*

   Arrivals come from a source called the "calling population." In the vast majority of queuing problems:

   a. the calling population is of infinite size; theoretically, any person or any item in the world can enter your service facility during operating hours.

   b. arrivals from the calling population are random and independent. Customers, for example, would enter a restaurant in parties of one, two, three, or more people who do not know one another, and enter on a staggered time basis.

   c. the pattern of arrivals is assumed to be Poisson-distributed, based on practical experience and extensive research. However, it must be confirmed by formal observation and statistical analysis (Chi-square goodness-of-fit test). An example of a Poisson probability distribution is shown below:

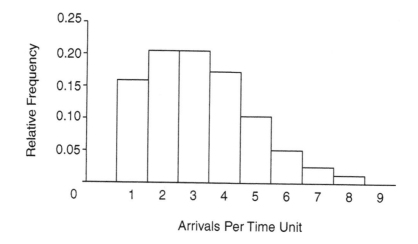

d. arrivals enter the facility at a constant average rate. Lambda (λ) is the symbol for the average arrival rate which is usually expressed in terms of the number of arrivals per hour to the facility.

Lambda is also the symbol of the estimated mean of a Poisson probability distribution. It is extremely important that the observed average hourly arrival rate (lambda) be statistically identical with the estimated mean of the particular Poisson arrival probability distribution observed. If the two lambda values differ, additional, more careful observations would need to be made. If the two lambda values continued to differ, the application of queuing theory would need to be abandoned in favor of computer-based simulation modeling.

Developing an accurate arrival rate can be difficult in a facility with surging and ebbing arrival rates, based on time of day. For example, fast food restaurants experience heavy demand during breakfast, lunch, and dinner, but very little demand in between. This might suggest the use of two separate queuing analyses: one for busy periods, and one for slow periods.

e. "queue discipline" must be maintained by arrivals into the service system. This means no balking, reneging, or jockeying will be tolerated.

(1) "balking" is the refusal of an arrival to join a waiting line, especially when that line is very long.

(2) "reneging" is the leaving of one's place in line before being served, especially when one has been waiting a very long time and the waiting line doesn't seem to be moving.

(3) "jockeying" is the act of joining a waiting line and then later crossing over to another waiting line that seems shorter or appears to be moving faster.

The Relationship Between Waiting Lines and Overall Facility Capacity

Waiting lines form because people or items arrive at the service facility faster than they can be served. This does not mean however, that the service facility is understaffed or does not have the overall capacity to handle the influx of arrivals. Waiting lines result because customers do not arrive at a constant, evenly-paced rate, nor are they all served in an equal amount of time. Thus, a waiting line is continually increasing or decreasing in length (and is sometimes empty), and approaches an average rate of arrivals and service time in the long run.

Decisions associated with waiting lines and their management are based on the above averages for arrivals and service times (mu and lambda). They are used in the queuing formulas to compute operating characteristics such as the average number of customers waiting in line, and the average time a customer must wait in line.

The Single-Channel, Single-Phase Model

A. *The SINGLE-CHANNEL/SINGLE-PHASE* or "Single-Server" system is the simplest form. It assumes an infinite calling population, a first-come, first-served queue discipline, a Poisson arrival rate, and negative exponential service times. Its operating characteristics are computed as follows:

a. the average number of customers in the system (where "system" is defined as all those who are being served *and* waiting to be served):

$$L = \frac{\lambda}{\mu - \lambda}$$

b. the average number of customers in the queue (only those who are waiting to be served):

$$Lq = \frac{\lambda^2}{\mu(\mu - \lambda)}$$

c. the average time a customer spends in the system (combined time waiting for service and receiving service):

$$W = \frac{1}{\mu - \lambda}$$

d. the average waiting time in the queue (only that time waiting for service):

$$Wq = \frac{\lambda}{\mu(\mu - \lambda)}$$

e. the percentage of time the service facility is utilized or "busy" (*at least* one customer or item in it):

$$\rho \ (\text{"Rho"}) = \frac{\lambda}{\mu}$$

f. the percentage of time the service system is idle (no customers or items):

$$P_0 = (1 - \rho) \ \text{ or } \ 1 - \left(\frac{\lambda}{\mu}\right)$$

g. the probability that there are more than "K" customers in the service system:

$$P(n > K) = \left(\frac{\lambda}{\mu}\right)^{K + 1}$$

Application Example

A store with one (1) check-out clerk on duty can serve thirty ($\mu = 30$) customers per hour on the average, but only gets twenty ($\lambda = 20$) customers per hour on the average. What are this system's operating characteristics?

a. $L = \dfrac{\lambda}{\mu - \lambda} = \dfrac{20}{30 - 20} = 2$ customers in the checkout area of the store on average.

b. $Lq = \dfrac{\lambda^2}{\mu(\mu - \lambda)} = \dfrac{20^2}{30(30 - 20)} = 1.33$ customers waiting in line to be served on average.

c. $W = \dfrac{1}{\mu - \lambda} = \dfrac{1}{30 - 20} = .10$ hours or 6 minutes that the average customer spends in the checkout area of the store (does *not* include shopping time)

d. $Wq = \dfrac{\lambda}{\mu(\mu - \lambda)} = \dfrac{20}{30(30 - 20)} = \dfrac{1}{15}$ hours or 4 minutes that the average time customer spends just waiting in line for service.

e. $\rho = \dfrac{\lambda}{\mu} = \dfrac{20}{30} = .67$ or 67% of the time, there's at least one customer in the checkout area of the store.

f. $P_0 = 1 - \dfrac{\lambda}{\mu} = (1 - \rho) = .33$ or 33% of the time, there are no customers in the checkout area of the store. In other words, the checkout clerk is idle.

g. the probability of more than "K" customers waiting in line or being served:

K	$P(n > K) = \left(\dfrac{\lambda}{\mu}\right)^{K+1}$
0	.667 or 66.7%
1	.444 or 44.4%
2	.296 or 29.6%
3	.198 or 19.8%

etc.

Multi-Channel Single-Phase Model

A line being serviced by more than one server. It assumes:

- An infinite calling population.
- A first-come, first-served queue discipline.
- A Poisson distribution arrival rate.
- Negative exponential service times.
- Additional parameters are:

(handwritten margin: $\sum^{\infty} \sum_{n=0} \sum_0$)

M = the number of servers or channels

Mμ = the mean effective service rate for the service facility

The operating characteristics are computed as follows:
  a. the probability that the service facility is idle:

(handwritten: upper limit / lower starting limit)

$$P_0 = \frac{1}{\left[\sum_{n=0}^{n=M-1} \frac{1}{n!}\left(\frac{\lambda}{\mu}\right)^n\right] + \frac{1}{M!}\left(\frac{\lambda}{\mu}\right)^M\left(\frac{M\mu}{M\mu - \lambda}\right)}$$

  b. the average number of customers in the system:

$$L = \frac{\lambda\mu\left(\frac{\lambda}{\mu}\right)^M}{(M-1)!\left(M\mu - \lambda\right)^2} \cdot P_0 + \frac{\lambda}{\mu}$$

  c. the average number of customers in the queue:

$$Lq = L - \frac{\lambda}{\mu}$$

  d. the average time a customer spends in the system:

$$W = \frac{L}{\lambda}$$

  e. the average waiting time in the queue:

$$Wq = W - \frac{1}{\mu} = \frac{Lq}{\lambda}$$

  f. the probability that a customer arriving in the system must wait for service (i.e., the probability that all the servers are busy) is:

$$Pw = \frac{1}{M!}\left(\frac{\lambda}{\mu}\right)^M \cdot \frac{M\mu}{M\mu - \lambda} \cdot P_0$$

Application Example

A bank has three (3) loan officers on duty, each of whom can serve four (4) customers per hour. Every hour, ten (10) loan applicants arrive at the loan department and join a common queue. What are the system's operating characteristics?

(handwritten margin: 3 loan officers = M / 4 cost/hr = μ / Mμ = 12 / λ = arrival rate = 10)

  a. $P_0 = \dfrac{1}{\left[\frac{1}{0!}\left(\frac{10}{4}\right)^0 + \frac{1}{1!}\left(\frac{10}{4}\right)^1 + \frac{1}{2!}\left(\frac{10}{4}\right)^2\right] + \frac{1}{3!} \cdot \left(\frac{10}{4}\right)^3 \cdot \left(\frac{3(4)}{3(4) - 10}\right)}$

  = .045 probability that no customers are in the loan department.

b. $L = \dfrac{(10)(4)\left(\dfrac{10}{4}\right)^3}{(3-1)!\left[3(4)-10\right]^2} \cdot (.045) + \dfrac{10}{4} = 6$ customers on the average in the loan department.

c. $Lq = 6 - \dfrac{10}{4} = 3.5$ customers on the average, waiting to be served.

d. $W = \dfrac{6}{10} = .60$ hours (36 minutes) average time in the loan department per customer.

e. $Wq = \dfrac{3.5}{10} = .35$ hours (21 minutes) average time waiting in line per customer.

f. $P\omega = \dfrac{1}{3!}\left(\dfrac{10}{4}\right)^3 \cdot \dfrac{3(4)}{3(4)-10} \cdot (.045) = .703$ or 70.3% probability that a customer must wait for service (i.e., that there are 3 or more customers in the loan department).

Summary of the Loan Department Operating Characteristics

- There is a 4.5% probability that no customers are in the loan department.
- There are six (6) customers on the average in the loan department.
- There are 3.50 customers on the average just waiting to be served.
- The average time spent per customer in the loan department is 36 minutes.
- The average time spent per customer in the loan department just waiting in line is 21 minutes.
- The probability that a customer must wait for service when they arrive is 70.3%.
- The probability that there are 3 or more customers in the loan department is 70.3% as well.

Decision-Making Implications from the Above Statements

Loan applicants must certainly be frustrated with the 21 minute wait and the 70% chance of waiting. If the bank were to add a fourth (4th) loan officer to the department, the average wait time would drop to just 3 minutes with only a 30% chance of waiting at all. The bank would need to consider the expense of the additional loan officer against the dramatic decrease in loan applicant waiting time (and waiting cost) in making a decision.

Undefined and Constant Service Time Model

Sometimes, it cannot be assumed that a waiting line system has an arrival rate that is Poisson-distributed, or service times that are negative-exponentially-distributed. For example, many manufacturing operations use automated equipment or robots that have constant (uniform) or undefined service times. The basic formulas for this system's operating characteristics are as follows:

a. $P_0 = 1 - \left(\dfrac{\lambda}{\mu}\right)$

b. $Lq = \dfrac{\lambda^2\sigma^2 + \left(\dfrac{\lambda}{\mu}\right)^2}{2\left(1 - \dfrac{\lambda}{\mu}\right)}$

c. $L = Lq + \left(\dfrac{\lambda}{\mu}\right)$

d. $Wq = \dfrac{Lq}{\lambda}$

e. $W = Wq + \left(\dfrac{1}{\mu}\right)$

f. $\rho = \dfrac{\lambda}{\mu}$

The key formula is "Lq" where μ and σ are the mean and standard deviation respectively for any general probability distribution with independent service times.

Application Example

A firm has one (1) copy machine which employees use randomly at an average of twenty (20) employees per hour. The time each employee uses the machine has a mean (μ) of two (2) minutes and a standard deviation (σ) of four (4) minutes. The operating characteristics of this system are as follows:

a. The probability that nobody is using the machine:

$$P_o = 1 - 20/30 = .33 \text{ or } 33\%$$

b. The number of employees waiting in line:

$$Lq = \dfrac{(20)^2\left(\dfrac{1}{15}\right)^2 + \left(\dfrac{20}{30}\right)^2}{2\left(1 - \dfrac{20}{30}\right)} = 3.33$$

Note: the standard deviation is 4 minutes or 1/15th of an hour.

c. Employees in line and employees using the machine (total number):

$$L = 3.33 + (20/30) = 4.0$$

d. Average wait in line:

$$Wq = 3.33/20 = .1665 \text{ hours} = 10 \text{ minutes}$$

e. Average time spent in the copy machine area:

$$W = .1665 + (1/30) = .1998 \text{ hours} = 12 \text{ minutes}$$

f. copy machine utilization:

$$\rho = 20/30 = .67 \text{ or } 67\%$$

Finite Calling Population Model

When there is a limited population of potential customers for a service facility, we need to consider a different queuing model. This model would be used, for example, if you were considering equipment repairs in a factory that has five (5) machines, or if you ran a hospital ward with twenty (20) beds. The model permits any number of servers to be considered.

The reason this model differs from others is that there is now a dependent relationship between the length of the queue and the arrival rate. That is, as the waiting line becomes longer, the arrival rate of customers or items into the system drops lower and lower. To illustrate, suppose a factory had five machines and all of them were broken and awaiting repair. In that case, the arrival rate would drop to ZERO!

This particular model has the following assumptions:

- The calling population, of course, is finite.

- Arrivals follow a Poisson distribution.

- Service times are exponentially distributed.

- Customers or items are served on a first-come, first-served basis.

- Here, there is only one (1) server.

- An additional parameter is introduced: N = size of the finite population.

Applications Example

A shop has fifteen (15) machines which are repaired in the same order in which they fail. The machines fail according to a Poisson distribution and service times are exponentially distributed. One (1) mechanic is on-duty. A machine fails, on average, every forty (40) hours. The average repair takes 3.6 hours.

$$N = 15 \text{ machines}$$

$$\lambda = 1/40\text{th of a machine per hour} = .0250 \text{ machines per hour}$$

$$\mu = 1/3.6\text{th of a machine per hour} = .2778 \text{ machines per hour}$$

$$P_0 = \frac{1}{\sum_{n=0}^{N} \frac{N!}{(N-n)!} \left(\frac{\lambda}{\mu}\right)^n} = \frac{1}{\sum_{n=0}^{15} \frac{15!}{(15-n)!} \left(\frac{.0250}{.2778}\right)^n}$$

$$P_0 = .0616 \ (\% \ \text{idle time})$$

$$Lq = N - \left[\frac{\lambda + \mu}{\lambda}(1 - P_0)\right] = 15 - \left[\frac{.0250 + .2778}{.0250}(1 - .0616)\right]$$

$$= 3.63 \ \text{machines waiting}$$

$$L = Lq + (1 - P_0) = 3.63 + (1 - .0616)$$

$$= 4.57 \ \text{machines in the system}$$

$$Wq = \frac{Lq}{(N-L)\lambda} = \frac{3.63}{(15 - 4.57)(.0250)}$$

$$= 13.94 \ \text{hrs. waiting for repair}$$

$$W = Wq + \frac{1}{\mu} = 13.94 + \frac{1}{.2778}$$

$$= 17.54 \ \text{hrs. in the system}$$

Summary of Shop Operating Characteristics

- The mechanic is idle, on the average, 6.16% of the time.
- There are, on average, 3.63 machines broken and awaiting repairs.
- There are, on average, 4.57 machines "out of service" (both waiting for repairs and/or being repaired).
- The average broken machine spends 13.94 hours just waiting for repairs.
- The average broken machine spends 17.54 hours "out of service."

Decision-Making Implications

The mechanic is busy 94% of the time repairing machines. This infers that there is very little time available for preventative maintenance or safety inspections! Of the fifteen (15) machines, an average of 4.57 or 30% are broken down, waiting for repair or under repair. Each broken down machine is idle, on average, 17.54 hours (or over two entire working days). The firm cannot afford to tolerate this situation. A second mechanic is probably necessary. However, a cost tradeoff analysis should be done first. That said, two days of lost machine productivity—which can never be recouped—is probably worth more than a second mechanic's salary!

In actual practice, operations staff can usually avoid tedious hand-calculations by accessing standard reference tables for queue characteristics. The only data required are the system's single-channel utilization rate* (rho) and the actual number of channels (M) in the system.

---

*The single-channel utilization rate is used, *regardless* of the actual number of channels existing within the service system.

Queuing Theory Behavioral Considerations

Most textbooks on queuing theory focus exclusively on the mathematical and cost aspects. Unfortunately, the time and cost of waiting may not be the only, or even significant yardsticks of customer aggravation.

- For many services, customers have some threshold of waiting. For waiting times below this threshold, aggravation is small and increases slowly. For waiting times above this threshold, aggravation increases rapidly. For example, a person may be very patient while waiting for tax return assistance, but very impatient while waiting to get gasoline for a car. In both cases, once the threshold is reached, customers may cease to patronize the firm for good. Similarly, a 10-minute response time to a house fire may result in five (5) times more damage than a 5-minute response time. It would therefore be absurd to compare response systems solely on the basis of average response time.

- Willingness to wait is higher if customers know that other customers are waiting their turn.

- Willingness to wait is a function of what is perceived to be reasonable. Someone who only wants to buy a can of soup at the grocery store does not expect to wait as long as someone with a full shopping cart.

- If customers are kept busy doing other things like filling in surveys, or required forms, or being entertained, their waiting may not be construed as wasted time.

- Waiting lines that are always moving are perceived as less painful than ones that are not.

- Accurate information on expected waiting time allows customers to adjust their expectations and hence reduce their aggravation.

- Customers should be allowed to perform the services that they can easily provide for themselves. Many people willingly pump their own gasoline, check their account balances via touch-tone telephone systems, and fill their own beverage cups at fast-food restaurants, in order to speed up service.

- Customers should be rewarded with discounts or gifts if they must wait in the queue beyond a certain period of time. It shows customers that the firm values their time, and is willing to pay them for it if the wait is too long.

The queuing process consists of two major aspects:

1. *The queue itself*

   The vast majority of queuing formulas are based upon the assumption that the queue may have unlimited length.

   a. the queue may consist of arrivals that entered on a "first-come, first-serve" (FCFS) basis (alias "first-in, first-out" FIFO).

   b. the queue may also consist of arrivals that entered on a "last-in, first serve" basis (although this would not be recommended for lines consisting of people!).

   c. no "crashing" of the queue by VIPs, celebrities, etc. is permitted. The formulas are invalid when a priority system is employed that correlates with serving time.

2. *The service facility*

   Two major subsets:

   A. *Its Configuration*

the service facility must be based on a combination of "channels" and "phases."

(1) *channel*: a service point or facility

(2) *phases*: the number of service points that must be encountered before a customer may leave the facility.

Example

(a) If a single line of students were waiting to be registered for courses at one table, the configuration would be a SINGLE-CHANNEL, SINGLE-PHASE one.

(b) If a single line of students were waiting to be registered for courses at two registration tables, the configuration would be a DUAL-CHANNEL, SINGLE-PHASE one.

(c) If a single line of students were waiting to be registered for courses at two registration tables, each with two additional tables behind them for additional administrative requirements such as parking permits and activity fees, the configuration would be a DUAL-CHANNEL, TRIPLE-PHASE one.

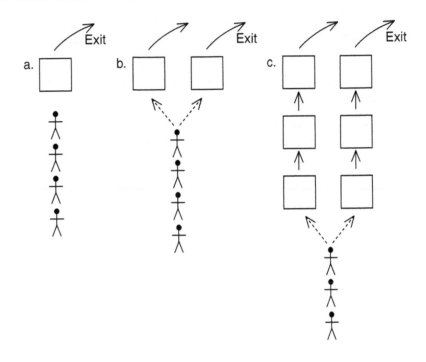

(d) The number of channels and phases that a service facility possesses is critical in determining the precise queuing formulas that must be used. Currently, queuing formulas exist for any combination of eight channels and/or eight phases. If a service facility possesses more channels and/or phases than current formulas can accommodate, computer-based simulation modeling must be employed to determine waiting line operating characteristics.

B. *The Service Facility's Service Times*

a. service times per customer may be exact.

b. service times per customer may also follow a negative exponential probability distribution. It would be advisable to clock some service times and determine if they follow this distribution (or any distribution with the same general characteristics).

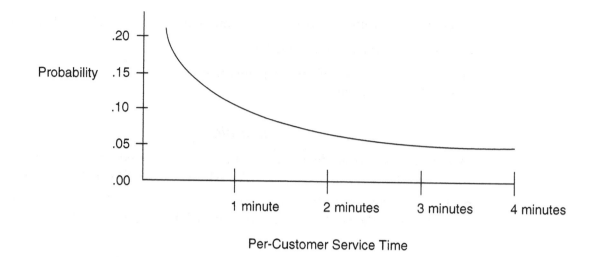

Per-Customer Service Time

Example of a Service Time Negative Exponential Distribution

(denotes that the chances of serving a customer's needs within one minute or less are very high, and that almost all customers' needs can be served within two minutes or less)

    c. service time must also have a known average rate. Mu (μ) is the symbol for the average service time which is usually expressed in terms of the number of customers (arrivals) served per hour.

    d. the average service rate (μ) must always exceed the average arrival rate (λ). Otherwise the queue would grow to infinity ($\mu > \lambda$).

P

A

R

T

3

Strategic Decisions in P/OM

Chapter 7

Process Strategy

Chapter 7 discusses the manufacturing spectrum which embraces all types of manufacturing processes (and parallel service sector processes as well).

When most people think of manufacturing, they envision an assembly line of sorts with a constant stream of automobiles, appliances, or toys emanating from it. This type of manufacturing however, accounts for no more than 25% of total manufacturing activity. In reality, products can range from hand-crafted, one-of-a-kind items such as heirloom furniture, to barrels of refined petroleum, with very different processes, equipment, and labor involved.

It is vitally important for a company to identify its position on what is called the "manufacturing spectrum," so that it can make intelligent and coordinated decisions in regard to equipment selection, labor selection and training, process layout, production planning and scheduling. Similar benefits will also accrue to service sector companies whose activities parallel the manufacturing spectrum.

A Process Layout Example

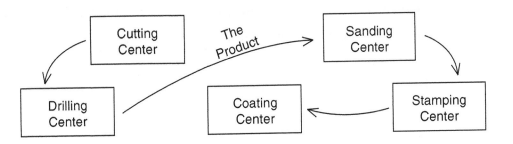

Intermittent Flow Operations (or "Job Shop" Operations) can only take place within a PROCESS LAYOUT. Here, major manufacturing processes are segregated into work centers, each with its own specially-trained workers, dedicated equipment, and supplies. Every product (or batch of products) requiring "cutting" work, for example, must physically be moved to the cutting work center. The product will then be moved to whatever other centers are required to complete it. Each product or batch of products will have its own unique moving sequence (or "route") through the process layout. Even within the same product batch, individual products may need to be routed through the same work center several times before they can meet the firm's quality standards.

Process Layout Examples

| –tool and die shop | –custom furniture shop | –any repair shop |
| –hospital | –physician's office | –university |

Characteristics:

- low product volume
- large product mix (heterogeneous)
- products made-to-order
- general-purpose equipment
- labor-intensive operations
- interrupted product flow
- work flows not standardized (even for the same product)
- varying rates of output
- low productivity per-square foot (due to large WIP inventory and frequent underutilization of some machines and equipment)
- frequent schedule changes
- skilled craftsmen with high flexibility
- no close management supervision
- support staff must possess highly-developed skills for:
  1. scheduling and expediting
  2. materials handling
  3. production and inventory control
- materials handling varies by type and volume
- duplication of handling due to waits between operations or shortages
- low turnover of raw materials and work-in-process inventories
- relatively LOW Fixed Costs
- relatively HIGH Direct Labor and Direct Materials Costs
- HIGH material handling costs
- work centers grouped together by function (department)
- similar machines are grouped together

The Manufacturing Process Spectrum

Job Shop (Intermittent Flow Opns)	Batch Flow	Worker-Paced Line-Flow / Machine-Paced Line-Flow (Repetitive Flow Opns)	Mass Production (Continuous Flow Opns)

Job Shop / Batch Flow (Intermittent Flow Opns)

- occurs within a PROCESS LAYOUT
- examples: machine tool shop, furniture shop
- much variety (heterogeneous product mix)
- low volume
- custom-made (one or few units)
- WIP inventory moved by people
- estimated job costing
- highly-trained labor (highly paid)
- low equip. utilization
- high inventories of raw materials (always "leftovers")
- worker is at a functional work center, processing many types of products
- very complex planning, scheduling, and executing
- this is "true manufacturing" since it is conversion of a raw material into a good, i.e., ore into steel; oil into gasoline and plastics; wood into furniture; stones into gems
- very slow WIP movement (months, possibly "years") caused by long lines of different jobs waiting to be processed at each work center

Worker-Paced Line-Flow / Machine-Paced Line-Flow (Repetitive Flow Opns)

- examples: appliances, engines
- others: standard-fare "fast-food" restaurants
- some worker training
- product movement is in hours and days
- WIP is moved by conveyor belts
- product made to forecast (week or month)
- JIT systems reduce inventory to near zero
- costs are known in advance
- workers are able to shift over from one product to another product with similar parts and technology, on the same production line
- this is *not* true manufacturing, but merely the assembly of pre-made parts, frequently ordered from an outside vendor

Mass Production (Continuous Flow Opns)

- examples: chemical refinery and paper mill
- takes place in a PRODUCT LAYOUT
- no product variety (or very little homogeneous product mix)
- high product volume
- less skill and training
- low raw materials
- made to stock (monthly, quarterly)
- made to intermediate forecast
- swift product movement through the process (in minutes and hours)
- WIP inventory travels by pipeline and fast chutes
- costs depend on capacity utilization
- worker is at a work station processing a very small part of the product
- also represents "true manufacturing," i.e., conversion of raw materials into goods
- only stops for scheduled maintenance and accidents

A Product Layout Example

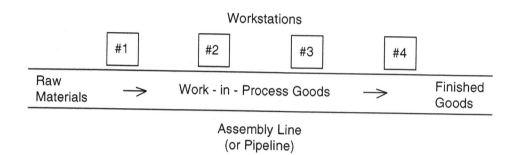

Workstations

| #1 | #2 | #3 | #4 |

Raw Materials → Work - in - Process Goods → Finished Goods

Assembly Line
(or Pipeline)

Continuous Flow Operations (some worker-paced line flow, all machine-paced line flow, and all mass production operations) take place only within a PRODUCT LAYOUT. Here, all raw materials and/or pre-made parts enter an assembly line (or pipeline) and leave as assembled or manufactured goods. The same assembly line is utilized by all of the firm's product offerings. Workstations scattered along the assembly line employ workers, computers, robots, or a mix of all three. Each workstation has a specialized role in product build-up.

Examples

–automobile assembly plant   –oil/chemical refinery   –bottling plant

–automatic car wash   –physical examinations for military recruits

Characteristics:

• high product volume

• small product mix (homogeneous)

• standardized products made-to-stock

• special-purpose equipment (dedicated)

• capital-intensive operations

• uninterrupted product flow

• same sequence of operations on each product (95% of time)

• stable rates of output

• straight-line product flow

• high productivity per square foot

• few schedule changes

• labor performs routine, repetitive tasks at machine-imposed rate

• labor tasks (jobs) have highly-specialized work content

• support staff is large and indirect:

  1. schedules the inputs of labor and materials into the system

  2. performs work and value analysis; capital budgeting, etc.

  3. performs scheduled and non-scheduled maintenance

- material flows are predictable, systematized, and often automated

- high turnover of raw materials and work-in-process inventories

- relatively HIGH fixed costs

- relatively LOW Direct Labor and Direct Materials costs due to economies of scale

Fixed Position Layout (A Specialized Layout)

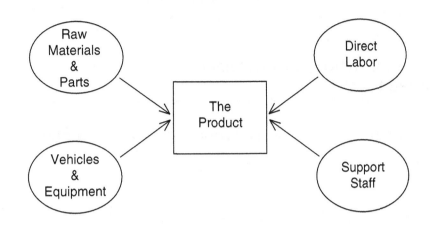

A third major type of layout is FIXED-POSITION. It does not represent any particular manufacturing operation. It is employed whenever it is not feasible to move the product due to its size, handling characteristics, weight, shape, or nature. All necessary resources are brought to the product build-up site.

Examples

–highway construction   –farming   –shipbuilding

–skyscraper construction   –oil drilling   –homebuilding

                             –aircraft production

Characteristics:

- product remains in one location

- each unit of the product is unique

- little or no product flow

- low volume

- tools, equipment, and labor brought to the site as needed

- labor must possess high degree of task flexibility

- specific work assignments vary

- support staff must possess high scheduling and coordinating skills

- low materials handling (may require heavy-duty general-purpose handling equipment)

- general-purpose production equipment that is mobile

- the duration of the production cycle determines the velocity of inventory turnover
- rate of productivity is LOW (indoors) per-square foot
- rate of productivity is N/A (outdoors)
- relatively LOW Fixed Costs
- relatively HIGH Direct Labor and Direct Materials Costs
- if the product needs to be moved, giant overhead cranes or flat-bed trucks are employed
- labor must be cross-trained in many tasks. (an oil-rigger for example would probably be proficient in first-aid, cooking, drilling, repair).

Combination (or Hybrid) Layout Example (A Specialized Layout)

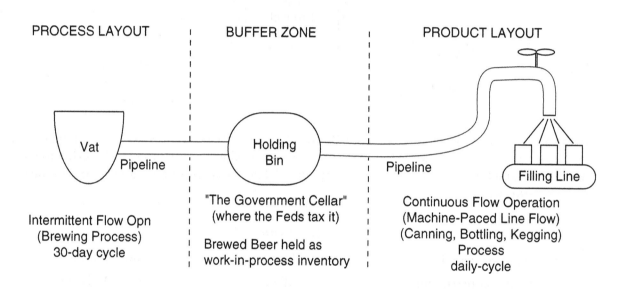

Although it is convenient to describe manufacturing operations in terms of "pure" layouts, the majority of those operations span two or more layouts, as can be seen in the above brewery example. Each "pure" layout must be physically separated from others via work-in-process inventories. This is necessary because each layout employs a very different planning and scheduling cycle, differently skilled employees, different management philosophies and practices, and different equipment. It almost goes without saying that the brewing operation in our example, would need to produce sufficient quantities of beer to sustain the canning/bottling operation for at least the next 30 days.

Work Cell (Group Technology) Layout (A Specialized Layout)

An increasingly popular successor to traditional process layout is the "work cell" or "group technology" layout. (see opposite chart). It involves the repositioning of major functional workcenters into workstations or cells along an assembly line.

Benefits:

1. the elimination of continual "back and forth" product or part trips between major work-centers, with their attendant waits in workcenter queues for hours, days, or weeks.

2. all major fabrication operations are done at once, providing greater and simplified control, as well as higher quality.

3. little or no idle time is experienced at the workcenters since all jobs are forced to take the same route through the job shop. Less idle time means better utilization of available machine capacity.

4. less work-in-process inventory in the shop at any given time means less materials handling which in turn, means higher quality, less shop clutter to mask operational problems, and better safety conditions.

5. Faster work-in-process inventory throughput means increased flexibility to changes in demand, lower costs, faster customer delivery, and increased productivity.

6. a more efficient collection of shop operating statistics due to a simpler data collection system.

7. the work cell arrangement forces the adoption of quicker set-up times between jobs, reduced tooling requirements, and reprogrammable robotics.

8. the elimination of substantial design and development costs through the integration of existing workcell-produced components into new products.

9. better cost reduction is possible via production of modular (interchangeable) parts for most or all existing products.

10. bulk material purchasing becomes possible with resulting quantity discounts. (Each work cell buys and receives its own materials direct.)

Additional Comments:

- group technology layouts can only be developed in job shop environments where all components, assemblies, and products share similar processing requirements, materials, shapes, and handling requirements.

- any special parts that demand unique setups, materials, shapes, and handling requirements can still be accommodated in one of three ways:

  1. via traditional process (job shop) layout maintained within a small portion of the shop.

  2. via scheduling such parts in the work cells, on a "space-and-time-available" basis.

  3. via subcontracting which may prove to be less expensive, since the subcontractor may specialize in their fabrication, or is able to combine similar orders from other customers for economies of scale.

- special parts fabrication may also be eliminated in a shop's production schedule by phasing out the products that contain them. In general, firms are tending toward production of rather limited product offerings to better serve (and dominate) specialized market segments.

Guidelines for Selecting the Appropriate Layout for the Firm

1. Estimate anticipated product volume over the immediate-, and long-term.

2. Consider the degree of product standardization in your current line of product offerings.

3. Consider the physical characteristics of your product offerings: their features, shared components, size, weight, handling characteristics.

4. Consider available alternative manufacturing technologies. Different technologies may call for different layouts as well.

5. Consider the availability of adequate short-term and long-term financial resources. Adequate funding permits a faster transition to continuous flow operations (product layout).

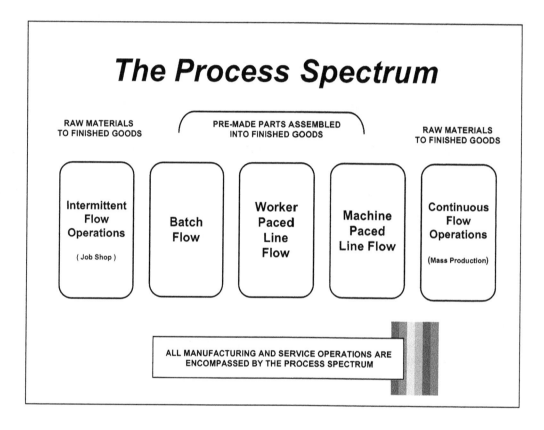

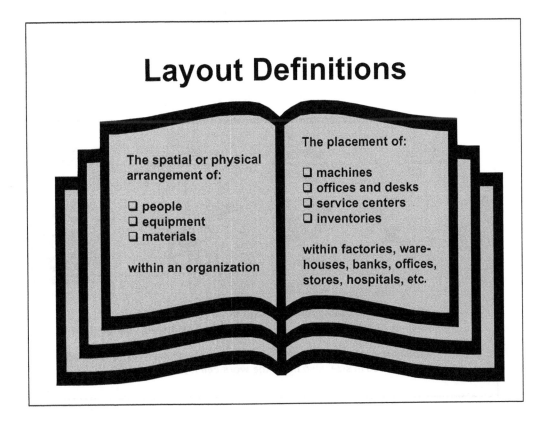

Layout Definitions

The spatial or physical arrangement of:

❑ people
❑ equipment
❑ materials

within an organization

The placement of:

❑ machines
❑ offices and desks
❑ service centers
❑ inventories

within factories, warehouses, banks, offices, stores, hospitals, etc.

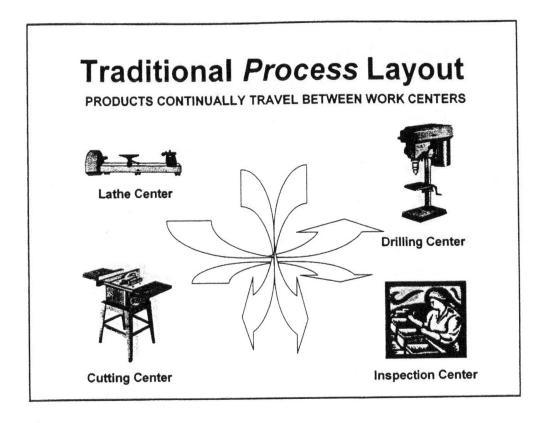

Traditional *Process* Layout

PRODUCTS CONTINUALLY TRAVEL BETWEEN WORK CENTERS

Lathe Center

Drilling Center

Cutting Center

Inspection Center

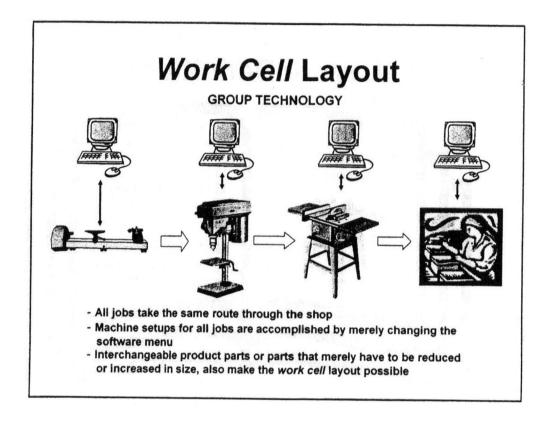

Other Layout Models/Techniques

Fixed Position Layout

As discussed in an earlier chapter, a fixed-position layout is one where the project remains in place while workers, materials, and equipment are brought to it. Examples are ships, highways, and buildings. Fixed-position layout techniques are not well developed and are complicated by three factors: limited space, the need for different materials at different construction stages, and the changing rate of material need.

Different industries address the above problems in different ways. The construction industry, for example, usually has a "meeting of the trades" to assign space for various time periods. Ship-yards have loading areas adjacent to the ship which are reserved for future material/equipment arrivals in a specified order by a master scheduling department.

Because problems with fixed-position layouts are so difficult to solve efficiently on-site, an alternate tact is to build as much of the project as possible off-site, on nearby assembly lines.

Warehouse Layout

The objective of a warehouse layout design is to find the optimum tradeoff between handling costs and warehouse space utilization. The greater the utilization of storage space, the greater the costs of moving and retrieving material, and vice-versa. Warehouse layout design also depends on the type of materials unloaded, what they are loaded from (i.e., trucks, ships), and where they are unloaded. In some firms, the receiving and shipping docks are the same, or receiving docks in the morning and shipping docks in the afternoon. There are three additional types of warehousing systems:

1. **Cross-Docking:**

   Labeled and pre-sorted loads are received directly at the dock for immediate rerouting, thereby eliminating formal receiving, stocking, and picking functions. Although cross-docking improves customer service and drastically reduces handling and carrying costs, it demands tight scheduling and accurate product identification, usually with bar codes.

2. **Random-Stocking:**

   The combination of automatic identification systems (usually in the form of barcoded inventories) and management information systems makes it possible to store and retrieve units anywhere in the warehouse on a random basis. This allows the potential utilization of the entire warehouse since space need not be reserved for each type of inventory. Random-stocking usually entails the following requirements:

   A. maintaining a list of available locations in the warehouse.

   B. maintaining accurate records of existing inventory and its locations.

   C. sequencing items on customer orders so as to minimize the travel time needed to "pick" those items.

   D. combining orders to reduce picking time.

   E. assigning certain items or classes of items to particular warehouse areas so that total distance traveled within the warehouse is minimized.

3. **Product-Customizing:**

   The additional use of warehouses for component assembly, customized labeling, packaging, and repairs. For example, a warehouse can put together customized computer systems from in-stock monitors, printers, CPUs, and software; package such systems for immediate retailer display; replace broken systems with repaired systems overnight; etc. This is a way of generating competitive advantage in markets with rapidly changing products. Increasingly, this type of work takes place adjacent to major airports in order to further lower costs and increase response.

Office Layout

Even though the movement of information is increasingly electronic, analyses of office layouts still requires a task-based approach. Managers must therefore examine both electronic and conventional communication patterns, separation needs, and other conditions affecting employee effectiveness. A useful tool is the Relationship Chart (or Proximity Chart) shown below. This chart indicates the relative importance of each combination of pairs.

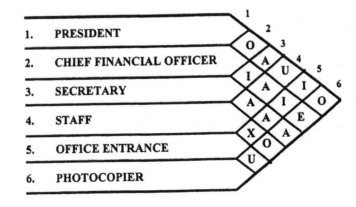

The chart is read in the same way as the mileage chart on a road map, except that letters rather than distances appear at the intersections. The letters represent the importance of closeness for each pair:

Code	Degree Of Importance
A	absolutely important
E	especially important
I	important
O	ordinary importance
U	unimportant
X	undesirable

In practice, the letters on the chart are often accompanied by numbers that indicate the reason for each assignment. For example:

1—the pair uses the same equipment or facilities

2—the pair share the same personnel or records

3—sequence of work flow

4—ease of communication

5—unsafe or unpleasant conditions

6—similar work performed

Input from analysts or managers is, of course, subjective and no optimizing algorithm exists, so trial-and-error alternatives must be developed and compared. Relationship charts are used when it is difficult to measure or estimate precise traffic flows or their costs among work centers. This is common when the primary flows involve people.

General office area guidelines suggest an average of one-hundred (100) square feet per person (including corridors). A major executive is allotted an average of four-hundred (400) square feet, and a conference room area is based on twenty-five (25) square feet per person up to thirty (30) people. Other layout considerations deal with working conditions, teamwork, authority, and status.

Capacity Planning
An Introduction

Managers are concerned about capacity planning for three reasons:

1. *They want sufficient capacity for meeting current demand*

   If demand exceeds capacity, the firm incurs "opportunity costs" in the form of lost revenues and profits.

   If capacity exceeds demand, the firm incurs the costs associated with excess inventories: carrying costs, taxes, obsolescence costs, finance charges.

2. *Available capacity affects operations efficiency*

   When the firm operates "below capacity," each produced unit must absorb more of the fixed overhead costs (administrative, utilities, depreciation, maintenance). *Result:* Higher product prices that run the risk of reduced market share.

When the firm operates "above capacity," each produced unit will also cost more and result in higher prices, due to:

- overtime labor rates
- sloppy quality control necessitating product rework or scrappage.
- soaring maintenance costs as equipment breakdowns caused by lapse preventative maintenance and overrunning occur.

3. *Capacity is an investment.*

Potential revenues and capacity costs must be carefully balanced if the firm seeks a good ROI (return on investment) or ROR (rate of return) on its operations.

$$\frac{\text{EBIT (earnings before taxes)}}{\text{Total Plant Investment}} \quad \frac{\$1,000,000}{\$10,000,000} = 10\% \text{ ROI}$$

but . . .

$$\frac{\$1,000,000}{\$5,000,000} = 20\% \text{ ROI}$$

. . . is better!

Definitions of Capacity

Design Capacity: the maximum output that can possibly be obtained. This "paper" capacity is under ideal conditions, and is not sustainable over time (*theoretical; no breakdowns, no worker fatigue, no mistakes, no late vendor deliveries*).

Effective Capacity: the maximum possible output given a product mix, scheduling difficulties, machine maintenance, quality factors, etc. It is always less than Design Capacity. Other factors affecting it are lunch and coffee breaks, and line-balancing problems (*built-in organizational constraints*).

Actual Output: the rate of output actually achieved. It cannot exceed Effective Capacity, and is often less than it, due to machine breakdowns, defective output, shortages of materials, absenteeism, and all factors beyond the control of a local manager's control (*daily random constraints*).

Measures of System Effectiveness

$$\text{Efficiency} = \frac{\text{Actual Output}}{\text{Effective Capacity}}$$

$$\frac{\text{Utilization}}{\text{(Effectiveness)}} = \frac{\text{Actual Output}}{\text{Design Capacity}}$$

It is quite common for managers to focus exclusively on efficiency.

Rated Capacity: The maximum usable capacity of a particular facility. It is always equal to, or less than "Design Capacity" (*a popular 4th type of capacity because it reflects how well (or how poorly) managers make use of the limited resources entrusted to them*).

It is equal to : (Design Capacity) × (Utilization) × (Efficiency)

Example: A firm's Design Capacity is always expressed as "1.00." If its utilization rate is 85% and its efficiency rate is 90%, then:

Rated Capacity = (1.00) (.85) (.90) = 76.5%★

★(rated capacity of 75% or more, is considered good)

The four definitions of capacity have been defined in general terms. In practice, every industry and firm has its own precise definition of each. Some major factors shaping capacity definition include:

- the number of shifts per work day

- the number of work days per week

- the number of hours per shift

The Measure of Capacity

The measure of capacity depends on the diversity of the product mix:

- when units produced are *identical,* the measure is "*units of output,*" i.e., tons of steel, number of vehicles, barrels of beer.

- when units produced are *diverse,* the measure is "*input measures,*" i.e., the number of attorneys in a law firm, available labor and/or machine hours in a tool and die shop (with hours being available per week, per month, or year). In a non-profit organization it would be funds available.

- *"Throughput" capacity* is the rate of input or output per time period, i.e., short-tons of cargo per day handled by a seaport, or 1,000,000 passengers per year serviced through Logan Airport.

Bottleneck Work Centers

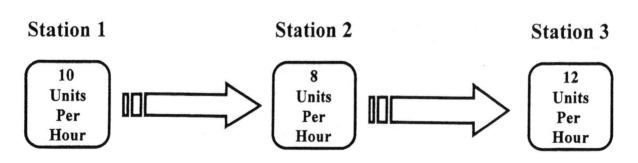

Station 2 is the bottleneck operation that limits overall capacity to 8 units per hour

Bottlenecks have less capacity than the prior or following work centers. They constrain throughput. Bottlenecks are a common occurrence because even well-designed systems are seldom balanced for very long. Changing products, product mixes, and volumes often create multiple and shifting bottlenecks. Consequently, bottleneck work centers occur in nearly all process-focused facilities, from hospitals and restaurants to factories. Successful operations managers deal with bottlenecks by increasing the bottleneck's capacity, rerouting work, changing production batch size, changing the work sequence, or accepting idleness at other work stations. Substantial research has been done on the issue.

To increase throughput, the bottleneck constraint must be maximized by imaginative management, well-trained employees, and a well-maintained process. Several techniques for dealing with the bottleneck are available:

- Increasing the capacity of the constraint. This may require a capital investment or more people, and take time to implement.

- Ensuring that well-trained and cross-trained employees are available to operate and maintain the work center causing the constraint.

- Developing alternate routings, processing procedures, or subcontractors.

- Moving inspections and tests to a position just before the bottleneck. This approach has the advantage of rejecting defects before they enter the bottleneck and add to the congestion.

The Process Flow Spectrum

	Project	Job Shop	Batch Process	Assembly Line	Continuous Flow
Flow	None	Jumbled	Disconnected & Dominant	Connected	Continuous
Flexibility	Very High	High	Moderate	Low	Very Low
Number of Products	Unique	Many	Several	Few	One
Capital Investment	Very Low	Low	Moderate	High	Very High
Variable Cost	Very High	High	Moderate	Low	Very Low
Labor Content	Very High	High	Moderate	Low	Very Low
Labor Skill	Very High	High	Moderate	Low	Very Low
Volume	One Unit	Low	Moderate	High	Very High

Capacity Modifications

Capital-Intensive Operations:

Long-Term: Essentially capacity is "fixed" over a one-year period. Then, you may add/delete "chunks" of capacity of up to 20%.

Short-Term: Temporary shutdowns or deletions of entire shifts during low demand. Around-the-clock operations during peak demand.

Labor-Intensive Operations:

During low demand periods, layoffs or the tolerating of idleness (so as to avoid layoffs and hard-to-find personnel).

During high demand periods, hirings and the paying of over-time pay to full-time workers.

Temporary or "Quick-Fix" Sources of Capacity

1. *Inventory:* stockpile finished goods during slow demand periods.

2. *Backlogs:* Appeal to the consumer to wait for the order to be completed after peak demand has passed.

3. *Work-Force Levels:* hire/fire in direct response to demand changes.

4. *Employee Training:* cross-train employees so that as skill requirements change throughout the organization, they can be rotated as needed (and not fired!).

5. *Process Design:* Perform work methods analysis to redesign the job contents at all work stations so as to increase productivity.

6. *Subcontract:* Allow (contract with) other firms to make the entire product or some of its parts during peak demand.

7. *Maintenance Deferral:* Temporarily discontinue routine, scheduled maintenance during peak demand periods, so that the facility can operate when it would have otherwise been idle.

8

Supply Chain Models

*C*hapter 8 looks at the major quantitative models used in locating new facilities within a firm's regional, national, or international distribution system.

Companies must frequently make location decisions for plants, warehouses, and retail outlets. When the planned facility is to have direct contact with the customer, decision responsibility usually falls to the MARKETING function. Here, revenues are considered more important than costs, and criteria such as customer convenience, high customer traffic exposure, and trading area "demographics" and "psycho-graphics" are closely evaluated.

When the planned facility is to have no direct contact with the customer (a warehouse, a factory, or the "back room" of a brokerage house) decision responsibility usually falls to the PRODUCTION/OPERATIONS function. Here, costs are considered more important than revenues, and criteria such as area workforce availability and skills, highway and rail access, favorable tax and regulatory climate, low land costs, and low utility rates are closely evaluated.

By far, the most important costs to be considered are those associated with transportation. They are beyond the direct control of production managers, yet represent the second largest influence on product pricing. It is not surprising then that most of the quantitative models developed for location decision-making, focus exclusively on the minimization of transportation costs.

The primary quantitative model used in location decisions is the Transportation Algorithm—a version of linear programming. This chapter is primarily devoted to its underlying assumptions, mechanics, and potential.

Facility Location Planning

Reasons for Location Changes:

- the need for additional capacity (i.e., sales may be increasing)

- changes in inputs may have occurred (i.e., the cost or location of labor, raw materials)

- shifts in geographical demand may have occurred

- mergers result in redundant facilities, some of which get phased out

- new product introductions may dictate location changes in order to economically reach new input resources and consumer markets

Unless local conditions have changed substantially, existing sites are favored because they are "known quantities." Many firms will expand or build nearby, especially smaller businesses that have been successful within their limited market area and have good but relatively few managers to assign to expanded territories.

Information Sources for Location Planning:

- local chambers of commerce

- Wall Street Journal

- trade publications

- Small Business Administration

- U.S. Census of Manufacturers

- Department of Commerce

- monographs*

*published pamphlets of states/countries breaking down, by city or town, such facts as:

- the tax base

- population characteristics

- major industries

- transportation network

- labor availabilities

- political structure

Where community reaction to firm's arrival is uncertain, Pilot Studies are recommended. Examples would be nuclear reactors, prisons, landfills, chemical plants.
Pilot studies accomplish two objectives:

1. assess community attitudes, and

2. develop strategies to gain acceptance if the above attitudes are negative.

When a few sites are equally attractive, *transportation costs* are pivotal in many industries. It is not surprising then, that the main focus of many quantitative models developed for location planning, are concerned with minimizing transportation costs.

The Gravity Location Model

- a mathematical technique used for finding the location of a distribution center that will minimize distribution costs.

- the method takes into account the location of markets, the volume of goods shipped to those markets, and shipping costs in finding the best location for a distribution center.

- the "center of gravity" is the best location for a single distribution point that services several stores or areas. It is determined by the following equations:

$$Cx = \frac{\sum dix\ Wi}{\sum Wi}$$

$$Cy = \frac{\sum diy\ Wi}{\sum Wi}$$

Cx = "x" coordinate of the center of gravity

Cy = "y" coordinate of the center of gravity

dix = "x" coordinate of location "i"

diy = "y" coordinate of location "i"

Wi = volume of goods moved to or from location "i"

Since the number of containers shipped each month affects cost, distance alone should not be the principal criterion. Fortunately, however, the simple median model assumes that shipping cost is directly proportional to both distance and volume shipped. The ideal location is that which minimizes the weighted distance between the distribution center and its retail outlets, where the distance is weighted by the number of containers shipped.

Example

A retail chain has six (6) locations which are now being supplied out of an old and inadequate warehouse located on the site of the chain's first store. Data on demand rates at each outlet are shown below:

Store Location	Monthly Number of Containers Shipped
Cincinnati	400
Knoxville	300
Chicago	200
Pittsburgh	100
New York	300
Atlanta	100

Requirement

1. Identify via "x" and "y" coordinates, the central location for the new warehouse.

Solution

We place the retail locations on a coordinate system. The origin of the coordinate system and the scale used are arbitrary, just as long as the relative distances are correctly represented. This can be done easily by placing a grid over an ordinary map as shown below:

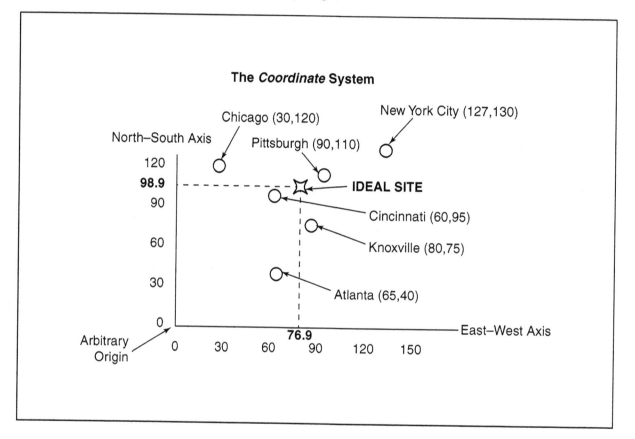

From the coordinate system, assuming that Cincinnati is location #1, we have:

$$d_{1x} = 60$$
$$d_{1y} = 95$$
$$W_1 = 400$$

From the coordinate system, assuming that Knoxville is location #2, we have:

$$d_{2x} = 80$$
$$d_{2y} = 75$$
$$W_2 = 300$$

and so on.

Using the data from the coordinate system and the retail outlet demand rate table, we find the "x" and "y" coordinates for the ideal warehouse site:

$$C_x = \frac{(60)(400) + (80)(300) + (30)(200) + (90)(100) + (127)(300) + (65)(100)}{400 + 300 + 200 + 100 + 300 + 100} = \frac{107,600}{1,400} = 76.9$$

Cincinnati   Knoxville   Chicago   Pittsburgh   New York   Atlanta

$$C_y = \frac{(95)(400) + (75)(300) + (120)(200) + (110)(100) + (130)(300) + (40)(100)}{400 + 300 + 200 + 100 + 300 + 100} = \frac{138,500}{1,400} = 98.9$$

Cincinnati   Knoxville   Chicago   Pittsburgh   New York   Atlanta

The ideal warehouse site is (76.9, 98.9) and is shown by the crosshair on the coordinate system. By superimposing a U.S. map over the coordinate system, we find this location is near Wheeling, West Virginia. It is important to note that the simple median model only identifies a general area for the facility from which a more detailed location analysis will be done. This is especially true in cases where the identified site is in the middle of a lake, miles from the nearest road and utility lines, or on rough terrain.

The Linear Scoring Rule Model

- appraises qualitative factors.

- also known as the factor-rating method.

- popular because a wide range of factors can be objectively included.

The LSR model has four steps:

1. Identify the factors important in selecting among alternative sites. Moreover, identify only those factors that differ markedly from one alternative site to another. In other words, if the availability of labor is equally important at all alternative sites, then it can be dropped from the analysis. Additionally, if an alternative is unacceptably poor in some dimension, i.e., the site is too small for building, it would be dropped from the analysis.

2. To each factor, assign a weight proportional to its importance in the decision. Thus, a factor with a weight of ".15" is considered 50% more important in the decision than a factor with a weight of ".10." Select weights so that they sum to "1.00."

3. Rate each alternative site with respect to each factor on a scale of 0–10, or 0–100. Exercise caution with respect to quantitative measures. For example, if the firm may only expect to need fifteen (15) acres of land, than a twenty-five (25) acre site and fifty (50) acre site would be assigned the same rating.

4. The overall rating for each site alternative is obtained by multiplying the rating on each factor by the factor weight and summing those values.

Example

Suppose a firm wants to evaluate three site alternatives: A, B, and C, employing a scale of 0–10 to rate each alternative against each factor:

Evaluation Factors	Factor Weights	Location Alternatives		
		A	B	C
Proximity to markets	.2	10	8	5
Transportation availability	.3	5	7	10
Environmental regulations	.1	4	6	10
Labor costs	.2	8	10	6
Proximity to suppliers	.1	10	6	3
Quality-of-life issues	.1	6	9	10
WEIGHTED TOTAL		7.1	7.8	7.5

In practice, dozens of factors may be important for a given decision. Some firms have workbooks listing hundreds of possible factors and convenient tables for performing the analysis. Oversights are eliminated, and a smoother process is possible. The LSR is applicable to many other business decisions such as which person to hire for a job or which type of computer to buy. The quality of the decision, however, will depend on the appropriateness of the decision factors, the factor weights used, and the accuracy of the factor assessments for the alternatives.

The Transportation and Assignment Algorithms

- proposed location sites are entered into the model, one at a time, and treated as actual sites.

- product sources (i.e., factories or warehouses) and product destinations (i.e., warehouses or consumer outlets) are identified.

- solution will be optimal and will specify shipping "x" number of units or truckloads of product from each source to each destination, so as to minimize total network transportation costs.

- model requires a shipping cost per unit or truckload from each specific source to each specific destination.

- model also assumes that only one mode of transportation is being used, i.e., all trucks, or all ships, or all trains.

- whichever site succeeds in reducing total network transport costs the most is the selected site.

Simulation Models

- allow management to assess the overall effects of a proposed location change on the entire network.

- effects can be measured, not only in transportation cost terms, but in other terms as well.

- can handle all types of variables including different modes of transport, different shipping rates based on traveled distances and times of day, different demands for the same product over time, one product shipped or a variety of products shipped, etc.

- widely-used (and originally used) for emergency facility location planning, i.e., fire stations, police stations, and ambulance services, where such variables as age of the general population area, regional insurance rates, proportion of buildings with wooden structures, emergency response time, and other factors are important.

Facility location planning may be conducted by MARKETING or PRODUCTION groups.

- It is a MARKETING function when the decision affects revenues more than costs, that is, consumer behavior and proximity to customers is primary.

- It is a PRODUCTION function when the decision affects costs more than revenues.

The Transportation Algorithm: An Example

Problem Statement

A firm has 3 factories and 3 warehouses. They are all located in different cities across the country. Each month, the factories produce product that is required by all 3 warehouses. Given the per-unit shipping costs between each factory and each warehouse, how many units should be shipped from each factory to each warehouse, in such a way as to fill each warehouse's product demand and also minimize total shipping costs for the entire distribution system?

A matrix known as the "transportation tableau" can be developed for this problem:

(destinations)
Warehouse

To / From	#1	#2	#3	Factory Capacity
A	$5.	4	3	100
B	8	4	3	300
C	9	7	5	300
Warehouse Demand	300	200	200	700 / 700

(sources) Factory

Interpretation

Cell "A1" represents the route from factory "A" to warehouse "1," and the per-unit shipping cost along this particular route is $5.00. All remaining cells are interpreted similarly.

"Factory capacity" in row "A" is "100" units. This represents the number of units produced by factory "A" during each period (usually monthly). Factory "A"'s units may be shipped to any warehouse in the system. All remaining rows are interpreted similarly.

"Warehouse demand" in column "1" is "300" units. This represents the number of units required by warehouse "1" during each period (usually monthly). Warehouse "1" is not concerned about which factory (or factories) supply it, as long as it receives its "300" units. All remaining columns are interpreted similarly.

The bottom right-hand cell "700/700" denotes the fact that total factory output exactly equals total warehouse demand for the period. A "balanced" problem is said to exist. If there were an inequality between supply and demand, a modification would need to be effected to the tableau. We will address that situation later in the chapter.

Development of the "First Feasible" Solution

Several techniques exist for developing the first solution, in a series of solutions, for this problem. They include a Vogel Approximation Method, Minimum-Cost Technique, and the Northwest-Corner Technique. The principal objective of all three techniques is to develop a preliminary solution that will be improved over subsequent solutions. The simplest technique to use is the Northwest-Corner one, although it may result in a longer overall solution time.

Northwest-Corner Technique Steps

Starting in the upper-left (or north-west corner) cell of the tableau:

1. proceed to allocate factory production from the *top-down* to the warehouse requirements.

2. proceed to satisfy warehouse requirements from *left to right*.

3. insure that all factory production has been allocated and that all warehouse requirements have been met.

Execution

A. Warehouse "1" requires 300 units. Factory "A" will ship its 100 units to warehouse "1." Factory "B" will ship its first 200 units to warehouse "1" to satisfy its remaining requirement.

B. Warehouse "2" requires 200 units. Factory "B" will ship its last 100 units to warehouse "2." Factory "C" will ship its first 100 units to warehouse "2" to satisfy its remaining requirement.

C. Warehouse "3" requires 200 units. Factory "C" will ship its last 200 units to warehouse "3" to satisfy all of its requirement.

The resultant tableau:

To / From	#1	#2	#3	Factory Capacity
A	(100) 5	4	3	100
B	(200) 8	(100) 4	3	300
C	9	(100) 7	(200) 5	300
Warehouse Demand	300	200	200	700 / 700

Note that each allocated cell (or route) in the tableau shows the allocated number of units within a node (or circle). These allocated cells are also referred to as "stepping-stones."

We can easily compute the total shipping cost of the first feasible solution as follows:

Cell	Units Shipped	×	Per-unit Cost	=	Total Cost
A1	100	×	$5.00		$500.00
B1	200	×	8.00		1,600.00
B2	100	×	4.00		400.00
C2	100	×	7.00		700.00
C3	200	×	5.00		1,000.000
				Total	$4,200.00

The Stepping-Stone Technique

To develop a second or any subsequent solution, we need to utilize a very different technique called the "stepping-stone." Its purpose is to evaluate the empty cells in the current solution for possible shipping cost savings. For example, it may be possible to transfer product into cell (route) "A2" from one or more of the currently allocated routes and realize a shipping cost reduction. Let's explore that possibility for cell "A2."

To / From	#1	#2		Factory Capacity
A	-1 (100) $5.	+1 ⌐4		100
B	+1 (200) 8	-1 (100) ⌐4		300
Warehouse Demand	300	200		700 / 700

Suppose we put one hypothetical unit into cell "A2" (shown by "+1"). By doing that, however, we would have to deduct one unit from cell "A1" in order to maintain the Factory "A" capacity balance of "100." We would also have to deduct one unit from cell "B2" in order to maintain the Warehouse "#2" demand balance of "200." Additionally, we would have to add one unit to cell "B1" in order to maintain the Factory "B" capacity balance of "300," and the Warehouse "#1" demand balance of "300."

The net effect (or impact) of these cell additions and deletions is a net cost increase:

	Cell "A2"	+	$4.00	Cell "B2"	–	$4.00
	Cell "B1"	+	$8.00	Cell "A1"	–	$5.00
Gross Increase or Decrease		+	$12.00		–	$9.00
Net cost Increase ("evaluation no.")		+	$3.00			

Conclusion: Since the net effect of putting one product unit in cell "A2" is a net increase in shipping cost of $3.00, we would never consider putting one or any other number of product units into cell "A2." This would just increase overall system shipping costs.

The "stepping-stone" technique is a much easier way of arriving at the same conclusion about cell "A2," if only because it spares the analyst from having to keep track of all "+" and "–" notations! The rules for the stepping-stone technique follow:

Rules, Tips, and Observations for the "Stepping-Stone" Technique used in the Transportation Algorithm

1. Every empty cell (route) in a given solution, must be evaluated for potential cost savings.

2. The "Stepping-Stone" technique is widely used for empty cell evaluation.

3. The evaluation path (or loop) begins in the empty cell which is to be evaluated.

4. The evaluation path that you develop *must* be as short as possible. There is usually only one evaluation path that actually is the shortest.

5. The evaluation path can be shaped like a "square," "rectangle," "L," upside-down "L," or a series of "steps."

6. There are at least four (4) cells involved in an evaluation path, and there may be more i.e., 6, 8, 10, 12, etc. (always in increments of "two").

7. You may move "clockwise" or "counter-clockwise" along an evaluation path.

8. You may only "land" on "stepping stones" (these are occupied cells), when you need to make a turn.

9. You bypass (and ignore) any "stepping stones" along the evaluation path, if you do not wish to make turns on them.

10. When you make turns, you turn at 90 degree angles, either to the "Left" or the "Right."

11. You may *not* move diagonally within the transportation tableau or the evaluation path.

12. The empty cell to be evaluated, must carry a "+" sign. The first occupied cell in the evaluation path carries a "−" sign. The second occupied cell in the evaluation path carries a "+" sign. The signage sequence is thus: + − + − + −, for as many cells as are in the evaluation path.

13. The empty cell with the highest potential cost savings is selected for the transfer operation. If there are "tie" cells, select one of these arbitrarily.

Execution

The evaluation path for Cell "A2" is: A2–B2–B1–A1, and its evaluation number is:

A2	+	4			B2	−	4
B1	+	8			A1	−	5
	+	12				−	9

+ 3 (no cost savings possible)

The evaluation path for Cell "A3" is: A3–C3–C2–B2–B1–A1, and its evaluation number is:

A3	+	3			C3	−	5
C2	+	7			B2	−	4
B1	+	8			A1	−	5
	+	18				−	14

+ 4 (no cost savings possible)

The evaluation path for Cell "B3" is: B3–C3–C2–B2, and its evaluation number is:

B3	+	3			C3	−	5
C2	+	7			B2	−	4
	+	10				−	9

+ 1 (no cost savings possible)

The evaluation path for Cell "C1" is: C1–B1–B2–C2, and its evaluation number is:

C1	+	9			B1	−	8
B2	+	4			C2	−	7
	+	13				−	15

− 2 (cost savings *possible*)

The "Transfer Operation"

Whenever one or more empty cells of the current solution are found to have negative evaluation numbers (which denote possible shipping cost savings), select the cell with the highest negative value (best possible savings) for the "transfer operation." If two empty cells are tied for the highest negative value, select one arbitrarily for the "transfer operation." The purpose of the transfer operation (for which no formal term exists) is to move as many units of product possible into the high cost-saving empty cell.

Execution

Since Cell "C1" is the empty cell with the highest potential cost savings, proceed as follows:

1. reconstruct cell "C1"'s evaluation path.

2. insert "+" and "–" signs in the appropriate cells of "C1"'s evaluation path.

3. identify those cells containing minus signs, and select the cell with the *smallest* unit allocation. (This would be Cell "C2" with 100 units.)

4. add "C2"'s 100 units to those cells having "+" signs.

5. subtract "C2"'s 100 units from those cells having "–" signs.

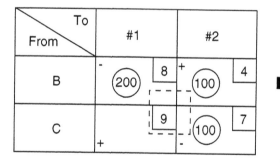

. . . and the tableau will now look like this:

To From	#1	#2	#3	Factory Capacity
A	(100) 5	4	3	100
B	(100) 8	(200) 4	3	300
C	(100) 9	7	(200) 5	300
Warehouse Demand	300	200	200	700 / 700

This is the second solution, and its total shipping cost can be computed as follows:

Cell	Units Shipped	×	Per-Unit cost	=	Total Cost
A1	100	×	$5.00		$500.00
B1	100	×	8.00		800.00
B2	200	×	4.00		800.00
C1	100	×	9.00		900.00
C3	200	×	5.00		1,000.00
					Total Cost $4,000.00

At this point, the stepping-stone technique would once again be employed to evaluate the second solution's empty cells for possible cost savings.

A third solution would have been obtained with a total cost of $3,900.00:

To From	#1	#2	#3	Factory Capacity
A	(100) 5	4	3	100
B	8	(200) 4	(100) 3	300
C	(200) 9	7	(100) 5	300
Warehouse Demand	300	200	200	700 / 700

At this point, the stepping-stone technique would once again be employed to evaluate the third solution's empty cells for possible cost savings. As it turns out, no further cost savings would have been possible, and therefore, the third solution would become the optimal solution.

Evaluation Number Points

A. if one or more empty cells of a current solution have *negative* evaluation numbers, there is at least one additional solution to follow, via the "transfer operation."

B. if one or more empty cells of a current solution have *zero* evaluation numbers, there is an alternate solution of the same cost via the "transfer operation."

C. if all the empty cells of a current solution have *positive* evaluation numbers, then the current solution is optimal.

Earlier in the chapter, it was noted that the transportation algorithm cannot be used unless total factory capacity equals total warehouse demand. If such is not the case (which it usually is), certain modifications need to be made to the tableau.

A. When factory capacity exceeds warehouse demand, create a Dummy warehouse (or other destination) that will fictitiously receive the excess capacity. Also assign a unit shipping cost of $0.00 to units shipped to this dummy from each factory.

To From	#1	#2	#3	#4	Factory Capacity
A	5	8	9	3	50
B	2	1	4	7	55
C	5	2	7	2	70
Warehouse Demand	30	60	20	40	175 150

becomes . . .

To From	#1	#2	#3	#4	Dummy #5	Factory Capacity
A	5	8	9	3	0	50
B	2	1	4	7	0	55
C	5	2	7	2	0	70
Warehouse Demand	30	60	20	40	25	175 175

Proceed to solve the problem as earlier shown, and if any units in the optimal solution are allocated to the dummy warehouse "#5," they will be interpreted as "unshipped" units from their respective factories.

B. When warehouse demand exceeds factory capacity, create a Dummy factory (or other source) that will fictitiously meet the excess demand. Also assign a unit shipping cost of $0.00 to units shipped from this dummy to each warehouse.

To From	#1	#2	#3	#4	Factory Capacity
A	5	8	9	3	50
B	2	1	4	7	30
C	5	2	7	2	70
Warehouse Demand	30	60	45	40	175 150

becomes . . .

To From	#1	#2	#3	#4	Factory Capacity
A	5	8	9	3	50
B	2	1	4	7	30
C	5	2	7	2	70
Dummy D	0	0	0	0	25
Warehouse Demand	30	60	45	40	175 175

Proceed to solve the problem as earlier shown, and if any units in the optimal solution are shipped from the dummy factory "D," they will be interpreted as "unfilled demand" at the affected warehouses.

A Location Decision Use

The transportation algorithm can also be used to select locations for individual factories, depots, warehouses, and retail outlets.

Sample Problem

A company has narrowed its choices for a new warehouse site to two cities: Atlanta and Denver. Presently the company has factories in Philadelphia, Chicago, and San Francisco; and warehouses in Phoenix, St. Louis, and New York. The unit-shipping costs for each route, factory capacities, and warehouse demands are known.

Which city should receive the new warehouse?

Solution Procedure

The company would develop a transportation tableau with the first location candidate (Atlanta) representing warehouse "#4." All unit-shipping costs from each factory to warehouse "#4" would be inserted in the appropriate column cells. An optional solution would be generated and total system costs computed.

The company would then develop a transportation tableau with the second location candidate (Denver) representing warehouse "#4." All unit-shipping costs from each factory to warehouse "#4" would be inserted in the appropriate column cells. An optional solution would be generated and total system costs computed.

Whichever proposed warehouse location succeeded in minimizing total system shipping costs would be selected.

Transportation Algorithm Assumptions

1. only one mode of transport may be used to ship units from sources to destinations. (For example, all units must be shipped by truck.)

2. there is a linear relationship between shipping cost and distance traversed. (For example, traversal of 1,000 miles is twice as costly as traversal of 500 miles.)

3. factory capacity and warehouse requirements may be stated in product units or truck-loads, ship-loads, car-loads, or containers.

4. A wide variety of products can be treated by the model, provided they travel in uniform-size shipping containers of equal weight and handling characteristics.

5. The model can only assess the impact of shipping costs on the distribution system. Variables such as shipping times, mixed transport modes, and multi-structured shipping rates can only be assessed within simulation models.

Layout Strategy

*C*hapter 9 focuses on the principal quantitative models used in developing and evaluating manufacturing layouts.

In an earlier chapter, the characteristics of the two major layouts (or configurations of labor, equipment, and materials) in operations, were discussed: PROCESS and PRODUCT.

The focus of this chapter is to develop, manipulate, and evaluate different versions of these layouts, in an attempt to reduce the firm's product/data movement costs, or production labor idle time.

Load-Distance models are used exclusively for PROCESS layout analysis, whereas Assembly-Line Balancing models are used exclusively for PRODUCT layout analysis.

The Load-Distance Model

- may only be employed with a PROCESS LAYOUT (i.e., "Job Shop" Operation)

- it is the oldest and most used quantitative model for process layout design. It involves a "trial and error" process.

- its purpose is to minimize the total cost of movement of materials or data within the firm by eliminating or reducing unnecessary traffic flows between departments (or work stations).

- the model assumes that the cost of movement is uniform per foot, or per yard between departments.

- the model also assumes that movement cost is a direct function of the distances traveled.

Example

Assume that the current layout of the firm consists of 4 uniform-sized areas, each 10 feet apart from each other. Movement cost has been determined to be 50¢ per foot traveled.

DEPT.	DEPT.	DEPT.	DEPT.
"A"	"B"	"C"	"D"

Step #1:   Determine the "LOAD": the number of daily communications* between all departments

_____

*(letters, memos, work-in-process inventory)

B	C	D	
10	25	20	A
	10	15	B
		5	C

Step #2:   Determine the "DISTANCE" between the departments, for the current layout.

B	C	D	
10	20	30	A
	10	20	B
		10	C

Step #3:   Determine the "WEIGHTED DISTANCE*" for the current layout.

   *(the number of daily communications × the distance between any two departments)
   The calculation of the weighted distance yields the total distances traveled daily within the firm.

B	C	D	
100	500	600	A
	100	300	B
		50	C

Σ Distances   =   1,650 feet
                  × .50/foot (travel cost)
                  $825.00 total movement
                          cost per day

if we change the layout to:

C	A	D	B

the distances between depts. becomes:

B	C	D	
20	10	10	A
	30	10	B
		20	C

and ∴ the total daily commo distance traveled is: (distance × commo)

B	C	D		
200	250	200	A	= 1200 feet
	300	150	B	× .50/ft
		100	C	$600.00 total movement costs per day

Conclusion: the proposed layout of "C–A–D–B" is more cost effective than the current layout of "A–B–C–D."

However, we should also evaluate other possible layouts such as:

A–C–B–D, B–D–C–A, or A–D–B–C

for even greater potential cost savings.

4! = number of potential
process layout designs
for this firm.

Some Limitations of the Simple Load-Distance Model

1. They ignore non-cost considerations such as noise levels, ventilation requirements, future expansion plans.

2. The sizes and shapes of the departments (work centers) may not be uniform in their dimensions. This complicates the cost analysis since the distances between various pairs of departments (centers) is not simply a multiple of one uniform distance.

3. They ignore special electrical and plumbing requirements. For example, a department must be near a drain or a high-power electrical service.

4. They can only handle one type of materials handling system in the cost analysis. If the firm employs cranes, hand trucks, conveyor belts, etc. the cost analysis is difficult if not impossible to perform.

5. There may be aisle restrictions between departments, resulting in the product not being able to pass through existing door frames.

6. There are lengthy computations involved, as the number of departments and material flows increase beyond *ten* departments, or when there is no dominant material flow pattern.

7. The L-D model may not yield a realistic design layout. Sometimes co-locating two departments for professional interchange purposes is more important than co-locating them for cost-cutting purposes.

8. Redesigned layouts resulting in the physical separation of paired departments may affect employee morale, leading to absenteeism, high labor turnover, and labor problems (i.e., an increase in worker grievances, lower productivity rates, and walk-outs).

SOME OF THE ABOVE LIMITATIONS MAY BE SUCCESSFULLY OVERCOME VIA USE OF COMPUTER-BASED LOAD-DISTANCE ALGORITHMS.

Cross-Chart, Flow Matrix, From-To Chart

This chart, which is known under three (3) different names (see above) is a required input to all manual and computer-based Load-Distance models. It shows the monthly or annual traffic volumes of materials or data between all pairs of departments. These volumes are estimated from (in order of best to worst):

1. PAST PRODUCTION CONTROL RECORDS: route sheets, work orders.

2. WORK FLOW ANALYSIS: "volunteered" staff count pallets of materials or data moving between departments for several weeks (to get a representative sampling).

3. AGGREGATE PRODUCTION SCHEDULES: Broad-based production schedules for all of the firm's products. These schedules must be disaggregated, decomposed, or "broken down" into individual finished products first. Then, the finished products must be broken down into specific assembly operations, and then further, into materials movements between departments. Time-consuming; tedious; least desirable.

Computer Assistance in Process Layout Planning

When a firm is faced with large and complex process-layout problems, computerized algorithms are available. These algorithms are classed as (1) those starting from scratch and developing a layout, or (2) those starting with a layout and systematically improving it.

One of the more popular "Class 2" models (algorithms) is CRAFT: Computerized Relative Allocation of Facilities Technique.

• it is a heuristic procedure (i.e., set of rules systematically applied).

• the objective is to obtain a "satisfactory" layout design, *not* an optimal design.

• it rearranges departments or work centers to reduce materials handling costs or communications cost.

• thousands of layout patterns can be evaluated in minutes.

• it will handle up to forty (40) departments of different shapes and sizes.

• individual departments can be specified as moveable or immovable.

• it considers differences in types and costs of materials handling (or communications) equipment between the various departments.

Requirements:

1. It needs the initial process layout, showing square footage, and all departments by size and location.

2. It needs a LOAD MATRIX (i.e., the volume of materials or communications flow between departments).

3. It needs a TRANSPORT COST MATRIX (i.e., the cost per distance unit (whether it be "per foot," "per yard," etc. and the cost of moving one unit of product or message unit between any two departments.)

The Output

CRAFT generates a process layout in the form of a block diagram, and a statement (just below it) of the associated materials handling costs, or communications cost.

*NOTE:*Further changes may be needed to obtain a realistic design. Human judgment, based on future plans of the firm and past difficulties, must be applied to any craft-generated solution.

Human Being vs. Computer-Based Models in Layout Design

Studies show that people developed more economical layout designs that did three of the most popular computer-based models: CRAFT, CORELAP (Computer Relationship Layout Planning), and ALDEP (Automated Layout Design Program). The reason? The human's ability to recognize and visualize complex patterns, whereas the computer-based models only utilize mechanical procedures. Source: Michael Scriabin + Roger Vergin, "Comparison of Computer Algorithms and Visual-Based Methods for Plant Layout," Management Science, October 1975.

Assembly Line Balancing

- done by industrial engineers

- a trial and error procedure

- there are no mathematical procedures for the *best* design

- the objective is to identify a "good" or "satisfactory" design

Any assembly line layout possesses a "good" design if it:

1. meets the desired output capacity (i.e., it is "effective")

2. establishes and maintains the proper task sequence (i.e., the basic manner in which the final end product is put together)

3. it is "efficient" (*i.e., usually 10% or less labor idleness at each work station*)

ASSEMBLY LINE BALANCING is the reapportioning of tasks among all work stations along the assembly line, in order to achieve the same (or as close to same) work performance times at all the work stations. The goal is to create a smooth, continuous flow along the assembly line with a minimum of idle time at each work station.

If production time at all work stations were *equal*, there would be *no* idle time in the line, and the line would be *perfectly-balanced*.

Six Steps to Line Balancing:

1. define the elemental tasks (smallest task reasonably assigned to one worker) and their performance times.

2. identify precedence requirements, that is, what tasks must take place before other tasks can follow. (This precedence relationship represents the MAJOR CONSTRAINT we face in assembly-line balancing).

3. calculate the minimum number of work stations needed along the line. (This requires "desired production output" and the calculated "cycle time").

4. apply an assignment heuristic for specifying the task content at each work station. (i.e., assign as many tasks as possible to each work station without exceeding the cycle time, or violating precedence relationships).

5. calculate the precise "effectiveness" and "efficiency" of the newly designed assembly line.

6. seek further improvement (i.e., increase the pace of the assembly line by changing the way in which tasks are performed, by redesigning the product, or by providing additional worker training, etc.).

"CYCLE TIME" can be interpreted in any of four (4) different ways:

1. the time interval between successive units of output.

2. the maximum period of time each product can spend in a work station before moving along to the next one.

3. the total time needed to produce one (1) finished product.

4. the pace (speed) of the assembly line.

Assembly line-balancing can be accomplished under two different approaches: the *maximum allowable cycle time* approach, and the *minimum allowable cycle time* approach. Many firms traditionally select the former because it guarantees that the daily production quota is achieved. There will be situations, however, where the employment of the *maximum allowable cycle time* approach will fail to achieve the minimum efficiency level. In such cases, the *minimum allowable cycle time* approach might very well develop a balanced line that not only meets the minimum efficiency, but also meets the daily manufacturing quota.

If neither approach proves to be efficient or effective, or both, management must pursue other measures that are beyond the scope of traditional line-balancing. These measures will be discussed later in the chapter.

Maximum Allowable Cycle Time Approach

Example

Work Task	Predecessor(s)	Time (in seconds)
A	none	60
B	A	80
C	none	30
D	C	40
E	B, D	40
F	none	50
G	F	100
H	D, G	70
I	E, H	<u>30</u>
		500
		seconds required to manufacture each unit

Assumptions

- the firm wants to achieve a production rate of 160 units per eight-hour day, utilizing a production line.

- The nine (9) work tasks must be assigned to work stations in such a way that they will be performed in the proper sequence.

- a rule is needed to guide the selection of tasks from the available list for assignment to the work station that is being loaded with work tasks.

FOUR COMMONLY USED HEURISTICS (rules):

1. The *"LOT" Rule:* assign tasks with the longest operation times first.

2. the *"MFT" Rule:* assign tasks with the greatest number of following tasks first.

3. the *"LFT" Rule:* assign tasks with the least number of following tasks first.

4. the *"Highest Sum"* RULE: assign tasks whose operation times and those of its followers sum to the highest time total.

Solution Procedure

1. compute the *total available production time per day.* (lunch and personal break time is excluded here for simplicity).

$$8 \text{ hr. shift/day} \times 60 \text{ min./hr} \times 60 \text{ sec./min.} = 28{,}800 \text{ seconds}$$

2. compute the *maximum allowable cycle time.*

$$\frac{\text{total available daily production rate}}{\text{daily management production quota}} = \frac{28{,}800 \text{ secs.}}{160 \text{ units}} = 180 \text{ seconds}$$

3. compute the *theoretical minimum number of work stations* required on this assembly line.

$$\frac{\text{total task time per unit}}{\text{max. allow. cycle time}} = \frac{500 \text{ seconds}}{180 \text{ seconds}} = \frac{2.77 \text{ or } 3 \text{ (must be}}{\text{rounded up)}}$$

As a result of steps 1, 2, and 3, a spreadsheet can be developed representing the three workstations and limiting each workstation's time on each production unit to 180 seconds before that production unit must move on to the next workstation.

	180 sec. avail	180 sec. avail	180 sec. avail	540 sec. (total)
	station #1	station #2	station #3	
Productive time				
Idle time				

4. *select a heuristic for the assignment of the nine (9) tasks* to the three (3) workstations. There are many heuristics or "rule-of-thumb" methods for accomplishing this. The "LOT rule"

assignment heuristic will be arbitrarily employed. This popular rule assigns the longest tasks to the workstations first.

What complicates the employment of any task assignment method is the constant threat that precedence relationships among the tasks may be inadvertently violated. The nature of the production process or the product itself usually dictates that certain tasks be completed before other tasks are allowed to begin. In automobile assembly operations, for example, the cabin must be built before the seats can be installed. The reverse sequence would be impossible.

An optional but extremely useful tool for avoiding precedence relationship violations is the "precedence diagram" which graphically shows the sequential relationship among all tasks as well as their performance times. This diagram will be used in assigning the nine tasks via the "LOT rule" heuristic.

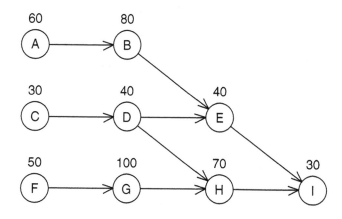

In the above precedence diagram, each work task is depicted as a node (circle) and the sequence requirements are indicated by arrows (arcs). The time required to perform each task is shown above its node. Among other data, the diagram shows that tasks "A," "C," "F" can start immediately because they have no predecessors. On the other hand, task "E" cannot begin until both tasks "B" and "D" have first been completed. Similarly, task "G" cannot begin until task "F" has first been completed.

Execution

Employing the "LOT rule" heuristic which assigns the largest tasks to workstations first:

candidates for 1st task in station #1

   A   (60 seconds)
   C   (30 seconds) "A" is assigned.
   F   (50 seconds)

candidates for 2nd task in station #1

   B   (80 seconds)
   C   (30 seconds) "B" is assigned.
   F   (50 seconds)

candidates for 3rd task in station #1

C (30 seconds) F (50 seconds) "C" is assigned (even though "F" is longest, station #1 can only accommodate "C" within its 180 second cycle time constraint).

candidates for 1st task in station #2

D (40 seconds)

F (50 seconds) "F" is assigned.

candidates for 2nd task in station #2

D (40 seconds)

G (100 seconds) "G" is assigned.

candidates for 3rd task in station #2

D (40 seconds) ("D" is not assigned because there are only 30 seconds of available cycle time in station #2).

candidates for 1st task in station #3

D (40 seconds) "D" is assigned.

candidates for 2nd task in station #3

E (40 seconds)

H (70 seconds) "H" is assigned.

candidates for 3rd task in station #3

E (40 seconds) "E" is assigned.

candidates for 4th task in station #3

I (30 seconds) "I" is assigned.

Task assignment is completed, and the spreadsheet looks like this:

	180 sec avail	180 sec avail	180 sec avail	540 sec (total avail)
	station #1	station #2	station #3	
	A (60)	F (50)	D (40)	
	B (80)	G (100)	H (70)	
	C (30)		E (40)	
			I (30)	
Productive time	170 secs	150 secs	180 secs	500 secs (total production time)
Idle time	10 secs	30 secs	0 secs	40 secs (total idle time)

Evaluation of the Newly-Balanced Assembly-Line

There are two ways of computing (as well as interpreting) the *efficiency* of an assembly line.

A. $\dfrac{\text{Total Productive Time Per Cycle}}{\text{Total Available Time Per Cycle}} = \dfrac{500 \text{ seconds}}{540 \text{ seconds}} = 92.6\%$

B. $\dfrac{\text{Total Idle Time Per Cycle}}{\text{Total Available Time Per Cycle}} = \dfrac{40 \text{ seconds}}{540 \text{ seconds}} = 7.4\%$ ★

★(the percentage of labor idle time that exists in any assembly line is called the "BDF" or balance delay factor).

Any assembly line with an efficiency equal to, or greater than 90%, or "BDF" equal to, or less than 10% is generally regarded as efficient.

The line is also *effective* because it meets management's daily production quota of 160 units. Actually, the employment of the maximum allowable cycle time (as opposed to the minimum allowable cycle time) in the balancing problem guaranteed daily quota compliance.

Further Improvement

A. line efficiency *cannot* be changed by using a different task assignment heuristic such as "MFT" or "LFT." These would just reshuffle the tasks among workstations. However, if management seeks a more equitable distribution of work among its employees, such heuristics may be useful.

B. line efficiency *may be changed* if management changes the cycle time basis from "maximum allowable" to "minimum allowable" or vice-versa.

C. any other tactics employed to improve efficiency would move the manager and engineer outside the "realm" of assembly-line balancing.

Other Considerations

Work tasks were assigned to work stations solely on the basis of the amount of time the tasks were expected to take. Sometimes other factors must be taken into consideration:

1. Tasks requiring different skills should not be assigned to the same person unless considerable staffing and training difficulty can be tolerated.

2. Regardless of the operator's skills, some processes are incompatible and should be performed in different areas. Grinding and painting, for example, should be separated. Assembly lines are sometimes zoned into areas and certain classes of work elements are assigned only within certain zones.

3. The worker's need for a sense of accomplishment suggests that the elements assigned to him/her be somewhat related and should make a recognizable contribution to the total job.

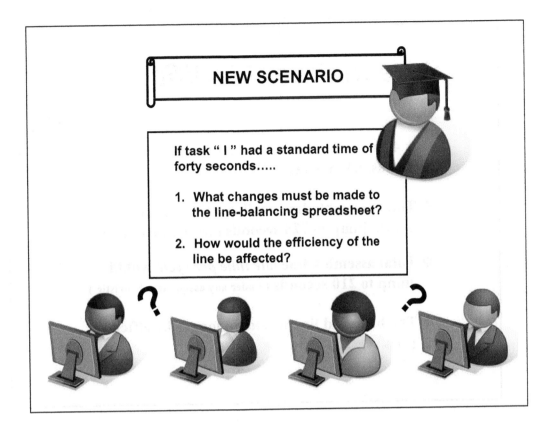

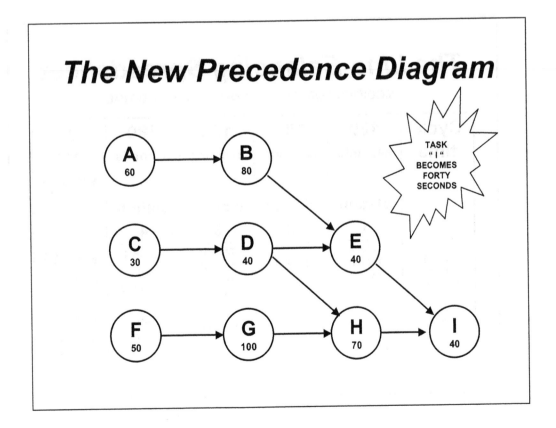

Spreadsheet Modifications

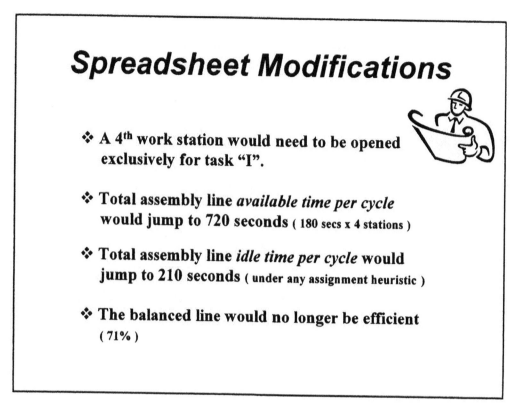

❖ A 4th work station would need to be opened exclusively for task "I".

❖ Total assembly line *available time per cycle* would jump to 720 seconds (180 secs x 4 stations)

❖ Total assembly line *idle time per cycle* would jump to 210 seconds (under any assignment heuristic)

❖ The balanced line would no longer be efficient (71%)

The Line-Balancing Spreadsheet

MODIFIED FOR TASK " I " NEW STANDARD TIME

Cycle time	180 seconds	180 seconds	180 seconds	180 seconds	Σ 720 seconds
	station 1	station 2	station 3	station 4	
Productive Time Per Cycle	TASK A TASK B TASK C 170 seconds	TASK F TASK G 150 seconds	TASK D TASK H TASK E 150 seconds	TASK I 40 seconds	Σ = 510 seconds
Idle Time Per Cycle	10 seconds	30 seconds	30 seconds	140 seconds	Σ = 210 seconds

Evaluating The Balanced Line

FOURTH STATION ADDED FOR TASK "I"

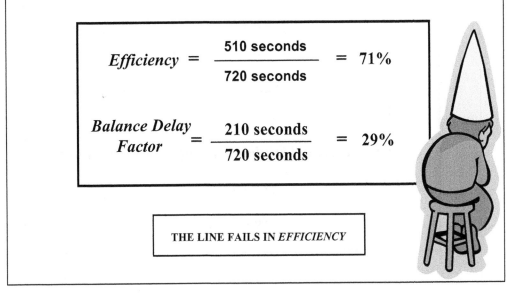

$$\textit{Efficiency} \;=\; \frac{510 \text{ seconds}}{720 \text{ seconds}} \;=\; 71\%$$

$$\textit{Balance Delay Factor} \;=\; \frac{210 \text{ seconds}}{720 \text{ seconds}} \;=\; 29\%$$

THE LINE FAILS IN *EFFICIENCY*

Minimum Allowable Cycle Time

THE "OTHER" CYCLE TIME

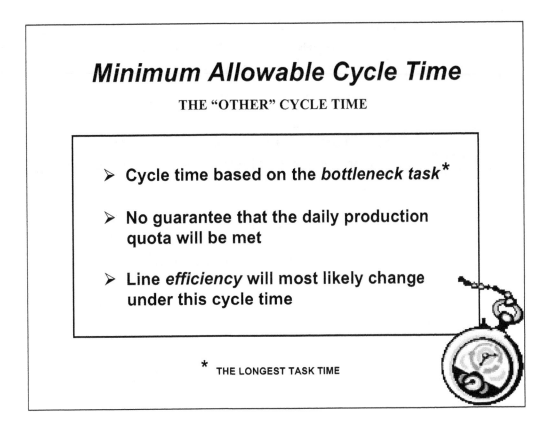

➤ Cycle time based on the *bottleneck task**

➤ No guarantee that the daily production quota will be met

➤ Line *efficiency* will most likely change under this cycle time

* THE LONGEST TASK TIME

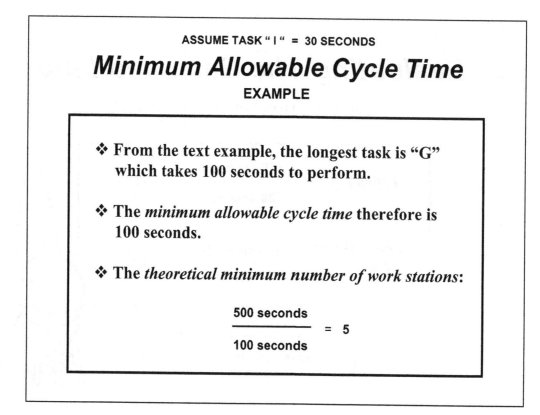

ASSUME TASK " I " = 30 SECONDS

Minimum Allowable Cycle Time
EXAMPLE

❖ From the text example, the longest task is "G" which takes 100 seconds to perform.

❖ The *minimum allowable cycle time* therefore is 100 seconds.

❖ The *theoretical minimum number of work stations*:

$$\frac{500 \text{ seconds}}{100 \text{ seconds}} = 5$$

ASSUME TASK " I " = 40 SECONDS

Minimum Allowable Cycle Time
LINE-BALANCING SPREADSHEET

Cycle Time	100 seconds	100 seconds	100 seconds	100 seconds	100 seconds	100 seconds	Σ 600 seconds
	Station 1	Station 2	Station 3	Station 4	Station 5	Station 6	
Productive Time Per Cycle	TASK A TASK C 90 seconds	TASK B 80 seconds	TASK F TASK D 90 seconds	TASK G 100 seconds	TASK H 70 seconds	TASK E TASK I 80 seconds	Σ 510 seconds
Idle Time Per Cycle	10 seconds	20 seconds	10 seconds	0 seconds	30 seconds	20 seconds	Σ 90 seconds

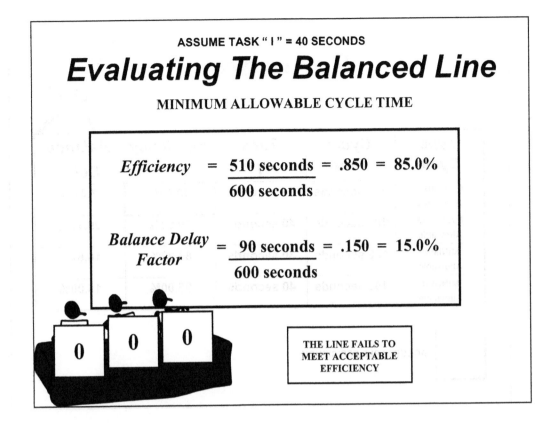

ASSUME TASK " I " = 40 SECONDS

Evaluating The Balanced Line

MINIMUM ALLOWABLE CYCLE TIME

$$Efficiency = \frac{510 \text{ seconds}}{600 \text{ seconds}} = .850 = 85.0\%$$

$$Balance\ Delay\ Factor = \frac{90 \text{ seconds}}{600 \text{ seconds}} = .150 = 15.0\%$$

THE LINE FAILS TO MEET ACCEPTABLE EFFICIENCY

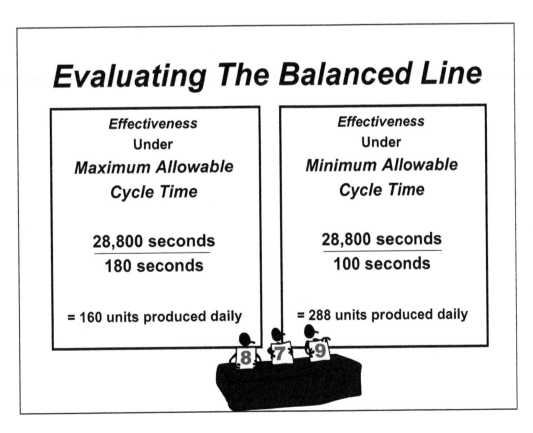

Evaluating The Balanced Line

Effectiveness Under *Maximum Allowable Cycle Time*	*Effectiveness* Under *Minimum Allowable Cycle Time*
$\dfrac{28{,}800 \text{ seconds}}{180 \text{ seconds}}$	$\dfrac{28{,}800 \text{ seconds}}{100 \text{ seconds}}$
= 160 units produced daily	= 288 units produced daily

Scoreboard

Type Cycle	Cycle Time	Task "I"	Efficiency	Balance Delay
MAXIMUM Allowable	180 seconds	30 seconds	92.59%	7.41%
MAXIMUM Allowable	180 seconds	40 seconds	70.83%	29.17%
MINIMIN Allowable	100 seconds	30 seconds	83.33%	16.67%
MINIMIN Allowable	100 seconds	40 seconds	85.00%	15.00%

ACCEPTABLE EFFICIENCY

The Behavioral Aspects of Layout

Product Layout (Assembly-Line)

- Routinization may lead to job dissatisfaction, absenteeism, and high labor turnover.

- Work becomes meaningless. Worker gets "lost" in the system. However some workers actually prefer routine tasks and seek self-actualization or personal challenges off the job.

- Managers must have the ability to find a good match between employees and work assignments.

Process Layout (Job Shop/Departmental Groupings)

- The departmentalization of activities by skill results in:

  1. group norms

  2. agreements about behavior

  3. the amounts of productive effort that its members generate.

- Group norms may or may not be compatible with the official corporate, management-set standards.

- Strong group affiliations are formed. A redesigned layout may disrupt existing group relations leading to:

  1. absenteeism

  2. high labor turnover

  3. labor problems (i.e., an increase in worker grievances, lower productivity rates, walk-outs).

- Different departments or groups may compete against one another, because a group's interests and loyalties are more inner-directed than outer-directed. Managers must be skilled at intergroup coordination, and be able to turn such interests and loyalties toward attainment of the firm's goals, i.e., have company sponsored sales contests, or "best-quality" production contests between groups.

Behavioral issues in layout design and the management techniques designed to deal with them are distinctly different, depending on whether the layout in question is PRODUCT or PROCESS. The issues and techniques are *not* interchangeable.

10

Human Resource Strategy, Work Measurement, and Learning Curves

Chapter 10 introduces management philosophies and specific techniques for designing, evaluating, and improving jobs.

Concepts such as "worker empowerment," "human resource management," "corporate restructuring," and "re-engineering" are nothing new. They are only new terms to describe a 100-year-old function called work design and analysis: a core responsibility of production/operations management.

In the early years, the sole pursuit of work design/analysis was cost reduction and higher productivity. During the 1960s, the additional goals of worker attitude improvement and personal development were added. Two very different management philosophies (or schools) shape work design/analysis. The first is the "micro-approach" or "Taylor school" (named for its founder Frederick Taylor) which stresses an industrial engineering approach and guarantees efficiency gains. The second is the "behavioral approach" which stresses a human approach with no such guarantees. Intelligent job design/analysis dictates the employment of both philosophies for the best long-term results.

This chapter also examines the "learning-curve phenomenon" where productivity gains increase exponentially over time, with significant implications for the scheduling, staffing, marketing, and purchasing functions.

Work Design and Analysis

Job (or Work) Design follows the planning and designing of the product, the process, and the equipment. It specifies *content* and determines the distribution of work in the firm.

Job Design is just one step of a series of steps toward development of performance standards for individuals and departments. They are:

PRODUCT PLANNING AND DESIGN

↓

METHODS ANALYSIS

(how you are going to create the product or service, i.e., manual, robotics, combination?)

↓

129

JOB DESIGN

(how the work to be done is distributed throughout the firm, i.e., who does what?)

↓

WORK MEASUREMENT

(the determination of the degree and quantity of labor in production/operations tasks)

↓

WORK STANDARDS

(the time or level of performance normally expected for completion of a task)

There are *two* (2) basic approaches to Job Design:

1. The *Micro-Approach (Technical/Physical):* This approach scientifically examines each detail of a job so that wasted effort is eliminated and productive output raised. It emphasizes task specialization, task repetition, reduction of skill requirements, and cost reduction. THE SOLE MOTIVATOR IS MORE MONEY.

2. The *Behavioral Approach (Socio-psychological):* This approach is concerned with the psychological and socio-psychological aspects of job design. It encourages the use of Job Enlargement, Job Enrichment, and Job Rotation techniques, as well as employee participation in job design. It *can,* that is, it has the potential to result in improved productive output over and above that output achieved through the Micro-Approach. However this usually only occurs in jobs that possess many opportunities for improvement in the areas of challenge, responsibility, and personal growth. For example, a high-level executive probably wouldn't respond positively to the Behavioral Approach because his or her position already has enough challenge, responsibility, and growth potential in it. THIS APPROACH ATTEMPTS TO FILL THE WORKER'S NEED FOR RECOGNITION, SELF-ESTEEM, AND SELF-ACTUALIZATION.

Changes in mgmt's style, practices, and the work environment.	→	(hopefully) positive attitude toward firm and its goals	→	(hopefully) increased productivity. (*not* 100% (guaranteed)

The Three Techniques of the Behavioral School

Job Enlargement: (*adds interest to the job*): redesigning jobs so as to make the worker feel more involved in, and responsible for, his or her work. There are two aspects to job enlargement:

1. *horizontal job enlargement:* adding more tasks of the same nature and skill to the job.

2. *vertical job enlargement:* adding more tasks of different natures and skills to the job.

Job Enrichment: (*more profound goals and more difficult and time-consuming to implement*): redesigning jobs so as to provide more meaning and enjoyment to the worker, by involving him or her in the planning, organizing, and controlling of that work.

A common example of job enrichment is giving a worker responsibility for quality control, and equipment maintenance.

There are two (2) pre-conditions for Job Enrichment: 1. Management must supply information to the workers on the firm's corporate goals and performance. 2. The proper organizational climate must exist, that is, no excessive control of individual behavior. You can tell someone what to do, but don't tell them how to do it.

Management must reorient its thinking when attempting to use Job Enrichment techniques. It must view every employee as a "manager" who plans, organizes, and controls his or her own job. Management must also attempt to make work like "play." Workers should be working at the firm because they want to be working there; firm provides meaningful, visible goals; firm might sponsor contests between departments to pick the best quality control or lowest cost manufacturing group or department; management provides the workers with immediate feedback on the company's activities and performances.

Not every job can be enriched:

— some workers don't want to be "managers" of any sort

— enriched jobs might reduce social interaction among workers

— some jobs cannot be improved, i.e., toll booth attendant, ditch digger

— some workers do not accept middle-class values and goals of job enrichment, i.e., they don't want responsibility, they don't enjoy work for the sake of work.

Job Rotation: (*when all else fails!*): A last-resort technique for jobs that cannot be (or further) improved through enrichment or enlargement. It involves reduction in boredom, i.e., two workers swap their jobs for one day, a worker on the "graveyard" shift gets to work during daytime hours for several weeks.

Occasionally, firms will take the additional step of hiring the mentally-challenged for elementary assembly work, basic maintenance, simple monitoring, or even grocery-cart retrieval at a shopping mall.

Remember that job enrichment, enlargement, and rotation are not replacements but *supplements* to sound work measurements and traditional (micro) job design.

Traditional Job Design Steps

1. Identify the operations "problem area" and specific job(s) that seem to be causing problems, i.e., high percentages of defects, bottlenecks, high number of worker union grievances, etc.

2. Analyze and document how the work is currently being done.

3. Analyze the content of individual jobs and their elements, i.e., reaching, grasping, joining, bending, etc.

4. Develop/Implement new work methods.

Methods Techniques

Engineers and technicians use a variety of charts to find ways of improving jobs that might have been overlooked by managers, supervisors, and the employees themselves. These charts attempt to reduce idle time by eliminating unnecessary tasks and/or changing task sequences. They are not mandatory methods of job analysis but they are useful.

1. *Flow Process Charts*

   • examine many jobs, but none in-depth (called "inter-job" analysis)

   • used in manufacturing and service sectors

   • portray flows of the overall production/service process from beginning to end

   • analyze inter-station or inter-department activities

   • reveal unnecessary product/data/document movements, or duplication of effort

- classify product movement into five (5) major elements or functions:

    A.   operations   ○

    B.   Transport   ➡

    C.   Storage   ▽

    D.   Inspection   ☐

    E.   Delay   ᗡ

- flowcharting flows frequently serves as the basis for software programming which automates the entire operation.

Example #1

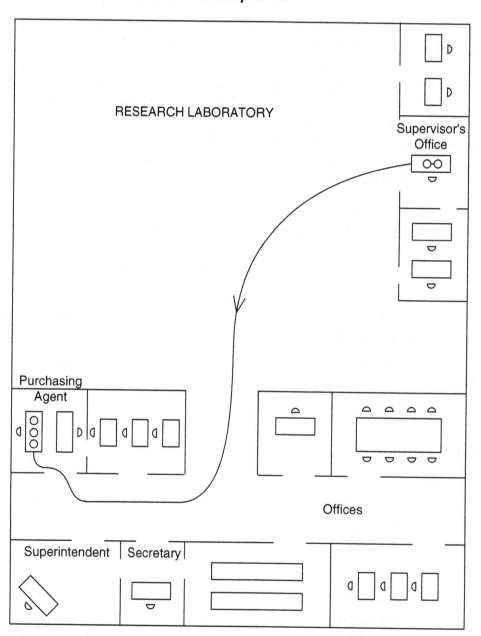

Flow diagram of an Office Procedure—Proposed Method. Requisition is written in triplicate by supervisor and approved by purchasing agent. *Source:* R. M. Barnes, *Motion and Time Study,* New York: John Wiley, 1968, pp. 78–79. Copyright © 1968 by John Wiley & Sons. Reprinted by permission.

Example #2

Present Method ☐	PROCESS CHART				
Proposed Method ☒					

SUBJECT CHARTED   Requisition for small tools
Chart begins at supervisor's desk and ends at purchasing agent's desk

Date _____
Chart By __J.C.H.__
Chart No. __R 149__
Sheet No. __1 OF 1__

DEPARTMENT   Research laboratory

DIST. IN FEET	TIME IN MINS.	CHART SYMBOLS	PROCESS DESCRIPTION
		● ⇨ ☐ D ▽	Purchase order written in triplicate by supervisor
		○ ⇨ ☐ D ▽	On supervisor's desk (awaiting messenger)
75		○ ⇨ ☐ D ▽	By messenger to purchasing agent
		○ ⇨ ☐ D ▽	On purchasing agent's desk (awaiting approval)
		○ ⇨ ■ D ▽	Examined and approved by purchasing agent
		○ ⇨ ☐ D ▽	On purchasing agent's desk (awaiting transfer to main office)
		○ ⇨ ☐ D ▽	
		○ ⇨ ☐ D ▽	
		○ ⇨ ☐ D ▽	
		○ ⇨ ☐ D ▽	
		○ ⇨ ☐ D ▽	
		○ ⇨ ☐ D ▽	
		○ ⇨ ☐ D ▽	
		○ ⇨ ☐ D ▽	
		○ ⇨ ☐ D ▽	
		○ ⇨ ☐ D ▽	

	SUMMARY			
		PRESENT METHOD	PROPOSED METHOD	DIFFER-ENCE
Operations ○		3	1	2
Transportations ⇨		4	1	3
Inspections ☐		2	1	1
Delays D		8	3	5
Distance Traveled in Feet		105	75	30

DIST. IN FEET	TIME IN MINS.	CHART SYMBOLS	
75		1 1 1 3	Total

Process Chart of an Office Procedure—Proposed Method for the Flow Diagram in Figure

2. *Activity Charts*
   - known by several names to include:
     1. Operator-machine analysis chart
     2. Multiple-Activity chart
     3. Man-Machine chart
     4. Gang chart.
   - analyzes a particular job (called "intra-job" analysis).
   - divides the task or job into major segments done by a worker and machine.
   - allows the analyst to identify and compute the idle time for both worker and machine, so as to address means of reducing or eliminating it.

- in order to justify the cost of analysis, the activity chart should only concentrate on routine, repetitive tasks with worker-machine interaction and long cycle times (2 minutes or more). There should also be many people in the firm performing the identical job.
- used in moderate/high production environments.
- *typical use results:*
  1. positioning a machine between two workers so that it is always being utilized.
  2. devising additional tasks for a worker who must wait for a machine to run through its cycle.

Example

Operation : _____   SOUTHERN TECHNICAL INSTITUTE
Equipment : _____   MARIETTA, GEORGIA 30080
Operator : _____
Study No. : _____ Analyst : _____   ACTIVITY CHART

	MAN		MACHINE	
	TIME	%	TIME	%
WORK	6	43%	14	100%
IDLE	8	57	0	0

Subject   Semi–Auto Machine   Date 11-6
(Present)
Proposed   Dept.   Sheet Of   Chart by LSA

Time	Operator	Time	Machine	Time
2	Load Machine		Being Loaded	
4				
6				
8	Idle		Run	
10				
12				
14	Unload		Being Unloaded	
16	Load Machine		Being Loaded	
18				
20				
22	Idle		Run	
24				
26				
28	Unload		Being Unloaded	
30	Load Machine		Being Loaded	
32				
34				

Cycle

Activity Chart. *Source:* Adapted from L. S. Aft, *Productivity Measurement and Improvement,* © 1983, p. 67. Reprinted by permission of Prentice-Hall, Inc., Engelwood Cliffs, N.J.

3. *Operations Charts*

- known by several names to include:
  1. Simo chart.
  2. Simultaneous Motion chart.
  3. Left-Hand/Right-Hand chart.

- analyzes a particular job (called "intra-job" analysis).
- divides the task or job into elementary motions of the right and left hands.
- the worker is positioned at a work space, and may only move away at times to draw materials.
- allows the analyst to identify and compute the idle time for both the right hand and the left hand, so as to address means of reducing or eliminating it.
- in order to justify the cost of analysis, the operations chart should only concentrate on routine, repetitive tasks with short cycle times (2 minutes or less). There should also be many people in the firm performing the identical job.
- used in low/moderate production environments.
- typical elementary motions of the hands include: reaching, carrying, grasping, pressing, turning, and positioning.
- *typical use results:*
  1. restructuring the job or enlarging it, in order to employ both hands of the worker.
  2. devising additional tasks for one hand while the other is engaged.

Example #1

LEFT-HAND / RIGHT-HAND CHART
SOUTHERN TECHNICAL INSTITUTE
MARIETTA, GEORGIA 30080

SUMMARY

SYMBOLS	PRESENT		PROPOSED		DIFFERENCE	
	LH	RH	LH	RH	LH	RH
O OPERATIONS	5	10				
⇨ TRANSPORTATIONS						
☐ INSPECTIONS						
D DELAYS	10	5				
▽ STORAGES						
TOTALS	15	15				

PROCESS __Bolt Washer Assembly__
STUDY NO. __1__
OPERATOR __SRA__
ANALYST _____
DATE __11/ 6 /82__ SHEET NO __1__ of __1__
METHOD (PRESENT) PROPOSED
REMARKS

LEFT-HAND ACTIVITY Present METHOD	DIST	SYMBOLS	SYMBOLS	DIST	RIGHT-HAND ACTIVITY Present METHOD
1 Reach for Bolt		●⇨☐DV	O⇨☐◾V		Idle
2 Grasp Bolt		●⇨☐DV	O⇨☐◾V		Idle
3 Move Bolt to		●⇨☐DV	O⇨☐◾V		Idle
Work Area		O⇨☐DV	O⇨☐DV		
4 Hold Bolt		O⇨☐◾V	●⇨☐DV		Reach for Washer
5 Hold Bolt		O⇨☐◾V	●⇨☐DV		Grasp Washer
6 Hold Bolt		O⇨☐◾V	●⇨☐DV		Move Washer to Bolt
7 Hold Bolt		O⇨☐◾V	●⇨☐DV		Assemble Washer on
		O⇨☐◾V	O⇨☐DV		Bolt
8 Hold Bolt		O⇨☐◾V	●⇨☐DV		Release Washer
9 Hold Bolt		O⇨☐◾V	●⇨☐DV		Reach for Nut
10 Hold Bolt		O⇨☐◾V	●⇨☐DV		Grasp Nut
11 Hold Bolt		O⇨☐◾V	●⇨☐DV		Move Nut to Bolt
12 Hold Bolt		O⇨☐◾V	●⇨☐DV		Assemble Nut to
		O⇨☐◾V	O⇨☐DV		Bolt
13 Hold Bolt		O⇨☐◾V	●⇨☐DV		Release Nut
14 Set Assembly		●⇨☐DV	O⇨☐◾V		Idle
Aside		O⇨☐DV	O⇨☐DV		
15 Reach for Bolt		●⇨☐DV	O⇨☐◾V		Idle

Operation Chart (Left-Hand/Right-Hand Chart) for Bolt-washer Assembly. *Source:* Adapted from L. S. Aft, *Productivity Measurement and Improvement,* 1983, p. 75. Reprinted by permission of Prentice-Hall, Inc., Englewood Cliffs. N.J.

Example #2

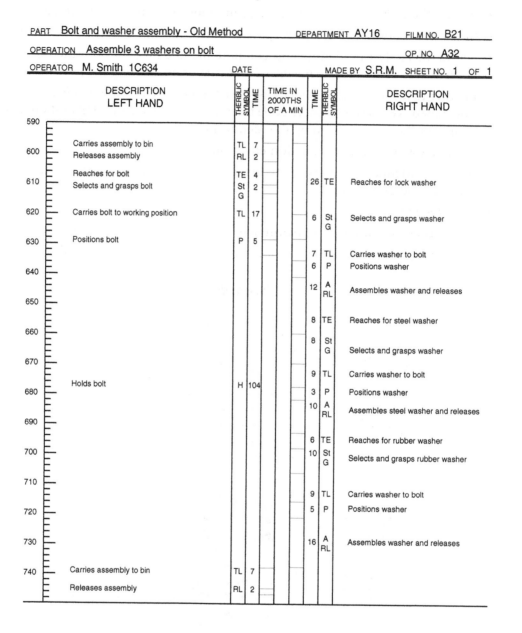

PART	Bolt and washer assembly - Old Method			DEPARTMENT AY16	FILM NO. B21

OPERATION	Assemble 3 washers on bolt				OP. NO. A32

OPERATOR M. Smith 1C634	DATE	MADE BY S.R.M. SHEET NO. 1 OF 1

	DESCRIPTION LEFT HAND	THERBLIC SYMBOL	TIME	TIME IN 2000THS OF A MIN	TIME	THERBLIC SYMBOL	DESCRIPTION RIGHT HAND
590							
600	Carries assembly to bin	TL	7				
	Releases assembly	RL	2				
	Reaches for bolt	TE	4				
610	Selects and grasps bolt	St G	2		26	TE	Reaches for lock washer
620	Carries bolt to working position	TL	17		6	St G	Selects and grasps washer
630	Positions bolt	P	5		7	TL	Carries washer to bolt
640					6	P	Positions washer
					12	A RL	Assembles washer and releases
650							
660					8	TE	Reaches for steel washer
					8	St G	Selects and grasps washer
670					9	TL	Carries washer to bolt
680	Holds bolt	H	104		3	P	Positions washer
					10	A RL	Assembles steel washer and releases
690							
700					6	TE	Reaches for rubber washer
					10	St G	Selects and grasps rubber washer
710							
720					9	TL	Carries washer to bolt
					5	P	Positions washer
730					16	A RL	Assembles washer and releases
740	Carries assembly to bin	TL	7				
	Releases assembly	RL	2				

Simo Chart for Bolt and Washer Assembly—Old Method. *Source:* R. M. Barnes, *Motion and Time Study,* New York: John Wiley, 1968, p. 177, copyright © 1968, by John Wiley & Sons. Reprinted by permission.

Principles of Motion Economy

- also known as Principles of Work Efficiency.

- general guidelines for analyzing and improving work arrangements, the use of human hands, legs, and torso; and the use of tools to increase efficiency and reduce fatigue.

- these principles can be applied to both manufacturing and service sectors.

All 22 Rules

These 22 rules or principles of motion economy may be profitably applied to shop and office work alike. Although not all are applicable to every operation, they do form a basis or a code for improving the efficiency and reducing fatigue in manual work.

Use of the Human Body	Arrangement of the Work Place	Design of Tools and Equipment
1. The two hands should begin as well as complete their motions at the same time. 2. The two hands should not be idle at the same time except during rest periods. 3. Motions of the arms should be made in opposite and symmetrical directions, and should be made simultaneously. 4. Hand and body motions should be confined to the lowest classification with which it is possible to perform the work satisfactorily. 5. Momentum should be employed to assist the worker whenever possible, and it should be reduced to a minimum if it must be overcome by muscular effort. 6. Smooth continuous, curved motions of the hands are preferable to straight-line motions involving sudden and sharp changes in direction. 7. Ballistic movements are faster, easier, and more accurate than restricted (fixation) or "controlled" movements. 8. Work should be arranged to permit easy and natural rhythm wherever possible. 9. Eye fixations should be as few and as close together as possible.	10. There should be a definite and fixed place for all tools and materials. 11. Tools, materials, and controls should be located close to the point of use. 12. Gravity-feed bins and containers should be used to deliver material close to the point of use. 13. Drop deliveries should be used wherever possible. 14. Materials and tools should be located to permit the best sequence of motions. 15. Provisions should be made for adequate conditions for seeing. Good illumination is the first requirement for satisfactory visual perception. 16. The height of the work place and the chair should preferably be arranged so that alternate sitting and standing at work are easily possible. 17. A chair of the type and height to permit good posture should be provided for every worker.	18. The hands should be relieved of all work that can be done more advantageously by a jig, a fixture, or a foot-operated device. 19. Two or more tools should be combined whenever possible. 20. Tools and materials should be prepositioned whenever possible. 21. Where each finger performs some specific movement, such as in typewriting, the load should be distributed in accordance with the inherent capacities of the fingers. 22. Levers, crossbars, and hand wheels should be located in such positions that the operator can manipulate them with the least change in body position and with the greatest mechanical advantage.

Source: R. M. Barnes, *Motion and Time Study*, New York: John Wiley, 1968, p. 220, copyright © 1968, by John Wiley & Sons. Reprinted with permission.

Work Measurement Techniques/
Time Standard-Setting Techniques

Work Measurement

- the determination of the degree and quantity of labor in production/operations tasks.

There are six (6) ways to establish a time (work) standard after a job or task has been measured:

1. ignore formal work measurement.
2. use historical data.
3. use direct time study.
4. use pre-determined time study.
5. use work sampling approach.
6. combining "2" through "5."

1st Method: IGNORE FORMAL WORK MEASUREMENT

- especially used in the service sector where work measurement is difficult.
- an informal standard is set by default, i.e., a boss's personal attitude toward you and your work.
- results in poor labor efficiency and poor morale.
- in better firms, rating scales might be used where a worker is rated on performance traits such as punctuality, attention to detail, receptiveness to constructive criticism, and cooperation.
- any system used depends on the supervisor's integrity to devote the necessary time and effort in generating meaningful results.

2nd Method: USE OF HISTORICAL DATA

- assumes that past performance equals normal performance.
- quick, simple, cheap.
- may reflect unusual working conditions or unusually capable or incapable workers.
- management must intuitively adjust the standard up or down to reflect changing technology, improved physical health via modern medicine, or improved training conditions.
- state and federal agencies have been especially successful in its use.
- for private industry, it is "better than nothing."

3rd Method: USE OF DIRECT TIME STUDY

- the most widely-used method in manufacturing operations.
- limited to existing jobs only.

- the performance standard is equal to the normal time to perform an operation plus time allowances for fatigue and personal needs (usually 10–15% of normal operation time).

- to compute the performance standard, the analyst must select the number of cycles to observe and the number of workers to observe.

- there is an accuracy-cost tradeoff in setting the performance standard, i.e., the more cycles and works observed, the more accurate the standard.

- the job studied must be repetitive in nature and performed by many individuals in order to justify its costs.

4th Method: USE OF PRE-DETERMINED TIME STUDY

- for current or planned (future) jobs.

- does not cause shop floor disruptions since it is used away from the shop floor.

- eliminates non-representative worker reactions such as found in direct-time studies.

- no PRs ("performance ratings") need to be computed because they are already "built-in."

- no AFs ("allowance factors") need to be computed because they are already "built-in."

- first step: identify the specific tasks required of a particular job.

- second step: decompose each task into a series of micro, basic, or elemental motions called "therbligs" (i.e., reaching, grasping, lifting, focusing).

- third step: reference the standard times that have been catalogued for each micro motion in available tables.

- fourth step: add all of the micro motion times, and the total becomes the pre-determined time standard for each task. Total task times, in turn, become the pre-determined time standard for the job.

- if certain micro motions are not identified or missing in the standard reference tables, they will distort the pre-determined time standard.

- any micro motions not found in standard reference tables must be measured by *direct-time study*.

- a "therblig" is also a term used for "TMU" (time measurement unit).

Example:

- there are 1,700 TMUs in one (1) minute (i.e., each equals .036 seconds).

- total micro motion time for a particular job equals 397.9 TMUs.

- 397.9 TMUs is the job's cycle time which can also be expressed as 14.32 seconds or .23838 minutes.

- since there are 60 minutes in one (1) hour, and each job cycle takes .23838 minutes to complete, 252 cycles should be expected of that job per hour by management.

- if each job cycle results in the production of one (1) unit of product, then standard output per hour would be set at 252 units.

5th Method: USE OF WORK SAMPLING APPROACH

- the most recently developed technique, based on random sampling techniques.

- estimates what proportion of time is devoted to a certain activity, i.e., work or idleness.

- the proportion can then be used as a performance standard, i.e., a librarian should be working (cataloging, servicing customers, and assisting researchers 80% of the times that he or she is randomly observed by management).

- particularly adaptive to service-sector jobs.

- accuracy depends on the sample size for the observations.

- for non-repetitive jobs such as secretary, nurse, police officer, social worker.

- the application of work sampling may span several days or weeks.

- if management is not satisfied with the actual proportion of time devoted to a certain activity or job, it may add or delete responsibilities as appropriate.

6th Method: USE OF TWO OR MORE METHODS

- in practice, two or more methods are used in combination as cross-checks on the accuracy of the time (work) standard.

- no one technique of work measurement is totally reliable.

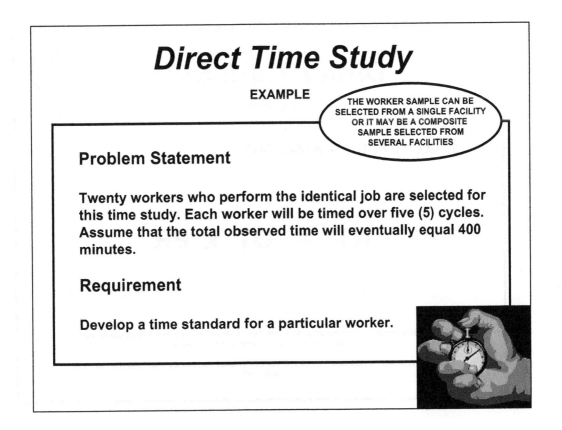

Direct Time Study

EXAMPLE

> THE WORKER SAMPLE CAN BE SELECTED FROM A SINGLE FACILITY OR IT MAY BE A COMPOSITE SAMPLE SELECTED FROM SEVERAL FACILITIES

Problem Statement

Twenty workers who perform the identical job are selected for this time study. Each worker will be timed over five (5) cycles. Assume that the total observed time will eventually equal 400 minutes.

Requirement

Develop a time standard for a particular worker.

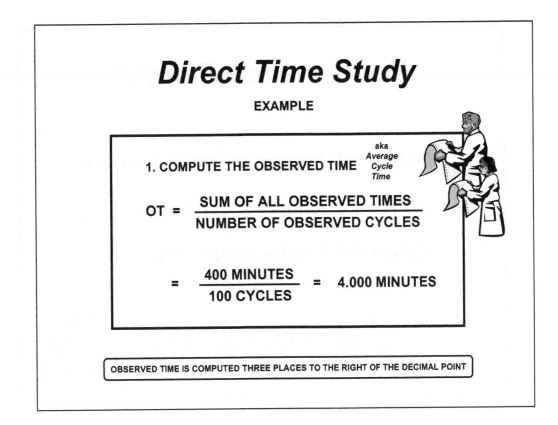

Direct Time Study

EXAMPLE

1. COMPUTE THE OBSERVED TIME *aka Average Cycle Time*

$$OT = \frac{SUM\ OF\ ALL\ OBSERVED\ TIMES}{NUMBER\ OF\ OBSERVED\ CYCLES}$$

$$= \frac{400\ MINUTES}{100\ CYCLES} = 4.000\ MINUTES$$

OBSERVED TIME IS COMPUTED THREE PLACES TO THE RIGHT OF THE DECIMAL POINT

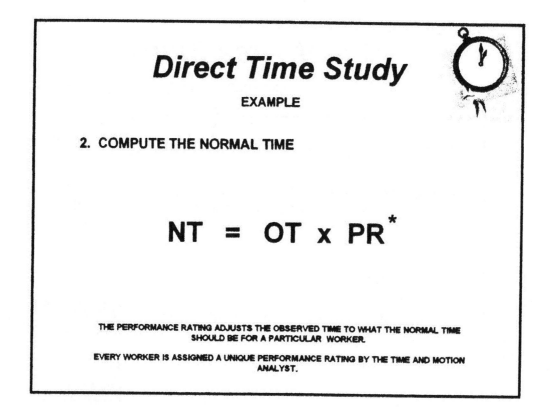

Direct Time Study

EXAMPLE

2. COMPUTE THE NORMAL TIME

$$NT = OT \times PR^*$$

THE PERFORMANCE RATING ADJUSTS THE OBSERVED TIME TO WHAT THE NORMAL TIME SHOULD BE FOR A PARTICULAR WORKER.

EVERY WORKER IS ASSIGNED A UNIQUE PERFORMANCE RATING BY THE TIME AND MOTION ANALYST.

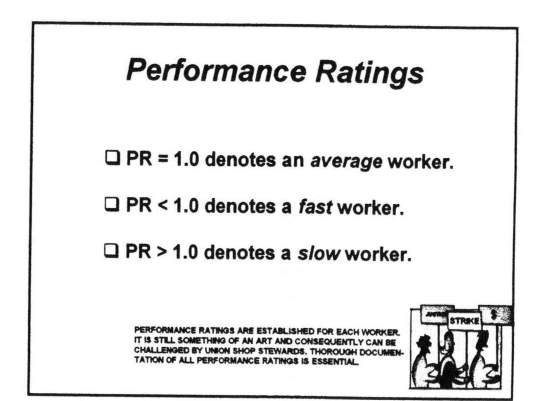

Performance Ratings

❑ PR = 1.0 denotes an *average* worker.

❑ PR < 1.0 denotes a *fast* worker.

❑ PR > 1.0 denotes a *slow* worker.

PERFORMANCE RATINGS ARE ESTABLISHED FOR EACH WORKER. IT IS STILL SOMETHING OF AN ART AND CONSEQUENTLY CAN BE CHALLENGED BY UNION SHOP STEWARDS. THOROUGH DOCUMENTATION OF ALL PERFORMANCE RATINGS IS ESSENTIAL.

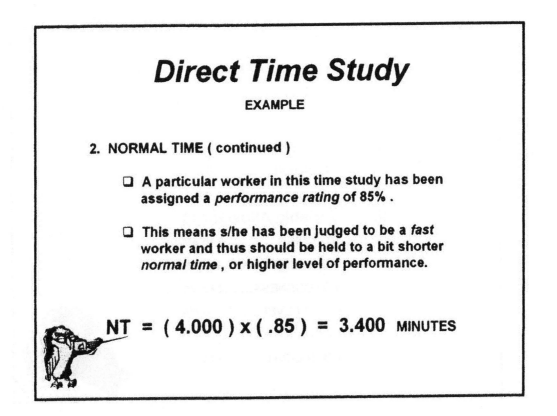

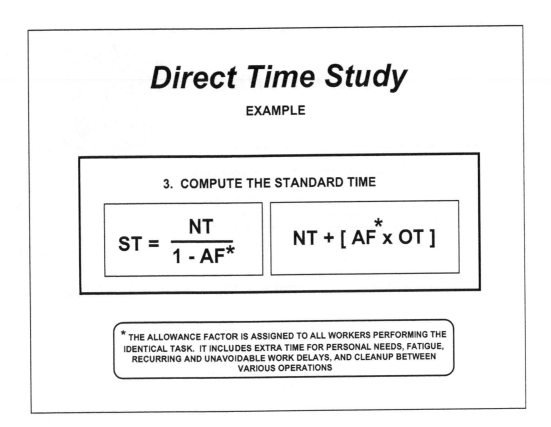

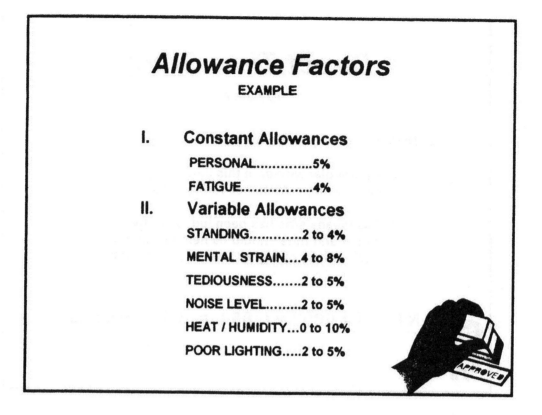

Allowance Factors
EXAMPLE

I.   **Constant Allowances**
    PERSONAL.............5%
    FATIGUE................4%

II.   **Variable Allowances**
    STANDING.............2 to 4%
    MENTAL STRAIN....4 to 8%
    TEDIOUSNESS.......2 to 5%
    NOISE LEVEL.........2 to 5%
    HEAT / HUMIDITY...0 to 10%
    POOR LIGHTING.....2 to 5%

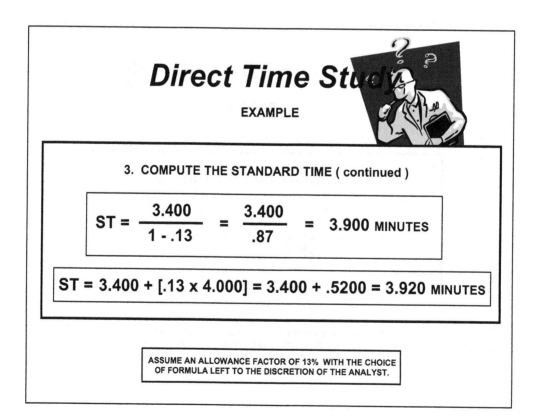

Direct Time Study
EXAMPLE

3. COMPUTE THE STANDARD TIME (continued)

$$ST = \frac{3.400}{1 - .13} = \frac{3.400}{.87} = 3.900 \text{ MINUTES}$$

$$ST = 3.400 + [.13 \times 4.000] = 3.400 + .5200 = 3.920 \text{ MINUTES}$$

ASSUME AN ALLOWANCE FACTOR OF 13% WITH THE CHOICE
OF FORMULA LEFT TO THE DISCRETION OF THE ANALYST.

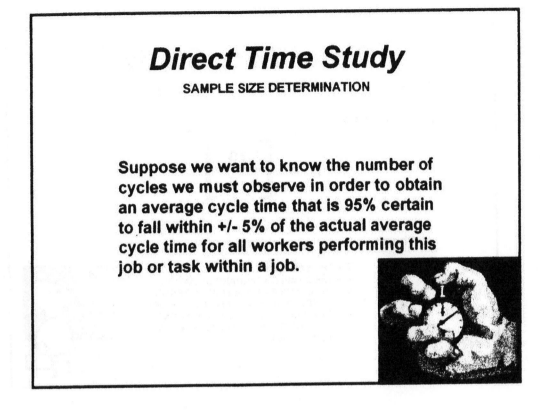

Direct Time Study

SAMPLE SIZE DETERMINATION

Suppose we want to know the number of cycles we must observe in order to obtain an average cycle time that is 95% certain to fall within +/- 5% of the actual average cycle time for all workers performing this job or task within a job.

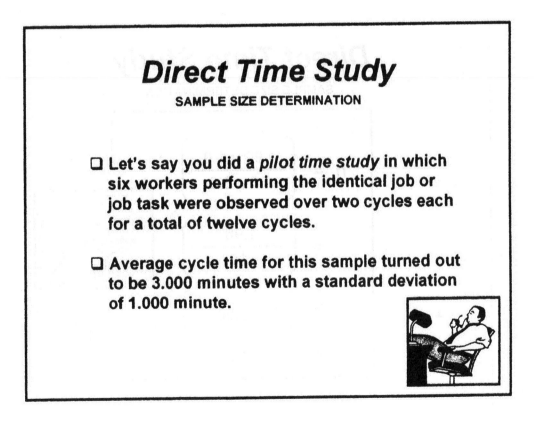

Direct Time Study

SAMPLE SIZE DETERMINATION

❑ Let's say you did a *pilot time study* in which six workers performing the identical job or job task were observed over two cycles each for a total of twelve cycles.

❑ Average cycle time for this sample turned out to be 3.000 minutes with a standard deviation of 1.000 minute.

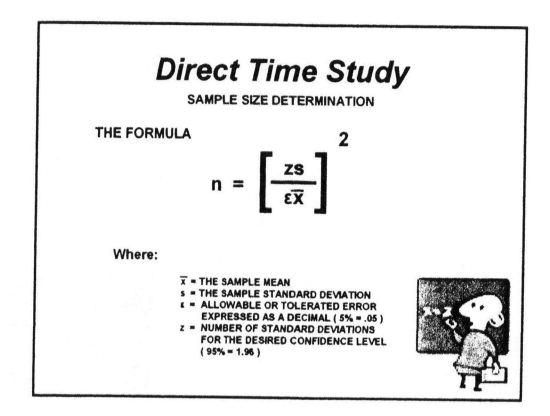

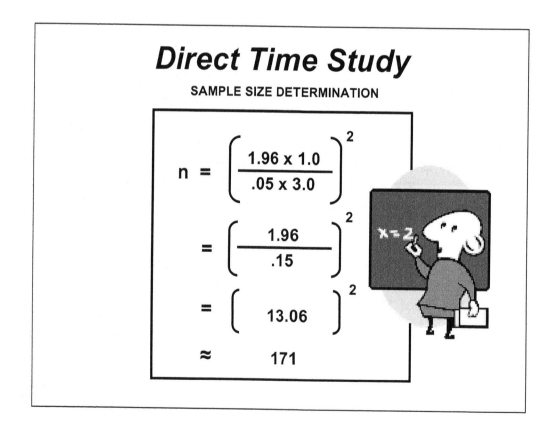

Direct Time Study

ADDITIONAL COMMENTS

- When observed times are not consistent, they need to be reviewed. Abnormally short or long times may be the result of an observational error and are usually discarded.

- Normal times (NT) are sometimes computed for each element of a job because the performance rating may vary for each element. In other words, the same worker may be fast on some tasks but slow or average on other tasks.

Intra - Job Performance Ratings

EXAMPLE

JOB ELEMENT	PERFORMANCE RATING
Drawing Materials	.99
Assembling Parts	1.08
Product Coating	.83
Product Inspection	1.20

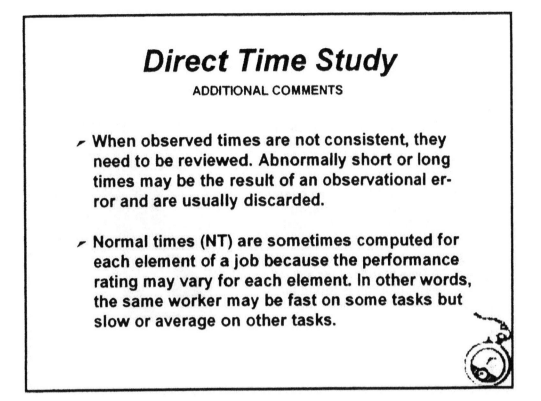

Predetermined Time Standards

- Repetitive, manual jobs are divided into basic motions of the human body.

- These motions have been studied under numerous conditions and assigned specific times.

- A time standard for a particular job is found by adding these basic motion times together.

Predetermined Time Standards

THERBLIGS

- Basic or elemental motions of the human body are called *therbligs*

- Term was coined by Frank Gilbreth *

- They include such activities as select, grasp, position, assemble, reach, hold, and inspect

- Time values for *therbligs* are specified in very detailed tables

GILBRETH SPELLED BACKWARDS WITH "T" AND "H" TRANSPOSED

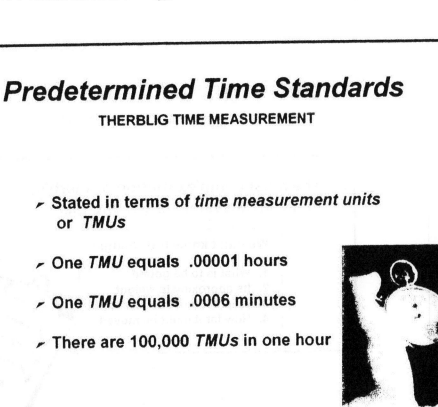

Predetermined Time Standards

THERBLIG TIME MEASUREMENT

➤ Stated in terms of *time measurement units*
   or *TMUs*

➤ One *TMU* equals .00001 hours

➤ One *TMU* equals .0006 minutes

➤ There are 100,000 *TMUs* in one hour

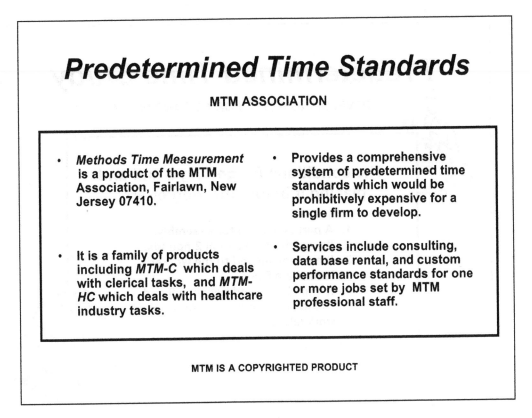

Predetermined Time Standards

MTM ASSOCIATION

- *Methods Time Measurement* is a product of the MTM Association, Fairlawn, New Jersey 07410.

- It is a family of products including *MTM-C* which deals with clerical tasks, and *MTM-HC* which deals with healthcare industry tasks.

- Provides a comprehensive system of predetermined time standards which would be prohibitively expensive for a single firm to develop.

- Services include consulting, data base rental, and custom performance standards for one or more jobs set by MTM professional staff.

MTM IS A COPYRIGHTED PRODUCT

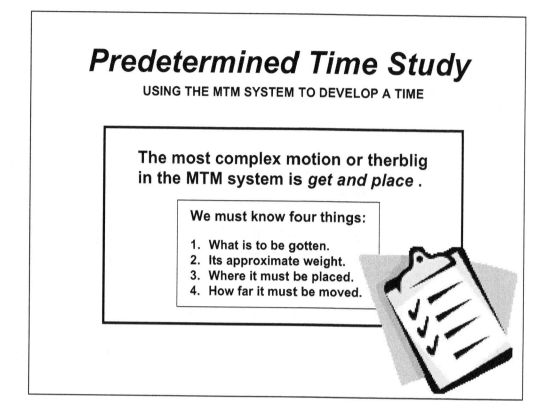

Predetermined Time Study

USING THE MTM SYSTEM TO DEVELOP A TIME

The most complex motion or therblig in the MTM system is *get and place*.

We must know four things:

1. What is to be gotten.
2. Its approximate weight.
3. Where it must be placed.
4. How far it must be moved.

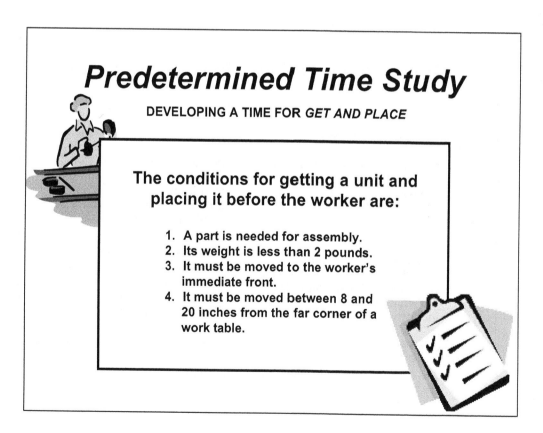

Predetermined Time Study

DEVELOPING A TIME FOR *GET AND PLACE*

The conditions for getting a unit and placing it before the worker are:

1. A part is needed for assembly.
2. Its weight is less than 2 pounds.
3. It must be moved to the worker's immediate front.
4. It must be moved between 8 and 20 inches from the far corner of a work table.

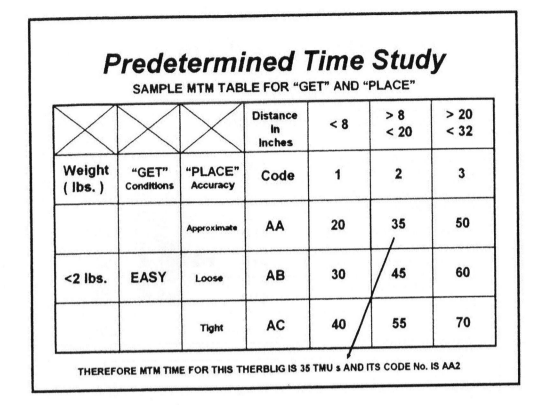

Predetermined Time Study

SAMPLE MTM TABLE FOR "GET" AND "PLACE"

			Distance In Inches	< 8	> 8 < 20	> 20 < 32
Weight (lbs.)	"GET" Conditions	"PLACE" Accuracy	Code	1	2	3
		Approximate	AA	20	35	50
<2 lbs.	EASY	Loose	AB	30	45	60
		Tight	AC	40	55	70

THEREFORE MTM TIME FOR THIS THERBLIG IS 35 TMU s AND ITS CODE No. IS AA2

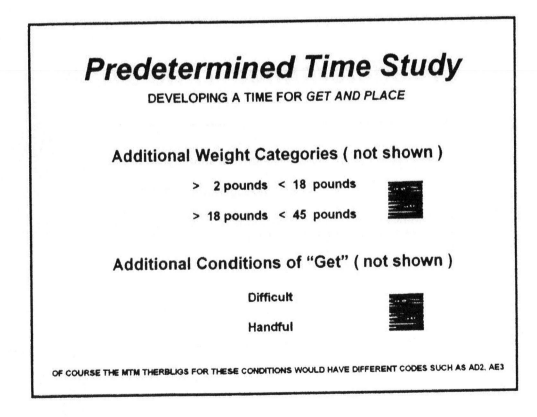

Predetermined Time Study

DEVELOPING A TIME FOR GET AND PLACE

Additional Weight Categories (not shown)

> 2 pounds < 18 pounds

> 18 pounds < 45 pounds

Additional Conditions of "Get" (not shown)

Difficult

Handful

OF COURSE THE MTM THERBLIGS FOR THESE CONDITIONS WOULD HAVE DIFFERENT CODES SUCH AS AD2, AE3

Predetermined Time Study

COMPLETE *MTM* JOB TIME EXAMPLE

JOB ELEMENT (THERBLIG)	JOB ELEMENT CODE	JOB ELEMENT TIME (in TMUs)
Draw item "A" from left corner of table	AA2	35
Draw item "B" from right corner of table	AC2	55
Assemble the two Items	AD2	45
Inspect the assembly	PT1	83
Place the assembly in a box	GB3	40
	$\sum$ TMUs	258

.0006 x 258 = .1548 *STANDARD MINUTES* FOR THIS COMPLETE JOB

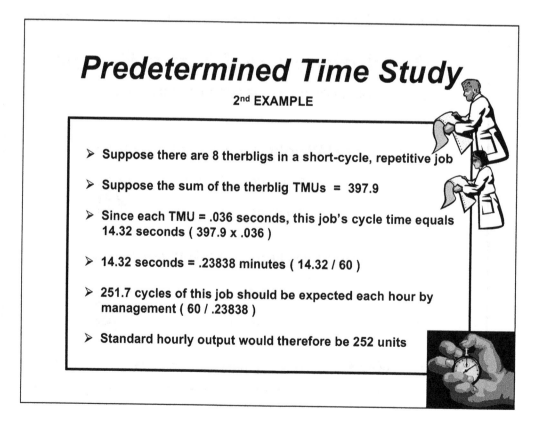

Predetermined Time Study

2nd EXAMPLE

➢ **Suppose there are 8 therbligs in a short-cycle, repetitive job**

➢ **Suppose the sum of the therblig TMUs = 397.9**

➢ **Since each TMU = .036 seconds, this job's cycle time equals 14.32 seconds (397.9 x .036)**

➢ **14.32 seconds = .23838 minutes (14.32 / 60)**

➢ **251.7 cycles of this job should be expected each hour by management (60 / .23838)**

➢ **Standard hourly output would therefore be 252 units**

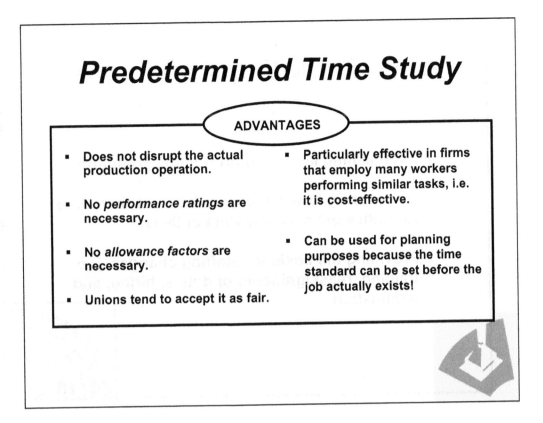

Predetermined Time Study

ADVANTAGES

- Does not disrupt the actual production operation.

- No *performance ratings* are necessary.

- No *allowance factors* are necessary.

- Unions tend to accept it as fair.

- Particularly effective in firms that employ many workers performing similar tasks, i.e. it is cost-effective.

- Can be used for planning purposes because the time standard can be set before the job actually exists!

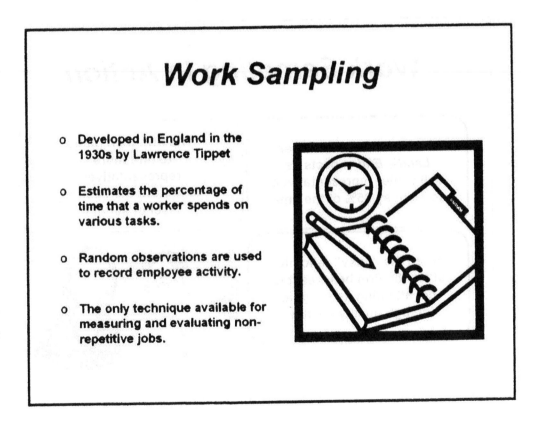

Work Sampling

o Developed in England in the 1930s by Lawrence Tippet

o Estimates the percentage of time that a worker spends on various tasks.

o Random observations are used to record employee activity.

o The only technique available for measuring and evaluating non-repetitive jobs.

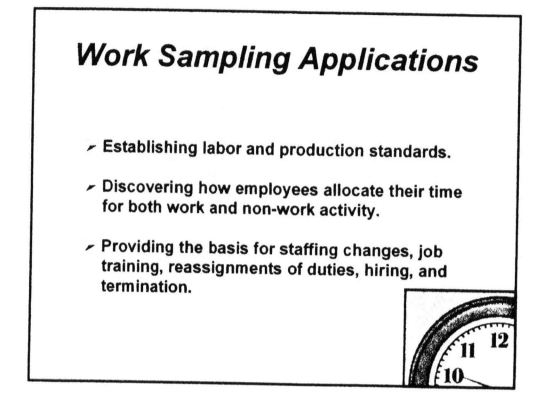

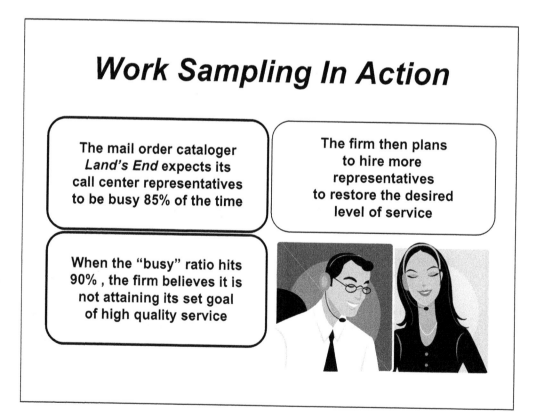

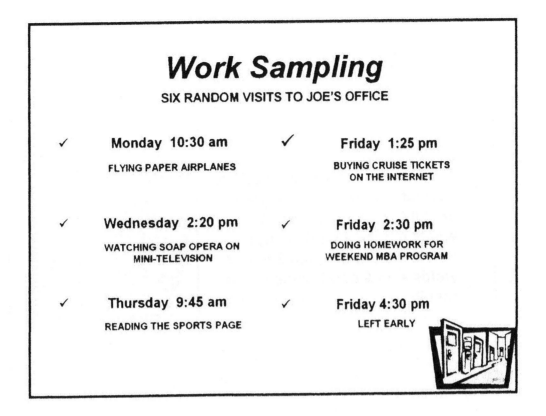

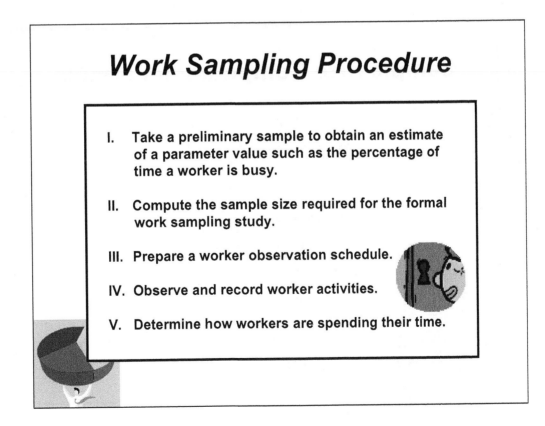

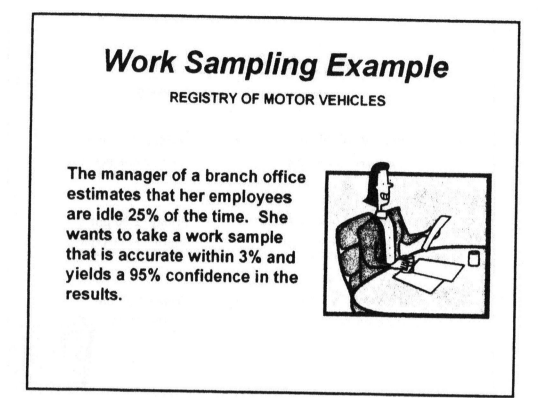

Work Sampling Example

REGISTRY OF MOTOR VEHICLES

The manager of a branch office estimates that her employees are idle 25% of the time. She wants to take a work sample that is accurate within 3% and yields a 95% confidence in the results.

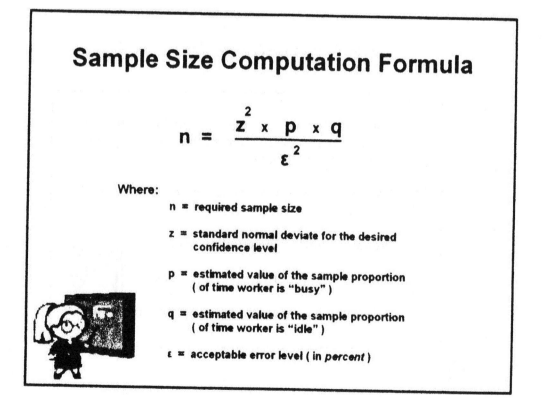

Sample Size Computation Formula

$$n = \frac{z^2 \times p \times q}{\varepsilon^2}$$

Where:

n = required sample size

z = standard normal deviate for the desired confidence level

p = estimated value of the sample proportion (of time worker is "busy")

q = estimated value of the sample proportion (of time worker is "idle")

ε = acceptable error level (in *percent*)

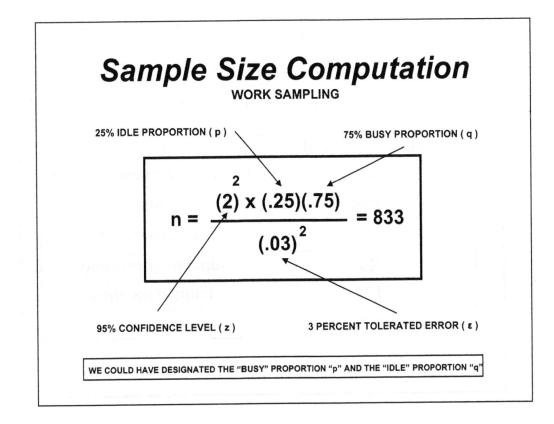

Sample Size Computation
WORK SAMPLING

25% IDLE PROPORTION (p)   75% BUSY PROPORTION (q)

$$n = \frac{(2)^2 \times (.25)(.75)}{(.03)^2} = 833$$

95% CONFIDENCE LEVEL (z)   3 PERCENT TOLERATED ERROR (ε)

WE COULD HAVE DESIGNATED THE "BUSY" PROPORTION "p" AND THE "IDLE" PROPORTION "q"

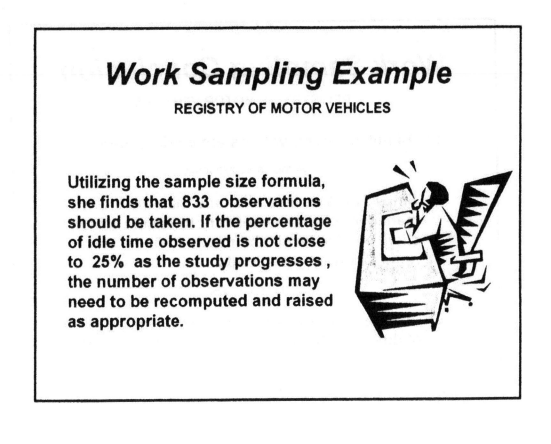

Work Sampling Example
REGISTRY OF MOTOR VEHICLES

Utilizing the sample size formula, she finds that 833 observations should be taken. If the percentage of idle time observed is not close to 25% as the study progresses, the number of observations may need to be recomputed and raised as appropriate.

Work Sampling Results

REGISTRY OF MOTOR VEHICLES

Number of Observations	Activity
485	on phone / meeting clients
126	idle
62	personal time
23	supervisor meetings
137	filing, data entry
$\sum$ = 833	

Work Sampling Conclusion

REGISTRY OF MOTOR VEHICLES

❑ All but 188 observations are work-related.

126 IDLE & 62 PERSONAL

❑ Since 22.6% is less idle time than the branch manager believes necessary to ensure a high client service level, she needs to find a way to reduce current work loads.

188 / 833 = 22%

❑ This could be accomplished via a reassignment of duties or the hiring of additional personnel.

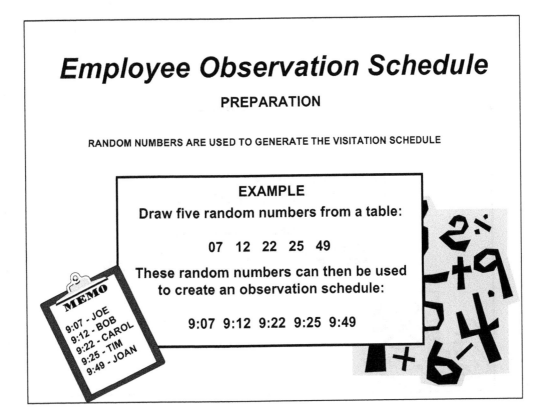

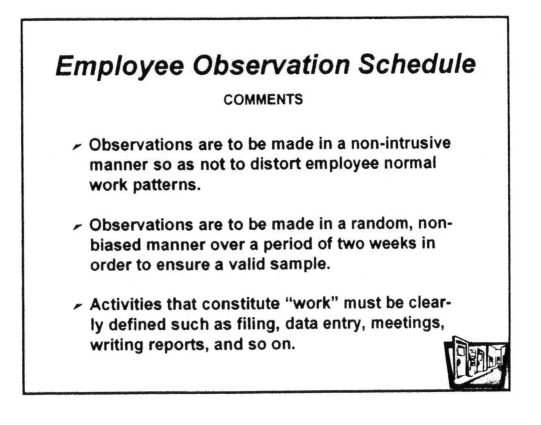

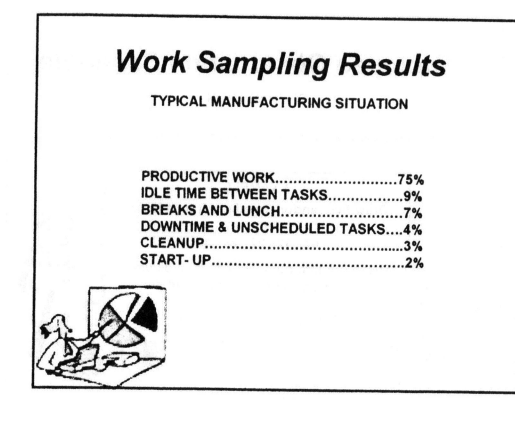

Work Sampling Results

TYPICAL MANUFACTURING SITUATION

PRODUCTIVE WORK..............................75%
IDLE TIME BETWEEN TASKS.................9%
BREAKS AND LUNCH...........................7%
DOWNTIME & UNSCHEDULED TASKS....4%
CLEANUP...3%
START- UP...2%

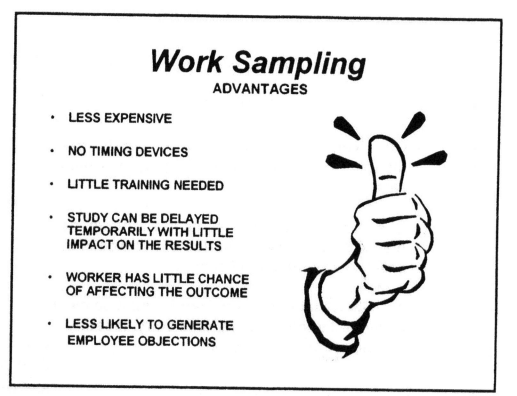

Work Sampling
ADVANTAGES

- LESS EXPENSIVE

- NO TIMING DEVICES

- LITTLE TRAINING NEEDED

- STUDY CAN BE DELAYED TEMPORARILY WITH LITTLE IMPACT ON THE RESULTS

- WORKER HAS LITTLE CHANCE OF AFFECTING THE OUTCOME

- LESS LIKELY TO GENERATE EMPLOYEE OBJECTIONS

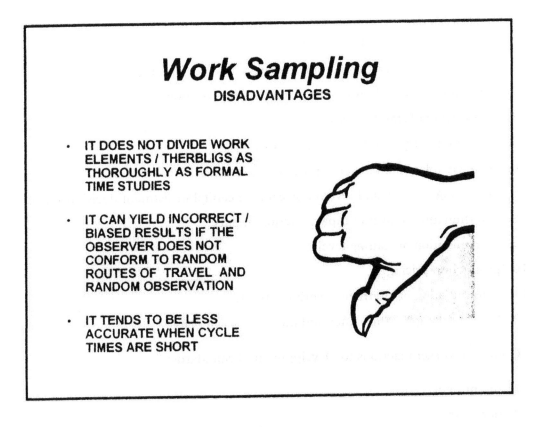

Standards

Production Standard: a criterion established as a basis for comparison in measuring or judging output.

A standard can be established for:

1. quantity.

2. quality.

3. cost.

4. any attribute of output.

Labor Standard: what is expected from an average worker under average conditions for a given period of time.

Standards must be revised due to:

1. changes in technology and technological processes.

2. changes in materials.

3. the physical characteristics of the workers themselves over successive generations.

4. changes in the products and services offered.

5. changes in work methods.

Uses for standards:

1. the basis for control of operations.

2. evaluating individual worker and departmental performance.

3. determination of subsequent supervisor compensation.

4. formulation of standard costs.

5. planning the types of labor skills necessary.

6. aggregate planning of overall production rates.

7. estimating expense and revenue streams in capital investment decision-making.

8. determination of overall capacity requirements.

9. determination of staffing levels.

10. production pricing.

11. determination of alternative work methods.

12. basis for compensation rates and incentive wage plans.

Common worker reactions to Development of Standards:

1. resentment

2. nervousness

3. slowing the work pace to "loosen" the standard

4. "padding" their jobs with extra tasks

To minimize the above:

1. repeated time study of the same workers over time.

2. stand by one worker, yet study the *adjacent* worker.

3. one-way mirrors.

4. closed-circuit television cameras in corners of the workplace.

5. study across several workers simultaneously.

Learning Curves

When a new model of product is introduced, the learning curve phenomenon can be useful in its production scheduling and planning. It has been observed that if a new task is performed repeatedly over time, its performance time will drop dramatically and then continue to drop at a slower rate until a performance time plateau (leveling off) is reached. This phenomenon applies to individual workers, departments, firms, and entire industries.

Actual labor performance on many different products over a long period of time, usually decades, is recorded. Regression analysis techniques are used to isolate the pattern of learning (the learning curve).

By convention, the learning curve is specified as a percentage. A "90%" learning curve, for example, means that each time cumulative productive output doubles, the newest unit of output requires only 90% of the performance time required of the "base" or reference unit:

If unit #1 requires 100 labor hours to complete, unit #2 will require only 90 hours (100 hours × .90).

If unit #2 requires 90 labor hours to complete, unit #4 will require only 81 hours (90 hours × .90).

If unit #4 requires 81 labor hours to complete, unit #8 will require only 72 hours (81 hours × .90).

If unit #8 requires 72 labor hours to complete, unit #16 will require only 63 hours (72 hours × .90), and so on.

The lower the percentage of the learning curve, the more efficient it is. An 80% learning curve is more efficient than a 90% one.

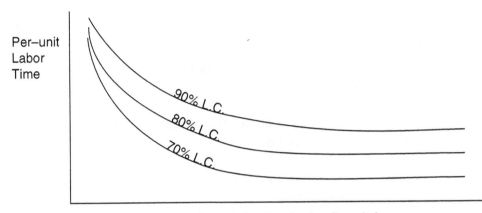

Cumulative Production (in units)

To employ learning curve analysis, two (2) parameters must be estimated:

1. the number of labor hours required to produce the first unit of output (which is *not* the prototype number of hours which is many times higher).

2. the learning index or rate of learning.

Slight variations from actual values can have serious repercussions on later production planning and scheduling. Estimates of labor hours for the first unit are based on staff experience and familiarity with the history of the production process. Estimation accuracy will be closely related to the degree of similarity between the new and previous product.

To dispel a popular misconception, the learning curve does not just reflect the effects of worker learning. It shows the synergistic effect of time improvements originating from:

–worker learning	–changes in work methods	–engineering modifications
–layout improvements	–equipment redesign	–worker training
–changes in labor policy		–equipment replacement
–changes in product materials		

Learning curve analysis is of greatest benefit for manpower planning and cash-flow planning which involves the timing of cash outlays and inflows associated with a new product.

A firm that "rides the learning curve" is one that enjoys higher productivity from fewer workers, greater profits from falling variable costs, and higher market shares based on its ability to lower prices. But there is a down-side risk as well. A firm whose workers' manufacturing skills and equipment capabilities are narrowly concentrated on a small line of aging, similar products is vulnerable to changing market tastes which could devastate its market share (and profits) in a very short time. For this reason, most firms today are content to "ride the learning curve" only partway, before "resetting" it for an all new product that will retain customer interest.

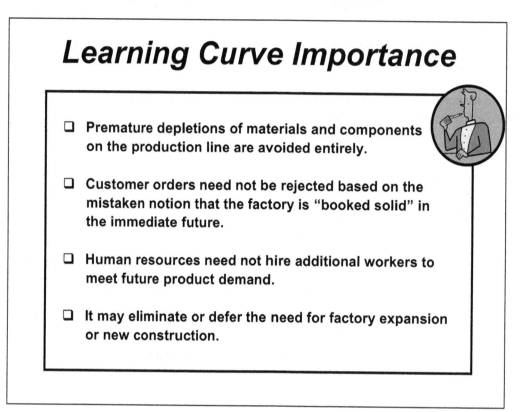

Learning Curve Importance

❑ **Premature depletions of materials and components on the production line are avoided entirely.**

❑ **Customer orders need not be rejected based on the mistaken notion that the factory is "booked solid" in the immediate future.**

❑ **Human resources need not hire additional workers to meet future product demand.**

❑ **It may eliminate or defer the need for factory expansion or new construction.**

Learning Curve Example

Problem Statement

Assume that a company has an "85%" learning curve historically. It now intends to introduce a new model. It is estimated that the 1st unit of production will require 3,000 labor hours. The company wants to know how many hours will be required to produce the fiftieth (50th) unit.

the general formula: $Y_n = Y_1 \cdot N^x$

Where Y_n = time required for a specified unit

Y_1 = time required for the first unit

N = the unit for which a time is sought

x = the learning rate

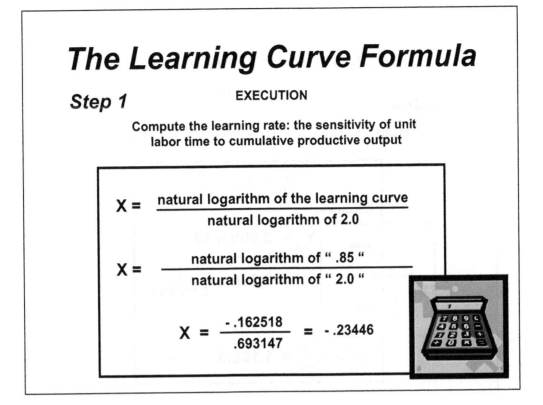

The Learning Curve Formula

Step 1   EXECUTION

Compute the learning rate: the sensitivity of unit
labor time to cumulative productive output

$$X = \frac{\text{natural logarithm of the learning curve}}{\text{natural logarithm of 2.0}}$$

$$X = \frac{\text{natural logarithm of " .85 "}}{\text{natural logarithm of " 2.0 "}}$$

$$X = \frac{-.162518}{.693147} = -.23446$$

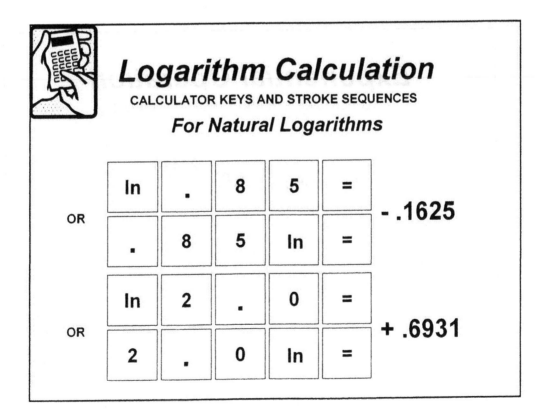

Logarithm Calculation

CALCULATOR KEYS AND STROKE SEQUENCES
For Natural Logarithms

| ln | . | 8 | 5 | = |

OR

| . | 8 | 5 | ln | = |

- .1625

| ln | 2 | . | 0 | = |

OR

| 2 | . | 0 | ln | = |

+ .6931

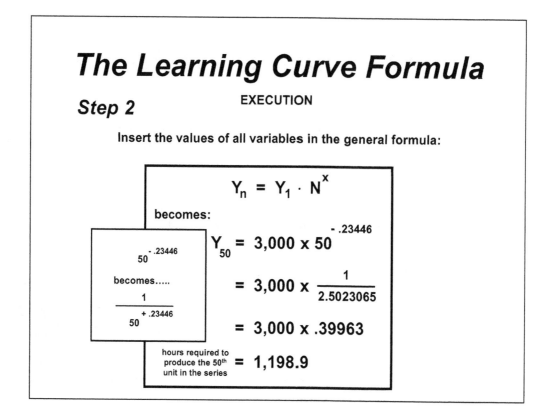

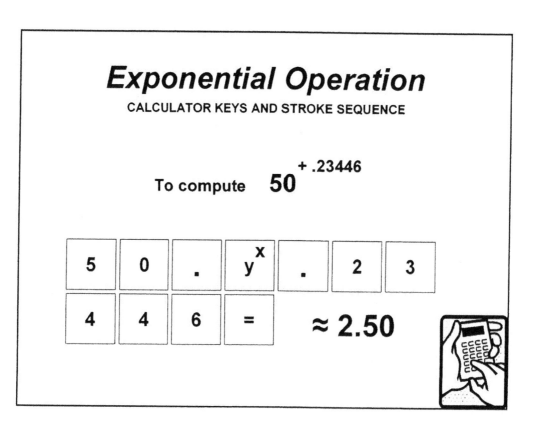

A Crude Estimation of the Learning Curve

Suppose that the labor content, in hours, for the first eight units of production were as follows:

Unit Number	Labor Content
1	41
2	34
3	29
4	26
5	24
6	24
7	23
8	21

For each pair of units: "n + 2n," we can compute the ratio of labor content:

	n 2n	Ratio
units	"1" and "2"	34/41 = .829
units	"2" and "4"	26/34 = .765
units	"3" and "6"	24/29 = .828
units	"4" and "8"	21/26 = .808

The average of the above ratios would then be an approximation of the learning curve for the firm:

$$\frac{.829 + .765 + .828 + .808}{4} = .807 \text{ or } 80\%$$

Choice of Production Units

A *production unit* need not be one (1) actual unit of production, i.e., a television set or automobile. For many items, the labor content of a single unit is so small that it is difficult to measure and not meaningful. Therefore, the *unit of production* could be "1,000" or even "1,000,000" actual units in the case of items such as nuts, bolts, screws, plastic caps, etc.

The definition selected for a *unit of production* is important because the learning curve will be different each time. The definition must be found through experience, and it will represent at least a few hours of production, and possibly the equivalent of a month or several months of production.

Experience Rates and Experience Curves

An *experience curve* looks, behaves, and can be used exactly like a *learning curve*, except it expresses the "cost per unit" as a function of cumulative productive output, rather than "labor content per unit."

"Cost per unit" includes labor cost, material cost, supplies, and depreciation, and is reduced by:

- process improvements
- better equipment

- better management

- better information flows

- economies of scale

- new plants and processes

- technological innovation

as cumulative production volume rises.

The *experience curve/experience rate* is not necessarily equal to the *learning curve/learning rate* for the same product. Accordingly, it should be derived separately.

An example of an *experience curve* is shown below:

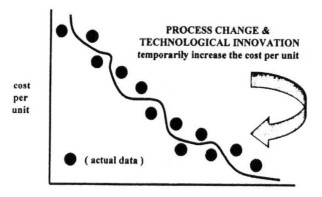

cumulative number of units produced

Chapter 11

Just-In-Time (JIT) Manufacturing and Service Systems

Chapter 11 addresses a relatively new approach to the manufacturing process and the manufacturer/supplier relationship. Just-in-Time manufacturing holds the promise of significant inventory cost savings, reduced manufacturing lead-times, empowered workers, and better quality.

In chapter 7, a particular type of manufacturing process called "repetitive manufacturing" was introduced. This process starts with the in-plant fabrication of basic components or their purchase from an independent vendor. These components in turn, are assembled into subassemblies, assemblies, and eventually, the finished product.

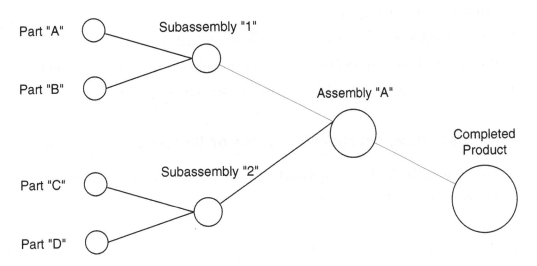

This flow-oriented process represents approximately 20% of all world-wide manufacturing activity, and typical applications are found in the toy, appliance, electronics, and automobile industries. Repetitive manufacturing has the capability of producing high volumes of a single product, several models of one basic product, or several kinds of products sharing the same basic components and manufacturing skill requirements—all on a common production line!

JIT reduces inventory to "0" and as such eliminates carrying costs.

There exist two very different approaches to repetitive manufacturing: the "push" system of the Western Hemisphere, and the "pull" system of the Asian Hemisphere. The answers to the questions of "when" and "how many" units to produce, will depend largely on the choice of system.

The repetitive manufacturing process has been the subject of myriad academic studies, professional journal articles, and even general media attention, because it has become the primary "battleground" in the continuing economic "war" between the world's two largest industrial titans: the United States and Japan. Beset by slumping worker morale, shoddy quality control, lagging productivity, mounting inventory costs, and longer set-up times between product runs, American manufacturing of the 1980s looked for solutions in its Japanese counterpart as a means of stemming declines in market share.

The purpose of this chapter is to introduce the principles of the "pull-system" which was originally developed in Japan during the 1930s and is also known as "kanban." The chapter will also examine the major differences between the "push" and "pull" systems, provide a brief operational example of kanban, list its vulnerabilities, and suggest ways in which American manufacturing can exploit them.

The "pull" system or "kanban" is the foundation of a broader manufacturing concept called JIT or "just-in-time" manufacturing. JIT brings all components and materials to the factory assembly line at the exact time and in the exact quantities to support production of the exact number of goods demanded by the factory's customers on a daily basis.

While cultural differences between east and west preclude total adoption, JIT is fast becoming the future of not only repetitive manufacturing, but of all manufacturing, as system analysts and computer programmers devise sophisticated applications of JIT to "job shop" and "mass production" operations.

Cornerstones of the Japanese Manufacturing System

1. Produce what the customer desires.

2. Produce those products only at the rate the customer wants them.

3. Produce with perfect quality.

4. Produce instantaneously, with zero unnecessary lead-time.

5. Produce with no waste of labor, material, or equipment: every movement has a purpose.

6. Produce by methods that allow for the development of people.

The Nine (9) Simple, yet Hidden Lessons of Japanese Manufacturing

1. Management Style (Leader is a leader among equals as well as a confidant)

2. Just-In-Time Production (JIT)

3. Total Quality Control

4. Horse-Shoe Plant Production Line

5. Flexibility

6. Purchasing Practices and Relationships

7. Self-Improvement of Work Quality

8. Striving for Simplicity in All Things

9. Zero Inventories (Raw Material, Work-in-Process, Finished Goods)

encourage worker accountability

Traditional Western Mfg Philosophy

- big, fast machines

- big, heavy products

- produce in huge volumes

- take huge amounts of time for planning future production operations

- implement production runs at all costs, and regardless of any arising problems on the production line

- treat labor as expendable items

- deliberately limit each worker's role in the manufacturing process (perhaps in order to avoid worker retaliation for management's treatment via product "sabotage")

Characteristics of Contrasting Approaches to Repetitive Manufacturing

Operations Characteristics	Push Systems (U.S.)	Pull System (Japan)
Major Orientation	Balanced, non-stop flows to meet predetermined schedule.	Flexibility & simplicity in responding quickly to actual demand.
Machines	Use single, specialized machines with production capacities in excess of anticipated needs. Large capital investment in machine & special tooling to perform a single purpose repeatedly.	Multiple copies of smaller, simpler, less expensive and perhaps slower machines with specially developed flexible tooling to facilitate shutdown, startup, and changeovers to different product models. Tools and attachments located conveniently at machine site to simplify setups & changeovers.
Material Handling Equipment	Extensive reliance on elaborate devices to move large lots or batches of raw materials, components and subassemblies between work stations & inventory storage areas.	Minimal use of conveyance equipment. Frequent use of manual transfer of components from worker to worker by locating work stations close together and producing in small batches or one at a time.
Inventory Posture	Extensive work-in-process inventories accumulate between work stations and stages of production. Produce large runs of components to spread high setup costs across many units, to avoid expensive changeovers, to hedge against equipment failures, and to compensate for defective components.	Avoid excess inventories. In general, the prevailing view is the inventories are dysfunctional because they mask or hide product problems. Produce only what is needed as it is needed. Instead producing ahead of need, produce just in time in small batches (one at a time) as frequently as necessary.
Relationships with Suppliers	Supply contracts often awarded on basis of price competition among suppliers who are geographically dispersed. Relationships between buyer & suppliers is transient. Materials purchased & delivered in large quantities and stored until use.	Close, long-lasting and team-like supplier-buyer relationships. Close purchase-delivery coordination, frequently on short notice in variable quantities, with suppliers located near customer's facility.

Operations Characteristics	Push Systems (U.S.)	Pull System (Japan)
Manpower Utilization	Features task specialization and strict division of labor in fixed work assignments with limited task scope. Limited transfer of employees across jobs with different work content and variety. Employees oriented toward performing specialized tasks on many units of one product with emphasis on keeping the line running.	Flexible labor oriented toward broader scope and view of work responsibilities. Concerned with discovering and correcting process weaknesses to ensure error-free production of every unit of product. Make equipment changeovers and set-ups at their own work stations needed to produce varieties of product models. Limited hiring and layoffs by transferring employees to diverse jobs as demand at their own workplace fluctuates. Production lines stop until any problems are corrected through efforts and ingenuity of workers.
Support Staff	Extensive investment in staff personnel for pre-production design of equipment, facilities, line balancing to a planned output rate, and job design for efficiency. Attempt to design production problems and bottlenecks out of the system to meet anticipated output levels. Extensive use of staffs for planning & controlling inventories, materials flows, and product quality during production. Foremen on production lines that are dedicated to a single product model ensure that each work station has the materials and people to meet the scheduled output. Foremen responsible for motivating a large number of employees.	Emphasis on improving production processes during as well as before production. Joint problem solving by engineering, workers, and managers as needed to address and resolve each problem as it arises. Foremen provide floor-level leadership for problem-solving and frequent rebalancing of lines in response to variable demands for mixed models of product. Constant emphasis on improving quality and reducing inventories and setup times. Strive for a single production line that can produce mixed models by rapid chang-overs to meet market demand.

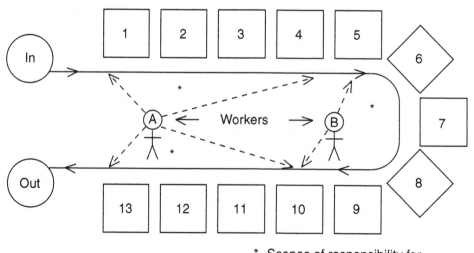

* Scopes of responsibility for both production workers

U-Shape Layout Under Pull-System (Japan)

Example (Above): Worker "A" works on the product batch moving through Stations 1, 2, 3, and 4. Worker "B" meanwhile adjusts equipment in Stations 5, 6, 7, 8, and 9 in anticipation of receiving that batch, and then actually works on it. Worker "A" turns around and prepares Stations 10, 11, 12, and 13 for the soon-to-arrive batch.

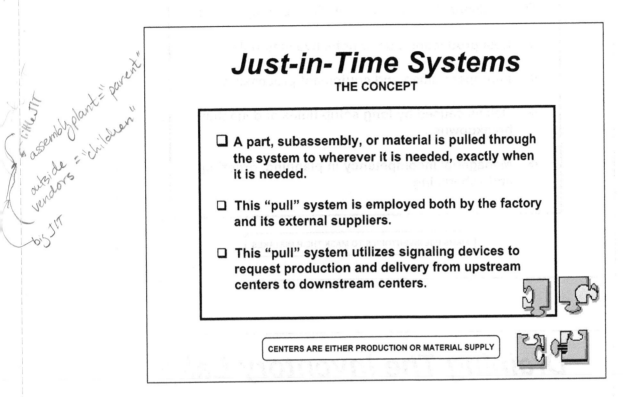

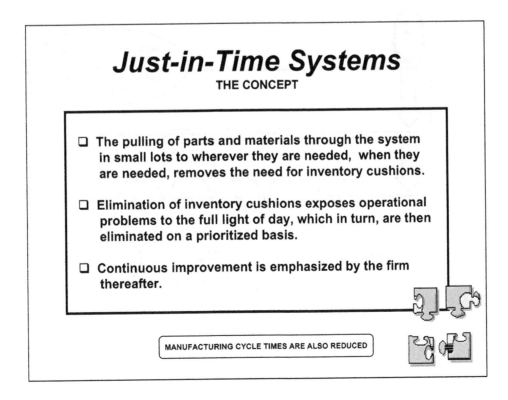

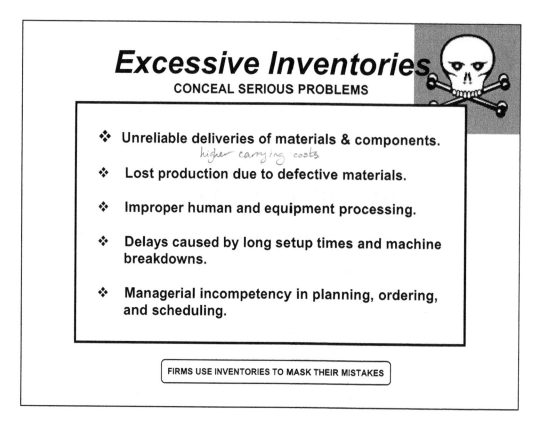

Excessive Inventories
CONCEAL SERIOUS PROBLEMS

❖ Unreliable deliveries of materials & components.

higher carrying costs

❖ Lost production due to defective materials.

❖ Improper human and equipment processing.

❖ Delays caused by long setup times and machine breakdowns.

❖ Managerial incompetency in planning, ordering, and scheduling.

FIRMS USE INVENTORIES TO MASK THEIR MISTAKES

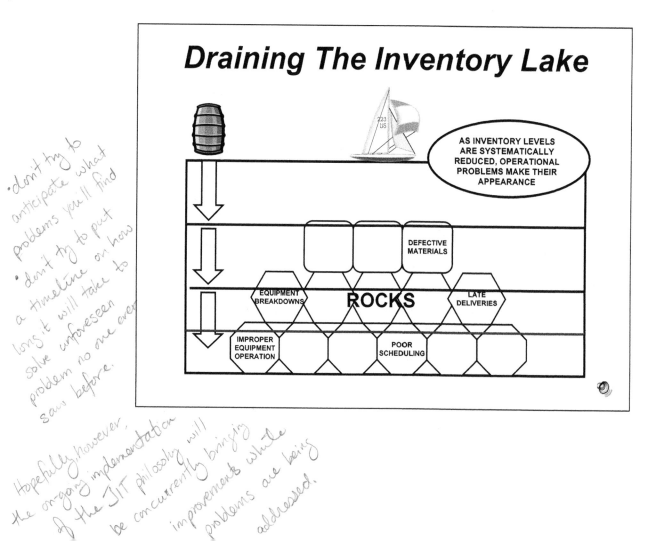

Draining The Inventory Lake

AS INVENTORY LEVELS ARE SYSTEMATICALLY REDUCED, OPERATIONAL PROBLEMS MAKE THEIR APPEARANCE

DEFECTIVE MATERIALS

EQUIPMENT BREAKDOWNS   **ROCKS**   LATE DELIVERIES

IMPROPER EQUIPMENT OPERATION   POOR SCHEDULING

• don't try to anticipate what problems you'll find

• don't try to put a timeline on how long it will take to solve unforeseen problem no one ever saw before.

Hopefully however, the ongoing implementation of the JIT philosophy will be concurrently bringing improvements while problems are being addressed.

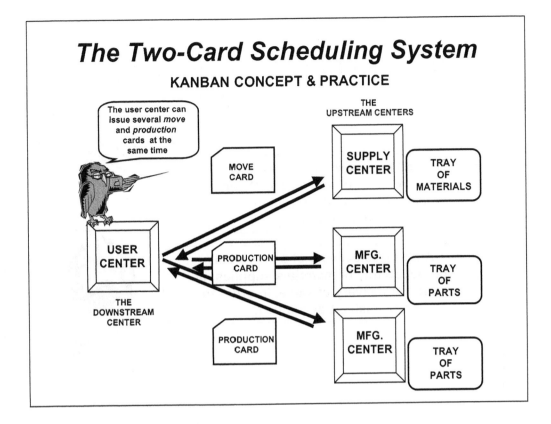

Kanban = 2-card → early name for JIT

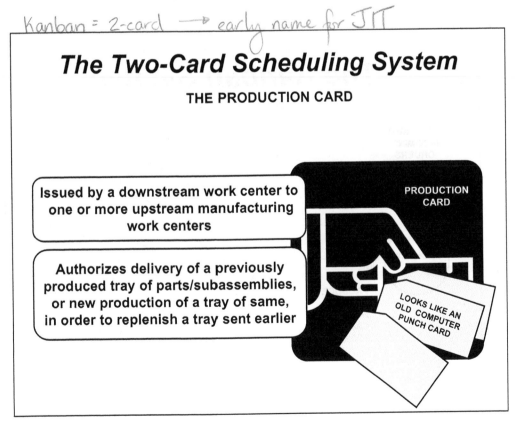

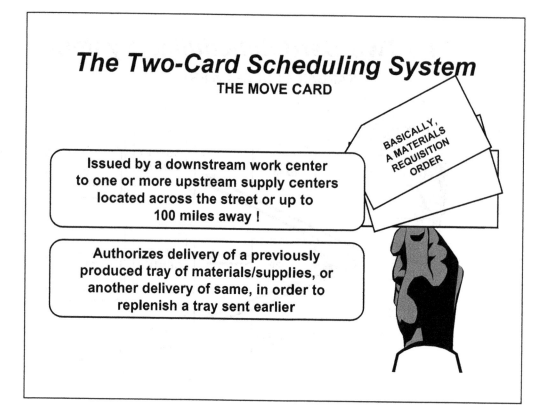

The Two-Card Scheduling System
THE MOVE CARD

BASICALLY, A MATERIALS REQUISITION ORDER

Issued by a downstream work center to one or more upstream supply centers located across the street or up to 100 miles away !

Authorizes delivery of a previously produced tray of materials/supplies, or another delivery of same, in order to replenish a tray sent earlier

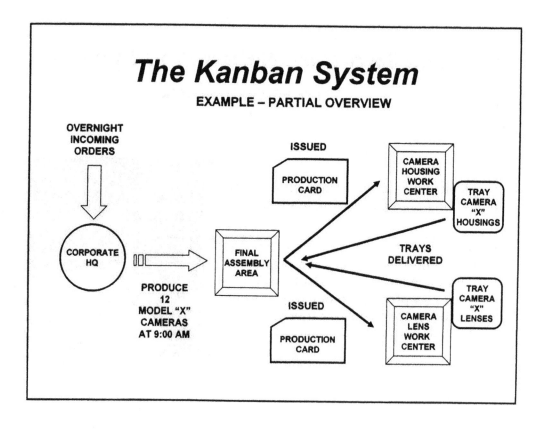

The Kanban System
EXAMPLE – PARTIAL OVERVIEW

OVERNIGHT INCOMING ORDERS

CORPORATE HQ

PRODUCE 12 MODEL "X" CAMERAS AT 9:00 AM

FINAL ASSEMBLY AREA

ISSUED
PRODUCTION CARD

ISSUED
PRODUCTION CARD

CAMERA HOUSING WORK CENTER

TRAY CAMERA "X" HOUSINGS

TRAYS DELIVERED

TRAY CAMERA "X" LENSES

CAMERA LENS WORK CENTER

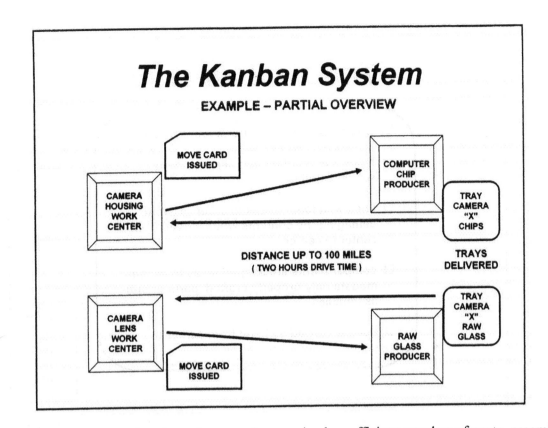

When a *downstream* (user) work center has received a sufficient number of parts, assemblies, or materials to meet its current production needs, it returns the empty tray(s) to its *upstream* (provider) work center or outside material vendor WITHOUT a move/production card attached.

The upstream work center or material vendor will then refill the tray(s) and retain it (them) until the next time it (they) are needed by the *downstream* work center.

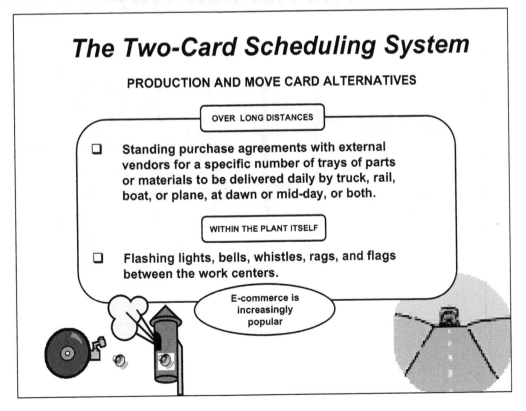

Classic JIT system has no conveyor belts it is all tray based & hand to hand

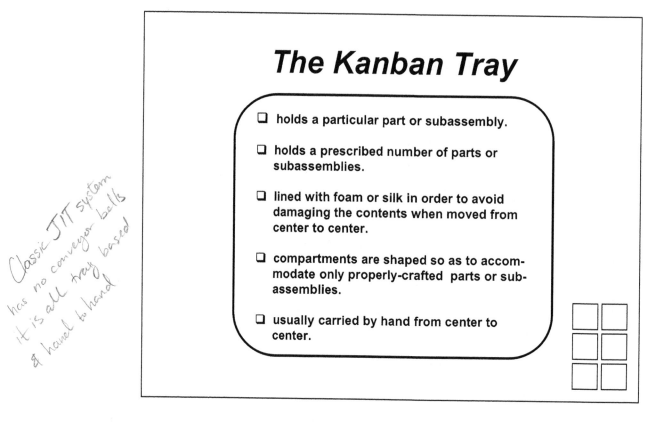

The Kanban Tray

- ❑ holds a particular part or subassembly.

- ❑ holds a prescribed number of parts or subassemblies.

- ❑ lined with foam or silk in order to avoid damaging the contents when moved from center to center.

- ❑ compartments are shaped so as to accommodate only properly-crafted parts or subassemblies.

- ❑ usually carried by hand from center to center.

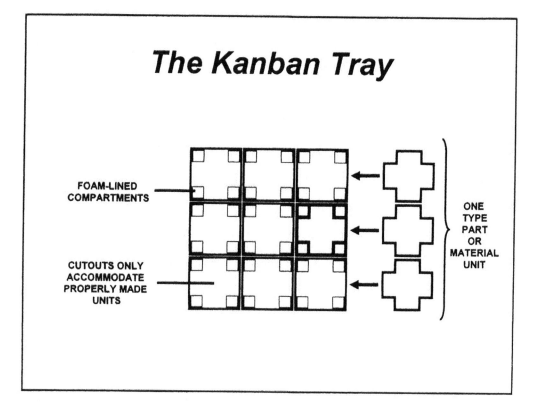

The Kanban Tray

FOAM-LINED COMPARTMENTS

CUTOUTS ONLY ACCOMMODATE PROPERLY MADE UNITS

ONE TYPE PART OR MATERIAL UNIT

The Kanban Tray / Bin
CALCULATING THE NUMBER REQUIRED

MANAGEMENT MUST FIRST
ESTABLISH THE NUMBER OF
COMPARTMENTS WITHIN
EACH TRAY / BIN AND ITS SIZE

The number of trays / bins
sets the amount of
authorized inventory
for a particular part
or material

It is based on the item's
daily demand, production
lead time, and safety stock
needed to compensate
for system uncertainty

Lead time = time required to prepare for a component production

lost time on "getting ready" for work (coffee chat, water cooler banter, etc.)

The Kanban Tray
THE NUMBER FORMULA

$x^2 + y^2 + 2dx + 2ey + f = 0$

$a = \pi r^2$

$$\text{Number of Trays} = \frac{\text{Lead Time Demand + Safety Stock}}{\text{Number of Tray Compartments}}$$

(extra units for the "shit happens" scenario)

FROM THE
CAMERA
EXAMPLE
(TEXT)

- DAILY DEMAND - CAMERA "X" = 12 UNITS
  THEREFORE.......
- DAILY DEMAND - CAMERA "X" LENS ASSEMBLY = 12 UNITS
- DAILY DEMAND - CAMERA "X" HOUSING = 12 UNITS
- PRODUCTION LEAD TIME = 30 MINUTES (1/2 HOUR) FOR EACH
- SAFETY STOCK = 3 UNITS FOR EACH

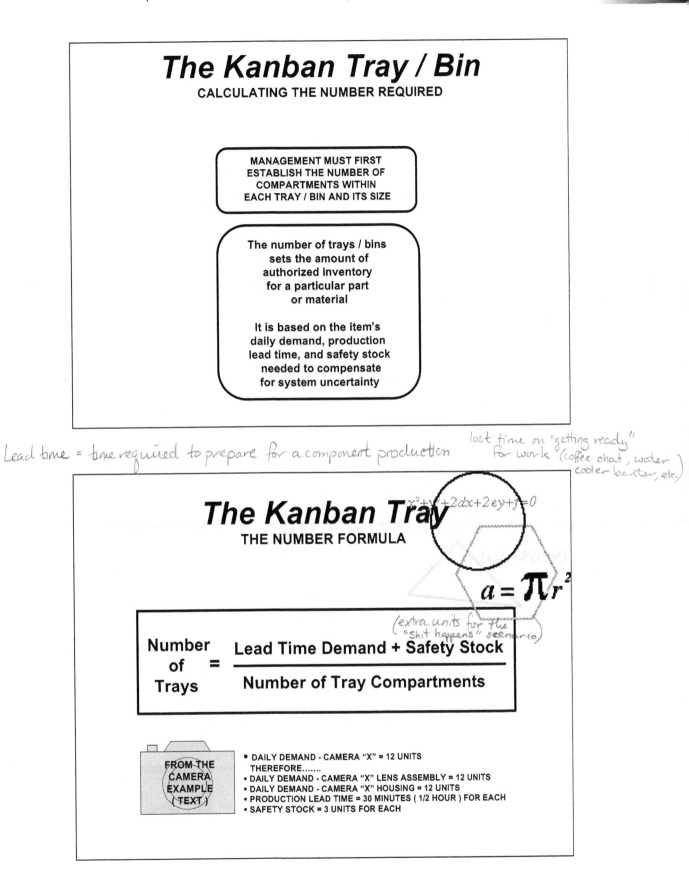

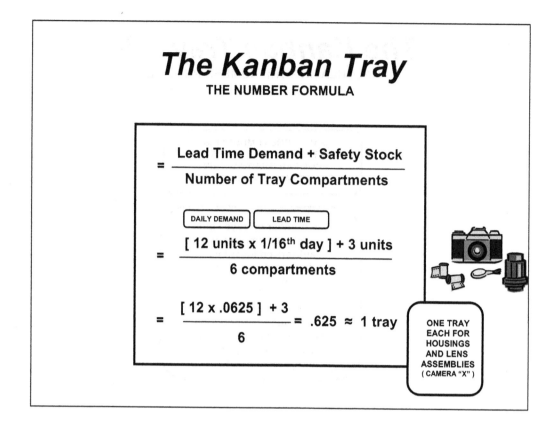

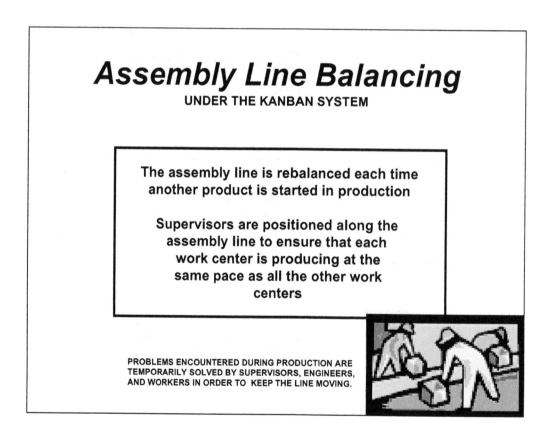

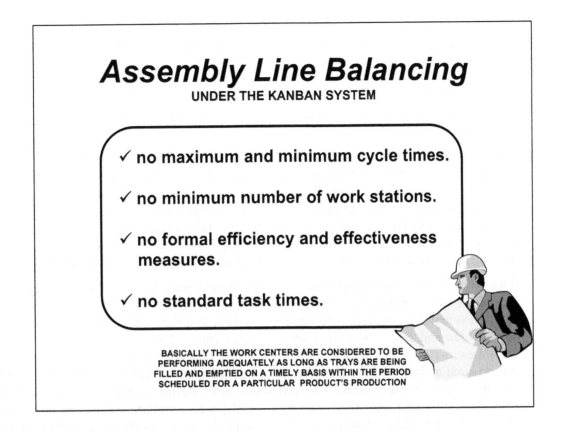

Limitations of the Japanese "Pull" System . . . and Beyond

1. It depends on the repetitive manufacture of a very small variety of models, sizes, styles, colors, or combinations of one basic product. This is a serious handicap in a marketplace dominated by multiple and changing consumer wants and needs.

2. It can only produce group-technology related products on its single assembly line, that is, products sharing the same basic components, labor training, knowledge, and skills (i.e., stereos and tape decks but *not* televisions or cameras as well).

3. The system depends on the close proximity of outside vendor firms to the manufacturing plant. In Japan, growing traffic congestion and poor roads have eroded vendor responsiveness to plant production schedule needs, even though the distances traveled remain the same. In the United States, Japanese "transplant" firms are thousands of miles away from their Japanese vendors, increasing the uncertainty of reliable and responsive resupply. Moreover, the shipment of these vendor supplies is becoming increasingly expensive as energy costs increase, and these supplies are levied with import fees and quota restrictions.

4. To counteract the disadvantages mentioned above, Japanese firms have attempted to "buy-out" American vendor firms in close proximity to their "transplant" firms. ("Keiretsu"—inner family-building where Japanese firms control all participants in an industry through horizontal and vertical integration by one or several Japanese firms working in concert.). "Keiretsu" violates U.S. anti-monopoly legislation and is being vigorously prosecuted. Result: Higher process on Japanese products to cover mounting legal fees and penalties.

5. The "PULL" System depends primarily on a dedicated workforce that puts work and quality above all else, including family. Japan's falling birthrate raises the spector of foreign

worker importation. Result: inherently lower quality in future products. In Japanese "transplant" firms located in the United States, the once youthful workforce has now aged, and they are making more mistakes on the assembly line due to failing eyesight and fatigue. Moreover, worker morale is falling due to the "glass ceiling" where American workers are limited as to how far up the corporate ladder they may climb. All top-level positions in "transplant" firms are held by Japanese nationals who are routinely rotated in and out every few years.

6. The belief system and traditional values of Japanese workers are changing. The youth do not possess the same drive as their parents, and the parents themselves have recently slowed down because they are exhausted after all these years. The average worker also feels that the major Japanese firms have benefited immensely at his/her personal expense. Recent efforts by the still infant Japanese labor movement have raised the average standard of living but have also resulted in much higher prices for Japanese goods and real estate at home and abroad. The situation abroad is compounded by a strong Yen in relation to the U.S. Dollar.

7. The "PULL" System must operate at a certain minimum level of output, around which it has been built. There is an extremely delicate balance between the market demand, the production scheduling of the manufacturing facility, and the vendor resupply activity. If the market demand falls below the eighty percent (80%) level, according to U.S. business school estimates, the "PULL" system collapses. This is nothing short of catastrophic in a nation such as Japan where there are no such things as worker furloughs, shortened work weeks, temporary shutdowns, or tolerated idle time. Result: workers released by the tens of thousands into unemployment roles in a country where welfare is non-existent and unemployment is a badge of shame that cannot be made known to those beyond the immediate family!

8. Japan's home market is limited in its ability to consume its total productive output. This forces Japanese firms to enter foreign markets, with a goal of total dominance. This is done through "dumping" (deliberately pricing goods at or below their actual production costs); highest quality manufacture, and incessant media advertising. Japanese firms are heavily subsidized by their government through the Japanese Ministry of Trade, as well as private Japanese banks. They derive additional funds through the avoidance of state and federal income taxes via "transfer-pricing." Transfer pricing works as follows: The Japanese imported part or finished product is sold to its "transplant" at a very high wholesale price (usually 85% to 90% of retail). After "cost-of-goods-sold" and "marketing" expenses are computed, the "transplant" firms report no profit on their foreign tax returns. The real profits on the other hand have already been sent back to the Japanese homeland!

Weakness of the Total Market Dominance Approach: If the foreign competition mounts a counter-campaign based on growing quality-control and cost-reduction, total market dominance may not be realized in the anticipated four to five-year timeframe. Losses mount, forcing the "transplants" to raise their prices, thereby making them vulnerable to loss of market share. If market share falls, Japanese firms have 3 options: 1) cut their losses and leave the foreign country, as some will, according to the Nomura Institute, a Japanese corporate "think tank" (some already have!); 2) allow their production facilities to hire more foreign workers and purchase their supplies from foreign vendors (which will reduce their costs in the long run) and be content with the reasonable profit returning to Japan (and inevitable unemployment at home); 3) enter into joint ventures with foreign firms. ("If you can't lick them, join them.")

9. Japan has only 17 computers per 100 workers, while the United States has 63! This disparity places Japan well behind the U.S. in annual productivity. Moreover, Japan has yet to

embark on significant corporate restructuring that could cut its manufacturing costs as a means of offsetting the damaging competitive effects of an overvalued Yen in relation to the U.S. Dollar.

10. With the notable exception of the automobile industry, there is an incredible lack of innovation and imagination in this highly-regimented, ethnically-pure society. Since World War II, Japan has earned the dubious distinction of world's greatest "replicator" of competitors' technology and products. The videocassette recorder, the video camera, the color television, the virtual-reality visor, the cordless telephone, the silicon chip, robotics, and a host of other revolutionary products were developed in the United States—not Japan. It should be noted in all fairness however, that several American companies, for their own selfish reasons, delivered these critical technologies to the Japanese. In some cases, technology transfers involved national security and bordered on treason. As a newly-aware U.S. Government and private sector take long-overdue steps toward safeguarding their basic and applied technology, Japan will be considerably hard-pressed to continue in its ways.

To summarize the above limitations, and to rephrase them in terms of American advantages, they are:

1. superior computer software and systems development for creating greater product variety and process applications within the context of JIT manufacturing.

2. the geographical advantage of closely-located suppliers literally adjacent to the client's factory or same metropolitan area.

3. a modern, efficient infrastructure of interstate highways, railroads, and air routes.

4. protection under government ant-trust laws from foreign business practices.

5. higher productivity and a devalued currency, resulting in lower prices for goods.

6. unparalleled advantage in innovation and entrepreneurship in both manufacturing and service sectors.

7. the steadily growing trend toward government deregulation and less taxation.

8. the ability to work "smarter" which can even offset emerging market labor rates in documented cases.

JIT Implementation

The JIT System View of Inventories

The JIT system appeals to firms not simply because it reduces inventories, but more important, because it recognizes that excessive inventories are symptomatic of more fundamental operations problems. In classic production systems, excessive inventories are frequently used to insulate the firm from unreliable deliveries of raw materials, lost production due to defective raw materials and processing, and delays resulting from long setup times and machine breakdowns.

The JIT system reduces inventories slowly at first, in order to "expose" these operations problems which are then solved by the firm on a priority basis. Inventories are subsequently, lowered even more, until no serious problems remain.

Successful JIT System Facilitators

From the very beginning, the founders of JIT realized that its advantages would be significantly impaired, or that the system might not work at all, unless certain preconditions were met. These include:

1. quick machine setups

2. reliable materials deliveries

3. better equipment maintenance and repair

4. better product and process quality

5. worker empowerment

Quick Machine Setups

In 1950, a Japanese employee at Mazda, Shigeo Shingo, discovered that setup operations consisted of two distinct activities: internal and external.

Internal activities are those that can be performed only when the equipment is stopped, i.e., changing an ink cartridge on a printing press. External activities are those that can be performed while the equipment is still operating, i.e., unpacking an ink cartridge from its carton. This discovery formed the basis of a procedure for reducing setup time called *SMED* (single minute exchange of dies), named after a particular consulting project involving die changes but applicable to almost any type of machine setup. SMED uses the following four-step procedure:

1. **Evaluate the current setup.** Construct activity and operations charts as described in chapter 10, in order to improve the setup.

2. **Separate internal from external setup activities.** Develop a plan wherein the preparation and testing of parts and tools, their movement to the machine, the gathering of materials to be processed, and the removal of products and waste are performed while the machine is operating. This alone will normally reduce setup times by 30% to 50%.

3. **Convert internal activities to external setup activities.** Activities that appear at first glance to be internal setup activities can sometimes be converted to external activities, i.e., pre-heating molds or materials to be processed, rather than doing all as internal setup.

4. **Simplify and streamline activities.** Reduce the time for internal setup tasks by standardizing the sizes and shapes of molds and other parts for easy insertion and removal, using the same fasteners for each setup, using pre-marked settings on dials and levers, etc.

Reliable Materials Deliveries

Late deliveries of supplies or deliveries of defective components will quickly immobilize the JIT system. Therefore, it is imperative that suppliers make reliable, on-time delivery of consistently good-quality materials and components, and still remain flexible. There are four ways to accomplish this:

1. **Share production schedules.** The customer-firm must make its production schedules (product volume, mix, and timing) known to the supplier-firm well in advance, so that the supplier-firm can more effectively adjust its production schedules to support the customer-firm.

2. **Include suppliers in product design.** Suppliers can often modify designs so that components will be easier to produce, with more consistent quality and lower cost.

3. **Assist suppliers in improving their production methods.** JIT-using firms are usually more sophisticated than their suppliers in terms of quality control, cost reduction, planning, and technology. By sharing its production expertise with its suppliers, a firm affords itself better quality components and materials at lower prices.

4. **Have spatially close facilities.** To eliminate uncertain deliveries due to traffic congestion, distance, bad weather, poor carriers, and so on, suppliers should locate near their major customers. In many cases, suppliers are situated in the same industrial park or inside the customer's production facility. Through advances in production technology, many components, assemblies, and materials can be made in small plants by as few as 100 workers as efficiently as in large plants. In order to encourage suppliers to participate in the four ways mentioned above, the customer must offer a guaranteed long-term purchasing commitment which, in some cases, may span 15 to 20 years or more.

The financial investment required of the supplier can only be recouped through large, dependable product volume over time. In addition, the customer should grant the supplier a guaranteed sole or nearly sole source status for the particular family of components, assemblies, or materials involved. It should be noted however, that sole sourcing is not without risks! Natural disasters, strikes, and major accidents at a supplier's production facility can stop production at the customer's plant within a few hours.

Better Equipment Maintenance and Repair

Poor maintenance leads to machine breakdowns which, in turn, adversely affect production in many ways. Production workers are idled, product shortages and late deliveries proliferate, production capacity is permanently lost, and defective products need to be scrapped or remade. The most common causes of machine breakdowns include:

1. inadequate preventative maintenance

2. overusing and operating machines at excessive speeds

3. dirt, oil, and chemical damage

4. incorrect machine setups

5. materials fed into machine incorrectly

1. **Maintaining excess capacity.** Most machines will wear out and fail more quickly when habitually operated at maximum speed. In addition, the precision and quality of work will deteriorate due to machine vibration or due to workers' inability to feed materials into the machine correctly or fast enough. Operating machines at 80% to 90% of their maximum speed makes failures less frequent, and over the long run, can actually result in higher product output. Lastly, JIT systems, as previously stated, produce for actual demand rather than forecasted demand. When moderate increases in demand occur, the production system must be capable of increasing production rapidly. One feature of JIT systems is that they are designed to operate normally at 80% to 90% of capacity, so that they can increase production rapidly when necessary. As long as these increases in production are of short duration, or are accompanied by additional preventative maintenance, machine wear and failures are not excessive.

2. **Cleanliness and orderliness.** A principal source of machine failures and poor product quality is the buildup of dirt, oil, and chemicals in machines or on materials. Cleaning machines should be a normal part of the preventative maintenance done by machine operators. Additionally, tools should be stored neatly in a designated place, materials arranged neatly, and aisles kept clear of clutter. This reduces accidents that can injure workers and damage machines.

3. **Proper machine setups.** Improper machine setups can lead to material jamming in the machine or other problems that can damage the machine. The methodical nature of *SMED*-driven setups almost guarantees that no setup task is omitted by accident.

4. **Work aids.** Human errors are a frequent cause of machine failure. Many can be reduced or eliminated by using mistake-proof devices to prevent materials from being fed into, or removed from, machines incorrectly, to prevent the wrong materials from being fed into a machine, and to ensure that the machine is operated at the correct speed. Emergency cut-off switches should be readily accessible to prevent small malfunctions from becoming major machine failures. Lubrication points should be painted with bright colors for easy identification, and so on.

Additional Maintenance Suggestions

a. Machine design should be kept as simple as possible for easier maintenance and higher reliability.

b. The variety of machines should be reduced for simpler maintenance.

c. Detailed records of machine failure causes and frequency should be kept in order to better allocate maintenance resources and more efficiently solve maintenance problems.

d. It is better to rebuild a machine by replacing all worn parts at once, instead of replacing them one by one, because when some parts are starting to wear, many others are wearing as well.

Quality and JIT Production

JIT production systems cannot tolerate stoppages due to poor quality any more than those due to machine failures. Good product quality depends on at least four factors:

1. The product should be designed so that it is easy to make.

2. Materials and components from suppliers should not be defective.

3. The production process should not introduce defects.

4. If defective items are produced, they need to be found quickly and the cause of the problem eliminated.

Because items are processed in small lot sizes (or batches) and not kept in any one processing center for long, defects occurring at one center are found there quickly, or at the next center. Production will then cease in order to find and solve the problem rather than continuing to produce defective items and then trying to either rework them or work around them. It is interesting to note that, in most cases, stoppages can be effected without disrupting delivery, because JIT systems habitually operate at only 80% to 90% of capacity and can easily make up the lost time.

Worker Empowerment and Continuous Improvement

A basic tenet of JIT is that regardless of how efficient the production system is, it can always be made better. The most successful continuous improvement systems are those that encourage the workers themselves to find ways of improving production methods and products. This can be done in three ways:

Employee suggestion systems. In use for over a century. Cash prizes are paid for them.

Quality circles. Small groups of workers who meet regularly to discuss and evaluate ways to improve productivity, quality, and safety.

Autonomous work teams. A group of workers who work together as a team to perform some aspect of production. They are often evaluated and rewarded as a team, and one aspect of the evaluation is performance improvement.

Guidelines for JIT Implementation

The ultimate success or failure of JIT production will depend on how it is implemented. Mistakes will be made, and a firm must be willing to backtrack and revise its plans. Some Suggestions:

A. **PATIENCE.** Five, ten or fifteen years could conceivably pass before the required changes to the production system's mechanics, the work of its employees, and the corporate philosophy and work culture would be completed. In the short term, productivity may actually decrease until workers gain proficiency. Inventories should be reduced slowly while making gradual reductions in setup time, batch sizes, defects, and machine breakdowns. That said, *inventory reductions in the order of 20% to 40%, and productivity improvements of 5% to 10% per year for each of the 1st two to three years are common!*

B. **CUSTOMIZED IMPLEMENTATION.** Every firm has a different level of experience and sophistication with regard to quality management, setup methods, job design, and maintenance methods. Therefore, the problems that become visible through inventory reduction will vary. For that reason, it may be wiser to wait for the most pressing problems to appear and respond to them quickly, rather than establishing improvement programs in advance.

C. **FLEXIBILITY.** There may be occasions when product demand jumps unexpectedly and the JIT system may need to respond, at least temporarily, by increasing inventories. This can be done by simply increasing the number of *production* and *move* cards for a particular product within the JIT system, or abandoning the JIT system temporarily before a seasonal surge in demand, so that inventory stockpiles can be built up.

D. **EXCESS CAPACITY.** As previously discussed, JIT systems function best when they are designed to operate routinely at 80% to 90% of capacity. This allows production to accelerate when demand surges. As also previously discussed, operating at 80% to 90% capacity makes it possible to halt production immediately to correct quality problems when they occur. This lower utilization rate also gives employees time to experiment with, and test improvements to the production process, which in turn, translates into greater productivity and capacity over time.

JIT in Service Industries

Although JIT production is most effective in manufacturing systems, it has also been effectively applied in service systems. For example, many retailers are using optical scanning and electronic data interchange (EDI) technologies to maintain real-time information on their merchandise inventories and to allow their suppliers to track their sales and inventories. The suppliers can then ship merchandise to the retailer as soon as inventories get low without waiting for the retailer to issue a purchase order. Further, by knowing the daily status of customer inventories, the supplier is also better able to plan its own production to deliver merchandise to the retailer "just-in-time." The net result is that retailers are able to maintain much smaller inventories while simultaneously reducing the risks of both stockouts and unsold goods. This linkage of retailers and manufacturers has been given various names, but a formal program called the *QUICK RESPONSE PROGRAM (QRP)* was initiated in the United States in the 1980s to help American manufacturers supply retailers more competitively than foreign suppliers.

Benefits

JIT systems use the smallest batch sizes possible.

Reduce avg. level of inventory

Pass thru system faster

Allow relatively early detection of quality problems

Help achieve uniform workload on the system

Simplify set-up

Potential Problems

Small batches ↑ # of setups & total setup costs

Setup cost & time is the same regardless of batch size

Equation like EOQ inventory model to find
optimum batch size $\sqrt{\dfrac{(2)(D)(s)}{h}}$ s = setup time
                                                        D = daily demand
                                                        h = processing time

Producers must select most
economical solution

Larger batch more economical
if setup time is really big

Batch Size notes
Formula notes

larger batches → higher inventory

Good JIT will reduce setup time for effectiveness.

↓ setup automatically reduces size of most economical batch.

P

A

R

T

4

Tactical Decisions in P/OM

Aggregate Planning

*C*hapter 12 discusses top-down operations planning and scheduling as a means of best managing a firm's limited resources and costs.

As discussed in preceding chapters, the firm's long-term or strategic planning generates three decisions that will fix the environment in which the production system must operate:

A. the design and mix of products

B. the location and capacity of facilities

C. the design of the production process

Directly below strategic planning is intermediate-term or aggregate planning. It determines the overall employment of the firm's facilities and other resources over the next 3 to 18 months, so as to satisfy customer demand for all goods and services at minimum cost, and certain corporate policy requirements, i.e., no layoffs, no overtime pay, no inventory stockouts.

At this level of planning, all products and services are abstractly defined in terms of "quasi-units" or representative output of all the firm's goods and services. Examples are "appliances" and "vehicles" in the manufacturing sector, and "meals" and "airline passenger miles flown" in the service sector.

A "quasi-unit" demand forecast is then developed for a period of up to one-and-one-half (1½) years. The firm then manipulates production rates, inventory levels, and workforce levels to generate a series of aggregate production plans that meet the demand forecast. Cost estimates are developed, and the lowest-cost plan adopted.

These plans may be developed on a trial-and-error basis, using pencils and graph paper or via computer-driven/mathematical models yielding optimal or satisfactory solutions.

Aggregate planning, by its very nature should only be conducted and supervised by seasoned managers who have intimate knowledge of their firm's operating and cost structures. Younger managers are groomed for these roles as assistants.

Once an aggregate plan has been selected, it is "decomposed" or "disaggregated" (broken down) into a series of MPS's (master production schedules) ranging from one month to one quarter. The MPS will specify the *exact* number of products and/or services by make and model, color,

and options to be generated on a daily and weekly basis, as consumer demand patterns material-
ize and economic conditions change.

By planning the mix and the timing of the use of its resources from the top-down, the firm can
more economically satisfy its demand and corporate policy requirements.

Aggregate Planning Goals

1. *PRIMARY:* to develop a plan that will meet aggregate demand over a specific time horizon,
   within resource limitations, at the lowest cost to the firm.

2. *SECONDARY:* to satisfy corporate policy requirements such as:

   a. a stable workforce

   b. 100% in-house production

   c. sufficient inventories to reduce the likelihood of stockouts to 5% or less.

   d. overtime labor hours not to exceed 10% of regular labor hours

   NOTE: Aggregate plans should be developed, *not* to minimize costs in each period (i.e.,
   month) but to minimize costs over the *entire* planning period.

Aggregate plans usually span 3 to 18 periods. A "period" is defined as one month, unless stated
otherwise. Beyond 18 periods, the number of possible alternative plans increases significantly; com-
putation time and costs become prohibitive; and the forecasts, upon which the aggregate plans so
critically depend, become less stable and accurate.

Three Principal Strategies

There are three (3) principal heuristics (guides) or strategies used to formulate aggregate plans.
Each one manipulates production, inventory, and workforce levels in a certain manner, thereby formulating a unique aggregate plan.

A. *INVENTORY CUSHION or LEVEL-WORKFORCE:*
   The labor force size and the production rate are fixed over the life of the aggregate plan.
   Consequently, inventories are built-up during "slow" demand periods, and drawn down
   during "high" demand periods. This strategy employs inventory as a "cushion" between
   steady production and variable external demand. Moreover, this strategy reduces inventory
   stockout costs and eliminates overtime pay, hiring, training, firing, sub-contracting, and production rate change costs.

B. *FORCE UTILIZATION or SKELETON FORCE:*
   The permanent labor force size is determined for a specific level of demand. Higher demand
   is met by scheduling overtime hours for the permanent labor force, hiring temporary workers, subcontracting production under license to other firms, etc. Lower demand is tolerated
   as paid idle time. Frequently, the permanent labor force is built around the lowest monthly
   forecasted quasi-unit demand, in order to hold the high cost of full-time employees (health
   insurance, retirement benefits, paid vacation time, etc.) to a minimum.

C. *CHASE or MATCHING:*
   This strategy calls for monthly adjustment of the labor force size as needed to match production to demand. It eliminates or drastically reduces inventory carry costs and inventory

stockout costs. It generates substantial employee hiring, training, and termination costs. Moreover, wage premiums may need to be paid to employees in exchange for lack of security, and productivity losses (an opportunity cost) may well result from poor employee morale and loss of company loyalty.

NOTE: None of the above strategies are cost-effective per se. A blend of two or three strategies will almost always result in an aggregate plan that yields the lowest overall production costs.

Regardless of the particular aggregate plan developed, each one should, as a minimum, specify a production rate, a level of inventory, and a level of labor force size for each period (month) that the plan will cover. In addition, possible other decision variables should be considered for inclusion in one or more aggregate plans such as:

- overtime labor hours

- part-time labor hours

- temporary labor hours

- production subcontracting

- extra shifts

- equipment and machine rental

- backordering (appealing to customers to wait for the product)

- various production rate changes

Elements of Aggregate Planning

Many different types of costs need to be identified and accurately estimated before actual planning begins. Examples are:

- the regular labor rate per hour

- the overtime labor rate per hour

- direct materials cost per unit

- direct labor cost per unit

- overhead cost per unit

- subcontracting cost per unit

- maintenance cost beyond normal production capacity

- inventory carry cost per unit

- inventory stockout cost per unit

- production rate change costs

- labor hiring and training cost per unit (when production must increase to meet rising demand)

- labor severance cost per unit (when production must decrease to meet falling demand)

- additional machine and equipment rental costs

Production staff strive to obtain as much input as possible from accounting and personnel since each of the three basic aggregate planning strategies and their variations requires very different amounts and forms of cost data.

Accounting and personnel in turn are usually most cooperative, to the point where they will construct custom charts depicting the behavior of selected costs over various production volumes, such as maintenance and production rate change costs. Other critical data, besides cost, that need to be assembled include:

- productivity rate per worker per day
- the number of production days in the planning period
- an accurate forecast of demand for the planning period, broken down by month
- machine processing hours per unit
- labor hours required per unit
- direct materials required per unit
- indirect materials and supplies required per unit
- existing production/service capacity at all the firm's facilities
- corporate policy regarding the use of overtime, subcontracting, backordering, inventories, etc.
- existing warehouse capacity at all the firm's facilities

Relevant Costs vs. Nonrelevant Costs

The identification and estimation of essential and potential aggregate planning costs is merely the first step. All costs must then be analyzed and classified as either "relevant" or "irrelevant." Relevant costs are those that will change from one developed aggregate plan to the next, thereby making each plan unique. Subcontracting is a typical relevant cost because it may be to a greater or lesser extent, included in one or more developed aggregate plans but not in all of them. Inventory carry (storage) cost is also a typical relevant cost because it is dependent on time period inventory levels which always differ from plan to plan.

Irrelevant or nonrelevant costs, on the other hand, are those that will *not* change from one developed aggregate plan to the next. Direct materials cost per unit produced is a typical non-relevant cost because it will not change over a broad range of productive output, especially when the forecasted demand for the firm falls squarely within that broad range. Overhead cost per unit produced is also a typical non-relevant cost because the firm's costs—on which it is based—will not change over a broad range of productive output.

Since they are identical in every developed aggregate plan, non-relevant costs are omitted entirely from each, saving valuable time and eliminating data redundancy, as the firm seeks to identify the most cost-effective plan.

Behavioral Aspects of Aggregate Planning

In its quest to meet demand at the lowest overall cost, aggregate planning may profoundly affect job design, performance standards, and worker attitudes for the worse. Its bias toward smaller, full-time workforces puts pressure on those employees to upgrade their skill levels, productivity, quality, and flexibility, while simultaneously forcing them to train and monitor more non-union, part-time, and temporary workers, involuntarily accept overtime hours on short notice, and agonize over prospects of some or much of their production being "out-sourced" to more competitive firms, etc. The firm should monitor its organizational climate on a continual basis for signs of job dissatisfaction, accidents, sliding productivity and quality, while developing aggregate plans that alienate its employees as little as possible. Corporate policies and/or collective bargaining agreements that stipulate no layoffs, limits on overtime hours, and guaranteed "in-house" production quotas are possible suggestions.

The Concept of Aggregation

Aggregate planning is essentially a "big picture" approach to planning which avoids focusing on individual products or services unless, of course, the firm has only one major product or service. Instead, aggregate planning focuses on defining the firm's existing capacity in aggregate or overall terms and assessing its ability to meet the forecasted aggregate or overall demand for its products and/or services over a specified time horizon.

It is useful to think of capacity in terms of labor hours or machine hours per month, or output rates per month, without worrying about how much of a particular make or model product will actually be involved. The reason for this approach is that it frees planners to make decisions about the use of resources in a general way without having to delve into the complexities of individual product or service requirements. Similarly, it is useful to think of forecasted demand in terms of aggregated units of output required, because fewer forecasts are needed, and they tend to be more stable and accurate than those for individual products.

The unit of aggregation is called the "quasi-," "pseudo-," or "composite"-unit. It is the "lowest common denominator" of the firm's overall product output, that is, it is a cross-representation of the firm's various product makes, models, colors, and options. It may take quite a bit of thought and time to define an appropriate "quasi"-unit. Some criteria include:

- a product that represents a family of individual products that are processed on the same equipment, by the same workers, and share the same general machine setup.

- a product that represents a family of individual products that have similar cost structures, carry costs per unit, and productivities (output rates).

- a product that represents a family of individual products sharing to a large extent, the same parts and assemblies, and physical characteristics.

Aggregate planning is normally done at the *facility* level, rather than at the corporate level, Accordingly, the definition of a "quasi"-unit frequently becomes a simple task, since all products made at a particular facility are merely variations of only one or two products.

Examples from Manufacturing

- "gallons" or "barrels" of beer (as opposed to individual brands)
- "tons" of steel (as opposed to ingots or beams of varying tensile strength)
- "appliances" (as opposed to washing machines, dryers, and refrigerators)

Extended Manufacturing Example

Consider an assembly plant that makes 2 types of cars and station wagons. A decision on the number of "vehicles" to be produced will be made without specifying two-door versus four-door cars, trim-levels, options, etc. Similarly, a decision on 6-cylinder and 8-cylinder engines will be made without concern for which engines will go with which cars and station wagons. The plant's staff will take into account the expected demand for it "vehicles" and "engines" and the available capacity for making those items. If expected demand and capacity are roughly equal, the staff will devote their efforts to meeting demand as efficiently as possible. If capacity exceeds demand, advertising and promotion might be realistic options or perhaps a capacity scale-back, plant closure, or assignment of a new or more popular line of "vehicles" to the plant by corporate headquarters.

If capacity is less than demand, subcontracting to a rival automobile company or a sister plant may be an option. In any event, the staff will be looking at aggregate measures of capacity and demand in making their decisions about levels of output, labor force, and inventories.

Examples from the Service Sector

- "passenger miles to be flown" at an airline, (as opposed to the number of flights by specific aircraft over specific routes).

- "faculty-to-student contact hours" in a university (as opposed to hours of classroom instruction, student advising, student testing, and supervision of student research projects).

- "square feet of display space available" in allocating percentages of available space to mens', womens', and childrens' in retailing (as opposed to what brand names will be offered or how much of mens' sportswear will be jackets).

Extended Service Sector Example

The MA. DPW is charged with the upkeep of the state and interstate highway system. The quasi-unit is a "maintained road mile." The agency would compute on a "per mile" basis, the annual requirements for snow removal labor hours, installations and repair labor hours, sand and debris removal labor hours, line-painting labor hours, equipment operation hours, and supervising/planning hours. The agency would then multiply the above hours by the approximately 20,000 miles of road that need to be maintained each year, in order to arrive at its aggregate maintenance requirements in labor and equipment hours. The agency would then evaluate its existing capacity in terms of available labor hours, vehicle hours, and equipment hours. Several different aggregate plans would then be formulated to meet the maintenance requirements by manipulating the mix of full-time, part-time, and subcontracted private firms and individuals, as well as state-owned and privately-owned vehicles and equipment. Costs would then be calculated for labor, subcontracting, equipment rental, etc. in order to identify the lowest cost plan, subject to seasonal constraints, i.e., no snow removal labor hours to be used in summer.

Possible Aggregate Plans

The Inventory Cushion (or Level Force) Strategy

Objective: To maintain a constant-size work force and uniform production rate over the specified planning period.

Assumptions:

- demand forecast of 6,200 quasi-units over the next six (6) months.
- one-hundred and twenty-four (124) available production days over the next 6 months.
- quasi-unit carry cost (warehouse storage cost) is $5.00 per unit, per month.
- each worker can produce five (5) quasi-units per day.
- each worker is paid $120.00 per day.

Month	Production	Forecast	Net Change	Ending Inv.
JANUARY	22 days × 50 = 1100	900	+200	200
FEBRUARY	18 days × 50 = 900	700	+200	400
MARCH	21 days × 50 = 1050	800	+250	650
APRIL	21 days × 50 = 1050	1200	–150	500
MAY	22 days × 50 = 1100	1500	–400	100
JUNE	20 days × 50 = 1000	1100	–100	0
	6200 units	6200 units		1850 units

(we must produce 6,200 units/124 days = 50 units per day to meet demand)

Total Costs: $158,050.00

- Inventory carry costs. . . . . $9,250.00 (1,850 units × $5.00 per unit)

- Overtime, Hiring, Firing, Subcontracting . . . . $0.00 (due to fixed work force size)

- Work force cost . . . . $148,800.00 (50 units/5 units = 10 workers; 10 workers × $120/day × 124 days = $148,800.00)

- Production rate change costs. . . . . $0.00 (due to uniform production rate)

The Skeleton Force or Cadre Strategy

Objective: To build a permanent work force around a specific level of demand, tolerating paid idle labor time during lower demand periods, and incurring the costs of overtime labor or subcontracting during higher demand periods.

Assumptions:

- the firm wants to build a permanent work force around the *lowest* period demand, in order to maximize savings on retirement benefits, health insurance premiums, paid vacation/leave, etc.

- February has the lowest forecasted, quasi-unit demand: 700 units.

- February has eighteen (18) available production days.

- the firm wants to subcontract production to an outside company whenever quasi-unit demand exceeds the permanent work force's capability.

- subcontracted quasi-units cost the firm 10.00 each.

The Calculations:

- Daily February Production: 700 units/18 days = 39 units per day.

- In-House Production: 39 units/day × 124 days in the aggregate plan = 4,836 units.

- Production to be Subcontracted: Total Demand = 6,200 units – 4,836 units = 1,364 units.

- Number of Workers Required: 39/5 units per worker per day = 7.8 (Permanent).

The Costs: $129,704.00

- Work force cost . . . . $116,064.00 (7.8 permanent workers $\times$ $120.00 per worker per day $\times$ 124 days)

- Subcontracting cost . . . . $13,640.00 (1,364 units $\times$ $10.00/unit)

- Overtime, Hiring, Training, Firing . . . . $0.00 (rejected options for meeting higher demand)

- Inventory Carry cost. . . . . $0.00 (demand is satisfied exactly by in-house production, and when necessary, by subcontracting)

The Chase or Matching Strategy

Objective: To hire or terminate personnel as needed, in order to closely or precisely match production to demand, period-by-period. This results in the elimination or drastic reduction of inventory carry and stockout costs.

Assumptions:

- each quasi-unit requires 1.6 hours of direct labor to produce.

- the cost of terminating personnel is $15.00 *per manufactured quasi-unit.*

- the cost of recruiting and training personnel is $10.00 *per manufactured quasi-unit.*

- each worker earns $15.00 per hour, on average.

Month	Demand Forecast	Production Costs	Forecast Change	Hire/Fire Cost	Total Cost
January	900	900 $\times$ 1.6 $\times$ $15 = $21,600	———	———	$21,600
February	700	700 $\times$ 1.6 $\times$ $15 = $16,800	(200) $\times$ $15	$3,000	$19,800
March	800	800 $\times$ 1.6 $\times$ $15 = $19,200	+100 $\times$ $10	$1,000	$20,200
April	1200	1200 $\times$ 1.6 $\times$ $15 = $28,800	+400 $\times$ $10	$4,000	$32,800
May	1500	1500 $\times$ 1.6 $\times$ $15 = $36,000	+300 $\times$ $10	$3,000	$39,000
June	1100	1100 $\times$ 1.6 $\times$ $15 = $26,400	(400) $\times$ $15	$6,000	$32,400
Total		$148,800		$17,000	$165,800

The costs: $165,800.00

- Regular labor costs.....$148,800. (6200 units $\times$ 1.6 hours of direct labor per unit = 9,920 hours $\times$ $15.00 per hour = $148,800.00)

- Hire/Termination costs......$17,000. ($8,000.00 in hiring costs and $9,000.00 in firing costs)

- Inventory Carry and Stockout Costs.... $0.00 (production exactly matches demand, period-by-period)

Possible Aggregate Plans (Comments)

1. If only three (3) strategies or plans were generated and evaluated, the firm would have to select plan number 2: Skeleton Force or Cadre, since it has the lowest projected total costs.

2. Direct materials cost, direct machine hour cost, and applied overhead cost per quasi-unit are identical in all three aggregate production plans. Hence, they are non-relevant costs which are routinely omitted from the analysis.

3. The mix of resources—work force size, production rate, and inventory, as well as subcontracting—and their timing allowed the development of three unique aggregate plan proposals and associated costs.

4. In strategy number 2, the firm chose to augment the capacity of its small permanent work force via subcontracting exclusively. Variations of strategy number 2 could be developed utilizing overtime hours or temporary labor exclusively, or a combination of overtime hours, temporary labor hours, and subcontracting.

5. Corporate policies may impose limitations on the use of subcontracting, overtime hours, inventory, production, machines, available production days, etc.

The Graph Method of Aggregate Planning

The *graph method* or *charting method* of aggregate planning is perhaps the most widely used. It works with a few variables at a time to allow planners to compare projected demand with existing production capacity. It is a trial-and-error approach that does not guarantee an optimal production plan, but it requires only limited computations and can be performed by clerical staff. Although mathematical models exist, they are not widely used. The average manager regards them as overly complex and untrustworthy. Moreover, managers need to make decisions quickly, based on the changing dynamics of the workplace. This may explain why the simple *graph method* is more generally accepted.

A Graph Method Example

Problem Statement:

- The firm forecasts an overall demand of 175,000 quasi-units for the calendar year.

- The annual forecast of demand has been broken down into monthly forecasts.

- The firm plans to operate two-hundred-and fifty (250) days during the calendar year, allowing for holidays, vacation periods, and scheduled maintenance shutdowns.

- The firm desires to first develop an *inventory cushion* plan which calls for a fixed labor force producing at a uniform production rate over the life of the plan.

Step 1: Develop a graph depicting "units produced/demanded" on the vertical axis, and the number of production periods on the horizontal axis.

Step 2: Plot the cumulative forecasted quasi-unit demand.

Step 3: Plot the cumulative planned quasi-unit production.

Step 4: Compare the cumulative forecasted quasi-unit demand plotting with the cumulative planned quasi-unit production plotting, in order to identify the duration and extent of inventory surpluses and inventory shortages.

Step 5: Calculate the costs of this plan:

   a. *for inventory surpluses:* [carry cost per quasi-unit] × [end-of-period inventory surplus balance] = period inventory surplus carry cost; and the total of the period inventory carry costs = the plan inventory carry costs.

   b. *for inventory shortages:* [stockout cost per quasi-unit] × [end-of-period inventory deficit balance] = period inventory stockout cost; and the total of the period inventory stockout costs = the plan inventory stockout costs.

   c. if the firm intends to eliminate inventory shortages altogether, end-of-period inventory deficit balances can be multiplied by:

   • [subcontract cost per quasi-unit]

   • [backorder cost per quasi-unit]

   • [overtime labor cost per quasi-unit]

   • [additional maintenance cost per quasi-unit]

   • [equipment rental cost per quasi-unit]

   • [part-time labor cost per quasi-unit]

   • [a mix of the above costs per quasi-unit]

Step 6: Modify the strategy, in an attempt to reduce costs further, by repeating steps "3," "4," and "5" with different types of resources, i.e., substitute subcontracting costs for in-house overtime labor costs.

   Attempt to reduce costs further by repeating steps "3," "4," and "5" with different strategies, as well.

Problem Execution:

Step 1: Construct the graph.

Since the forecasted demand is 175,000 quasi-units, "50,000-unit" intervals are appropriate for the vertical axis; and since the plan's time horizon is a calendar year, twelve "monthly" intervals are appropriate. In addition, for slightly more accuracy, tick marks for each available production day should be shown within each monthly interval.

Step 2: Plot the cumulative forecasted quasi-unit demand.

Demand is forecasted on a monthly basis, with cumulative forecasted demand computed as follows:

Period	Forecast	Cumulative Forecast
January	8,000 units	8,000 units
February	9,000 units	17,000 units
March	9,000 units	26,000 units
April	8,000 units	34,000 units

(and so on, for the next 8 monthly periods)

Step 3:   *Plot the cumulative quasi-unit production under the inventory cushion strategy, as follows:*

Day	*Daily Production	Cumulative Daily Production
Jan. 2	700 units	700 units
Jan. 3	700 units	1,400 units
Jan. 4	700 units	2,100 units
Jan. 5	700 units	2,800 units

(and so on, for the next 246 available production days)

NOTE: since 175,000 quasi-units need to be manufactured in 250 available production days, 700 units must be produced daily.

Step 4:   *Compare the cumulative forecasted unit demand plotting with the cumulative unit production plotting, in order to identify the duration and extent of inventory surpluses and inventory shortages:*

Problem Execution:

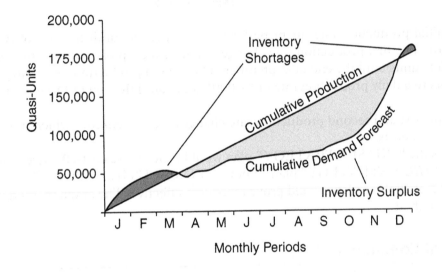

Step 5: Calculate the costs of this plan.

End-of-month inventory surpluses can be roughly estimated from the graph, using the vertical axis scale. Multiplying these end-of-month surpluses by the carry cost per unit (i.e., storage cost per unit), we obtain the monthly inventory carry costs which, when totaled, yield the inventory carry costs of the plan.

End-of-month inventory shortages can likewise be roughly estimated from the graph, using the vertical axis scale. Multiplying these end-of-month shortages by the stockout cost per unit, we obtain the monthly inventory stockout costs which, when totaled yield the inventory stockout costs of the plan.

If the firm intends to eliminate inventory stockouts in part, or in whole, the same end-of-month inventory shortages can be multiplied by overtime costs per unit, subcontracting cost per unit, or any other cost per unit used to eliminate anticipated inventory stockouts.

Step 6: Seek cost improvement.

Continuing this example, the firm might want to develop a "Chase Strategy" plan via the graph method, as it looks for ways of reducing the costs of inventory surpluses and inventory stockouts.

This plan would call for several production rate changes to more closely align production to current demand:

Problem Execution:

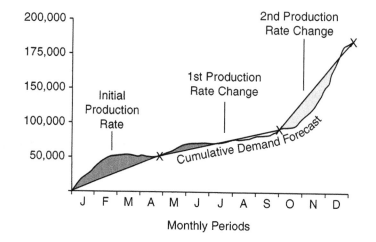

The initial production rate might be "900" units per day until the end of April. It is a *non-relevant* cost. The first production rate change might be a drop of 500 units to a daily production rate of "400" units until the end of September. The second production rate change might be a rise of 600 units to a daily production rate of "1,000" units until the end of December (and the end of the plan).

Both the first and second production rate changes are *relevant costs* which must be included in the plan's total costs.

Perhaps the "CHASE STRATEGY" plan would prove more cost-effective than the "*INVENTORY CUSHION* STRATEGY" plan. If not, a "FORCE UTILIZATION STRATEGY" plan or some hybrid of all three plans would prove more cost-effective. The graph method is indeed a trial-and-error method.

Additional Comments

- when computing the available number of operating days in the plan's time horizon, it is easier to close the facility for a common 2 to 3-week vacation period than to agonize over which workers are or not available each day, week, or month. This also eliminates the expense of fill-in workers.

- the carry (or holding) costs of inventory include security, obsolescence risk, warehouse depreciation, possible taxes, materials handling, and climate-control. These costs may be computed on a daily, weekly, monthly, or quarterly basis as the plan requires.

- good practice dictates postponement of overtime production until inventories approach zero, (overtime labor costs are much higher than inventory carry costs).

- production rate change costs are not a linear function. They increase exponentially (or decrease) with the magnitude of the rate change. For example:

rate change planned	cost
±1–200 units	$15.00/unit
±201–400 units	$40.00/unit
±401–600 units	$99.00/unit

- when demand is forecasted to fluctuate, the attempt should *not* be made to constantly match the labor force size to demand. It is too costly in terms of the rate changes. Instead, the production rate should be adjusted on a bimonthly, quarterly, or semiannual basis (but not monthly).

- the accounting function facilitates the planning effort by providing detailed cost data on operations as well as custom-designed charts and schedules.

- the finance function is better able to anticipate working capital needs via a well-considered aggregate plan.

- the marketing function has a better picture of when, how many, and what products will be available so as to intelligently plan its promotions and customer commitments.

- the personnel function will have better information on staffing needs on a period-by-period basis, so as to schedule recruiting and training programs.

- a mixed strategy, characterized by moderate inventory levels, moderate stockouts, and a small number of production rate changes, will usually be selected. This combination invariably produces the lowest total operating costs.

Mathematical Techniques for Aggregate Planning

A number of mathematical techniques have been developed over the past forty years to handle aggregate planning. They range from mathematical programming models to heuristic and computer search models:

A. *THE TRANSPORTATION METHOD*

   When an aggregate planning problem is viewed as one of allocating capacity to meet forecasted demand, it can be formulated in a linear programming format. The transportation method of linear programming will produce an *optimal* plan for minimizing costs. It is also flexible in that it can specify regular and overtime production in each time period, the number of units to be subcontracted, extra shifts, and the inventory carryover from period to period. The transportation method was originally developed by E.H. Bowman in 1956. Although it works well in analyzing the effects of holding inventories, using overtime, and subcontracting, it does *not* work with non-linear costs such as hiring and layoff. In such cases, the Simplex Method of linear programming must be used.

Example

A firm developed data that relate to production, demand, capacity, and costs at one particular plant:

	PERIOD (Month)		
	June	July	August
DEMAND	800	1,000	750
CAPACITY:			
regular	700	700	700
overtime	50	50	50
subcontracting	150	150	130
BEGINNING INVENTORY	100		

	COSTS
REGULAR TIME	$40 per unit
OVERTIME	$50 per unit
SUBCONTRACT	$70 per unit
CARRY COST	$ 2 per unit per month

The above data are then used to construct a transportation matrix (or tableau) and an initial (first) feasible solution as shown below:

	Demand / Capacity	June	July	August	Unused Capacity (Dummy)	Total Capacity Available
	Beginning Inventory	(100) 0	2	4	0	100
June	Regular Time	(700) 40	42	44	0	700
	Overtime	50	(50) 52	54	0	50
	Subcontract	70	(150) 72	74	0	150
July	Regular Time	X	(700) 40	42	0	700
	Overtime	X	(50) 50	52	0	50
	Subcontract	X	(50) 70	72	(100) 0	150
August	Regular Time	X	X	(700) 40	0	700
	Overtime	X	X	(50) 50	0	50
	Subcontract	X	X	70	(130) 0	130
	Total Demand	800	1,000	750	230	2,780 / 2,780

Comments

A. Carry costs are $2.00 per unit per month. Units produced in one month and held to the next month will have a $2.00 higher cost. Since carry costs are linear, units produced in one month and held for the next two months will have a $4.00 higher cost. So when you move across each row from left to right, regular time, overtime, and subcontracting costs are lowest when units are sold in the same month in which they are produced. If units are produced in one month and carried over to the next, carry costs are incurred.

B. Total capacity must equal total demand in transportation problems. Therefore, a dummy column called "unused capacity" has been added. The costs of not using capacity are zero.

C. Because backordering is not an option in this model, no production is possible in those cells that represent production in one month to satisfy demand in a past month, i.e., those cells with an "X."

D. Quantities in each column (circled numbers) designate the level of inventory needed to meet demand requirements. Demand of "800" units in June is met by using "100" units from beginning inventory, and "700" units from regular time.

E. To complete the table, allocate as much production as you can to a cell with the smallest cost without exceeding the unused capacity in that row or demand in that column. If there is still some demand left in that row, allocate as much as you can to the next-lowest-cost cell. You then repeat this process for July and August (and beyond, if necessary). When you are finished, the sum of all your entries in a row must equal the total row capacity, and the sum of all entries in a column must equal the demand for that month.

B. *THE SIMPLEX METHOD*

The simplex method of linear programming is an alternative to the transportation method of linear programming. It was originally developed by George Dantzig in 1947. However, the simplex method <u>must</u> be used in situations where there are non-linear costs involved such as hiring and layoff.

Minimum or maximum constraints can be placed on the desired amounts of regular labor, overtime labor, subcontracting, backordering, and many other factors on a monthly, bimonthly, quarterly, or semi-annual basis, for example. Unfortunately, constraint formulation is quite complex and the optimal solution virtually always must be obtained via computer, since there are usually dozens or hundreds of variables (decision, artificial, slack, surplus) involved.

Illustrative Example

A production manager must develop an aggregate plan for the next two quarters of the year. The plant produces computer terminals. The firm estimates that 700 terminals will need to be shipped to the customers in the first quarter and 3,200 in the second quarter. It is the policy of the firm to ship customers' orders in the quarter in which they are ordered. It takes an average of 5 hours labor to produce each terminal, and only 9,000 hours of straight-time labor is available in each of the two quarters. Overtime can be used, but the firm has a policy limiting the amount of overtime in each quarter to 10 percent of the straight-time labor available. Labor costs $12.00 per hour at straight-time rate and $18.00 per hour at the overtime rate. If a terminal is produced in one quarter and shipped in the next quarter, a carrying cost of $50.00 is incurred.

How many terminals should be produced on straight-time and overtime in each of the two quarters to minimize straight-time labor, overtime labor, and carrying costs?

The market requirements, straight-time labor availability, and overtime policy must be adhered to.

Formulation

Define the decision variables:

X_1 = number of terminals to be made on straight-time in the 1st quarter and shipped in the 1st quarter.

X_2 = number of terminals to be made on overtime in the 1st quarter and shipped in the 1st quarter.

X_3 = number of terminals to be made on straight-time in the 1st quarter and shipped in the 2nd quarter.

X_4 = number of terminals to be made on overtime in the 1st quarter and shipped in the 2nd quarter.

X_5 = number of terminals to be made on straight-time in the 2nd quarter and shipped in the 2nd quarter.

X_6 = number of terminals to be made on overtime in the 2nd quarter and shipped in the 2nd quarter.

Q_1 = the first quarter.

Q_2 = the second quarter.

Z = the total cost of the plan.

Define the objective function:

$$\text{Minimize } Z = 60X_1 + 90X_2 + 110X_3 + 140X_4 + 60X_5 + 90X_6$$

Comments:

1. In this aggregate plan, the direct materials cost per unit, and the applied overhead cost per unit are unchanged over the anticipated range of production. They are therefore, excluded from the objective function coefficients.

2. In the objective function, the term "$60X_1$" means that each terminal made on straight-time, in the 1st quarter, and shipped in the 1st quarter, will cost $60.00:

   [5 hrs. of labor] × [$12.00 per hour, straight-time labor cost]

3. In the objective function, the term "$90X_2$" means that each terminal made on overtime, in the 1st quarter, and shipped in the 1st quarter, will cost $90.00:

   [5 hrs. of labor] × [$18.00 per hour, overtime labor cost]

4. In the objective function, the term "$110X_3$" means that each terminal made on straight-time, in the 1st quarter, and shipped in the 2nd quarter, will cost $110.00:

   [5 hrs. labor] × [$12/hr. straight-time labor cost] + [$50.00 carry cost]

5. In the objective function, the term "$140X_4$" means that each terminal made on overtime, in the 1st quarter, and shipped in the 2nd quarter, will cost $140.00:

   [5 hrs. labor] × [$18/hr. overtime labor cost] + [$50.00 carry cost]

The constraint equations: (2 quota constraints and 4 resource constraints)

$$X_1 + X_2 \qquad\qquad\qquad\qquad\qquad \geq 700 \; Q_1 \text{ demand}$$

$$X_3 + X_4 + X_5 + X_6 \qquad \geq 3{,}200 \; Q_2 \text{ demand}$$

$$5X_1 + 5X_3 \qquad\qquad\qquad\qquad \leq 9{,}000 \; Q_1 \text{ straight-time labor}$$

$$5X_5 \qquad\qquad \leq 9{,}000 \; Q_2 \text{ straight-time labor}$$

$$5X_2 + 5X_4 \qquad\qquad\qquad \leq 900 \; Q_1 \text{ overtime labor}$$

$$5X_6 \qquad \leq 900 \; Q_2 \text{ overtime labor}$$

Comments:

1. The 1st constraint is a quota constraint. It stipulates that terminals made on straight-time and overtime, in the 1st quarter, must be able to meet or exceed a demand of 700 terminals, in the 1st quarter.

2. The 2nd constraint is also a quota constraint. It stipulates that terminals made on straight-time and overtime, in the 1st quarter, and shipped in the 2nd quarter, must, along with terminals made on straight-time and overtime, in the 2nd quarter, be able to meet or exceed a demand of 3,200 terminals, in the 2nd quarter.

3. The 3rd constraint is a resource constraint. It allows all terminals made on straight-time in the 1st quarter, and shipped in the 1st quarter, as well as terminals made on straight-time in the 1st quarter, and shipped in the 2nd quarter, to use no more than 9,000 straight-time labor hours, in the 1st quarter.

4. The 4th constraint is a resource constraint. It allows all terminals made on straight-time in the 2nd quarter, and shipped in the 2nd quarter, to use no more than 9,000 straight-time labor hours, in the 2nd quarter.

5. The 5th constraint is a resource constraint. It allows all terminals made on overtime in the 1st quarter, and shipped in the 1st quarter, as well as terminals made on overtime, and shipped in the 2nd quarter, to use no more than 900 overtime labor hours, in the 1st quarter.

6. The 6th constraint is a resource constraint. It allows all terminals made on overtime in the 2nd quarter, and shipped in the 2nd quarter, to use no more than 900 overtime labor hours, in the 2nd quarter.

The constraints rewritten as linear equalities:

$$X_1 + X_2 - S_1 + A_1 = 700$$

$$X_3 + X_4 + X_5 + X_6 - S_2 + A_2 = 3{,}200$$

$$5X_1 + 5X_3 + S_3 = 9{,}000$$

$$5X_5 + S_4 = 9{,}000$$

$$5X_2 + 5X_4 + S_5 = 900$$

$$5X_6 + S_6 = 900$$

Define the surplus variables:

S_1 = Excess 1st quarter production, beyond the 700 unit minimum.

S_2 = Excess 2nd quarter production, beyond the 3,200 unit minimum.

Define the slack variables:

S_3 = The amount of straight-time labor hours unused in the 1st quarter.

S_4 = The amount of straight-time labor hours unused in the 2nd quarter.

S_5 = The amount of overtime labor hours unused in the 1st quarter.

S_6 = The amount of overtime labor hours unused in the 2nd quarter.

Once the constraints have been converted into linear equalities, the Simplex Method is applied—a set of mathematical steps for solving a linear programming problem carried out in a table or matrix called a tableau.

Solution

X_1 = 580 terminals to be made on straight-time in the 1st quarter and shipped during the 1st quarter.

X_2 = 120 terminals to be made on overtime in the 1st quarter and shipped during the 1st quarter.

X_3 = 1,220 terminals to be made on straight-time in the 1st quarter and shipped during the 2nd quarter.

X_4 = 0 terminals to be made on overtime in the 1st quarter and shipped during the 2nd quarter.

X_5 = 1,800 terminals to be made on straight-time during the 2nd quarter and shipped during the 2nd quarter.

X_6 = 180 terminals to be made on overtime in the 2nd quarter and shipped during the 2nd quarter.

S_1 = 0 excess production in 1st quarter.

S_2 = 0 excess production in 2nd quarter.

S_3 = 0 unused straight-time labor hours in 1st quarter.

S_4 = 0 unused straight-time labor hours in 2nd quarter.

S_5 = 300 unused overtime labor hours in 1st quarter.

S_6 = 0 unused overtime labor hours in 2nd quarter.

Z = $ 304,000. total cost of the aggregate plan, where straight-time labor cost, overtime labor cost, and inventory carry costs are the only relevant variables. It is an optimal solution.

C. *The Linear Decision Rule (LDR)*

Another optimizing technique, the LDR was developed during the 1950s by Charles Holt, Franco Modigliani, John Muth, and Herbert Simon. It seeks to minimize the combined costs of regular payroll, hiring and layoffs, overtime, and inventory using a set of cost-approximating functions, three of which are quadratic (contain squared terms) to obtain a single quadratic equation. Using calculus, two linear equations (hence the name linear decision rule) can be derived from the quadratic equation. One of the equations can be used to plan the production output for each period in the planning horizon, and the other can be used to plan the work force size for each period. Although the model has found some applications, its chief function seems to be as a benchmark against which proposed techniques can be evaluated.

In practice, the model suffers from three (3) limitations:

1. a specific type of cost function is assumed.

2. considerable effort must usually be expended in obtaining relevant cost data, and developing cost functions for each organization.

3. the method can produce solutions that are not feasible or are impractical.

Example:

Regular Payroll Cost $\quad = \quad C_1 W + C_{13}$

$\qquad\qquad\qquad\qquad\qquad\qquad$ ↑ $\qquad$ ↑

$\qquad\qquad\qquad\qquad\qquad\qquad$ month no.

Overtime Costs $\qquad = \quad C_3(P - C_4 W_1)^2 + C_5 P - C_6 W_1 + C_{12} PW$

Hire/Fire Costs $\qquad = \quad C_2(W_t - W_{t-1} - C_{11})^2$

Inventory, Backorder & Setup Costs $\quad = C_7[I - (C_8 + C_9 O)]^2$

Total Cost For Any One Period $\qquad$ (assumes output as **"quasi-units"**)

$\qquad\qquad\qquad\qquad\qquad$ **Quadratic Composite Mathematical Cost Function**

$C_t - 340 W_t + 64.3(W_t - W_{t-1})]^2 + .20(P_t - 5.67\ W_t)$
$51.2\ P_t - 281\ W_t + .082(I_t - 320)^2$

Total Cost = Regular Payroll + Hire/Layoff + Overtime + Inventory

Restraint (no stockouts by end of period)

$\qquad I_{t-1} + P_t - O_t = I_t$

Where:

$\quad W_t$ = size of work force in period "t"

$\quad P_t$ = production in period "t"

$\quad I_t$ = net inventory in "t" (inventory – backorders)

$\quad O_t$ = order rate (i.e., demand forecast)

The composite cost function is differentiated by calculus methods to yield *two* linear mathematical functions: (together they form a decision rule to minimize "C," total cost in any period).

1st: for *PRODUCTION* in each period:

$$Pt = \begin{pmatrix} +.463\ O_t \\ +.234\ O_t + 1 \\ +.111\ O_t + 2 \\ +.046\ O_t + 3 \\ +.013\ O_t + 4 \\ -.002\ O_t + 5 \\ etc. \end{pmatrix} +.993\ W_{t-1} + 153 - .464\ I_{t-1}$$

2nd: for *WORK FORCE SIZE* in each period:

$$W_t = .743\ W_{t-1} + \left(2.09 - .010\ I_{t-1}\right) + \begin{pmatrix} .010\ O_t \\ .0088\ O_{t+1} \\ .0071\ O_{t+2} \\ .0054 + O_{t+3} \\ etc. \end{pmatrix}$$

Just before starting production each month, you, as plant manager, will calculate the employment level and the production rate for that particular month by substituting the forecasted demand for this month (i.e., O_t) in both equations.

You can also minimize costs even more by using moving average forecasting techniques, or by forecasting for an entire period (i.e., quarter) rather than monthly.

D. *MANAGEMENT COEFFICIENTS MODEL*

A heuristic model proposed by E.H. Bowman in 1963, the management coefficients model attempts to incorporate previous managerial planning, experience, and performance into a decision model. The rationale is based on improving performance rather than on trying to develop a "new" optimizing method. The procedure involves the use of multiple regression analysis of past production decisions made by managers. The regression line provides the relationship between variables, such as demand and labor, for future decisions. Any changes in management personnel invalidate the model.

E. *SIMULATION*

A computer model called "scheduling by simulation" was developed by R.C. Vergin in 1966. It uses a search procedure to look for the minimum cost combination of values for work force size and production rate. It can accommodate any type of cost—linear or non-linear—but no optimal solution is guaranteed, and the procedure is long and costly.

The Master Production Schedule (MPS)

- the selected aggregate production plan is dis-aggregated or "de-composed" into several master production schedules.

- the master production schedule calls for the production of specific makes, models, options, and colors of products.

- the products are scheduled for production (the "build schedule") in a logical and orderly sequence such as:

fully-equipped blue product "A"s—1st

fully-equipped red product "A"s—2nd

fully-equipped green product "A"s—3rd

basic-equipped blue product "A"s—4th

basic-equipped red product "A"s—5th

and so on. . .

- the firm's external suppliers are sent copies of all master production schedules in advance, so that they can align their component and material production schedules to its needs.

- the total time horizon of all MPSs must equal the time horizon of the selected aggregate plan parent.

- the total resource requirements of all MPSs must never exceed the total resource requirements of its selected aggregate plan parent.

- the capacity requirements of each MPS must never surpass the available capacity of its aggregate plan parent for the same period.

- the quasi-unit period forecasts of the aggregate production plan are fine-tuned as the plan moves forward in time, based on recent customer patterns, industry developments, and economic conditions.

4 Monthly Master Production Schedules

January		February		March		April	
(25 days)		(22 days)		(26 days)		(25 days)	
12,000		**10,000**		**14,000**		**12,000**	
9,000 Fusion	3,000 MKZ	7,000 Fusion	3,000 MKZ	8,000 Fusion	6,000 MKZ	6,000 Fusion	6,000 MKZ
6,000 3,000 gas hybrid	1,500 1,500 gas hybrid						
A/C 5,000 auto trans No A/C 1,000 manual trans / A/C 2,000 auto trans No A/C 1,000 manual trans / A/C 1,200 auto trans No A/C 300 manual trans / A/C 1,000 auto trans No A/C 500 manua ltrans 1st week / 2nd week / 3rd week / 4th week		Semi-Firm MPS ("slush") 80% Firm Dealer Orders 20% Open		Soft MPS ("water") 50% Firm Dealer Orders 50% Open		(not started) 100% Open	
Firm MPS ("ice") 100% Firm Dealer Orders		Orders accepted up to January 25th deadline		Orders accepted up to February 24th deadline			

COMMENTS

1. The above example illustrates a 4-period aggregate production plan that has been dis-aggregated into four (4) one-period master production schedules.

2. The above example comes from the Ford Motor Company plant in Hermosillo, Mexico. It produces the Ford Fusion sedan as well as the Lincoln MKZ sedan for the U.S. market.

3. Since the Ford Fusion and Lincoln MKZ are sisters, with only cosmetic differences such as grills, tail lamps, and badges, the quasi-unit "vehicle" is basically a single product for aggregate planning purposes.

4. The January aggregate plan calls for producing 12,000 "vehicles" in order to meet forecasted demand. A combination of incoming Ford and Lincoln dealer orders and historical sales data will decide what percentage of "vehicles" will become a Fusion or an MKZ, and more specifically, what percentage of each will become gasoline sedans and hybrids, as well as base and premium models.

5. The deadline for submission of dealer orders, and revisions to historical sales data based on late-breaking developments, is December 25th for the January MPS. The January MPS is now "firm," and not even the general manager of the plant or the vice-president of production has the authority to change it from that date onward.

6. Since the Fusion outsells the MKZ in virtually every period, it is logical to schedule Fusion production first, producing in the following order: premium gas sedans, basic gas sedans, premium hybrids, and base hybrids. This production sequence allows the plant's external suppliers to more intelligently plan for, and ship the appropriate materials and components for each make, model, trim level, and color.

Aggregate Planning in the Service Sector

Some service firms conduct aggregate scheduling exactly the same way as manufacturing firms and usually formulate mixed aggregate planning strategies. In such industries as banking and fast foods, aggregate planning may even be easier than in manufacturing. In service firms, the need to keep labor costs as low as possible is essential. It entails:

1. Some type of "on-call" labor pool that can be added or deleted to meet unexpected demand.

2. Individual workers with flexible skills who can be reallocated to various assignments.

3. Individual workers with flexible output rates and work hours to meet expanded demand.

All this may seem daunting, but it is routine in service industries where labor is the principal aggregate planning resource. For example:

- supermarket stock clerks switch to cashiers when checkout lines get too long.

- police and fire departments have arrangements for calling up off-duty personnel for major emergencies.

- excess capacity is used for study time and planning time by real estate sales agents.

- experienced waitstaff quicken their pace as crowds of diners arrive.

Approaches to aggregate scheduling differ by the type of service provided:

A. Businesses that offer a bundle of service and product

In high-volume fast-food restaurants, for example, aggregate scheduling focuses on smoothing the production rate and determining the workforce size. This usually requires the buildup of modest levels of inventory during slack periods and depleting that inventory during peak periods, but still using labor to meet the bulk of changes in demand. Although this scenario is similar to manufacturing, it should be noted that the product is most likely perishable and cannot be inventoried more than ten (10) minutes. Additionally, peak and slack periods may be measured in *hours*—not weeks or months.

B. Businesses that offer services with very little or no product

Financial, hospitality, transportation, and recreation services for example, provide high-volume but intangible (not physical) output. Here, aggregate planning focuses mainly on planning for labor requirements and managing demand, i.e., leveling demand peaks and finding ways of utilizing labor during forecasted low-demand periods.

Tactics to Stabilize Demand in the Service Sector

Aggregate planning, whether it be in manufacturing or services, has traditionally focused on manipulating resources to satisfy a forecasted demand at minimum cost. The starting assumption—*that the demand pattern was unalterable*—was not questioned, and actions affecting the demand pattern were considered beyond the domain of operations management.

We now recognize that aggregate planning should be viewed as a way to coordinate and match demand and supply (resources) over the intermediate term, and to *maximize* profit as well. In other words, aggregate planning should also include marketing tactics that create a demand pattern that can be served more efficiently and profitably.

Consider the demand pattern shown below:

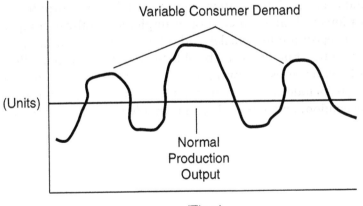

Demand regularly fluctuates above and below production capacity. During high demand, the firm must either incur overtime production costs, raise hiring costs, or use inventories, while during periods of low demand, it must either carry workers that produce at less than maximum capacity, lay off workers, or produce above the rate of demand and build inventories.

If however, the same total demand were spread more evenly over time, as in the demand pattern shown below, total cost could be reduced and customer responsiveness increased:

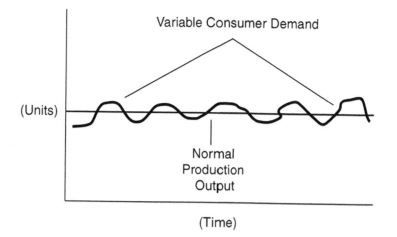

The following simple, yet effective tactics can improve both short-term and intermediate-term demand patterns:

- **Advertising, Pricing, and Promotion** Use heavy advertising, price discounts, coupons, and contests during periods of low demand. Use little or no advertising, price premiums, and no coupons or contests during periods of high demand. Additionally, service industries such as airlines and hotels can employ differential pricing among peak and off-peak seasons, and even days of the week.

- **Countercyclic but Similar Products** Produce products that share the same parts, facilities, and workers yet have countercyclic demand patterns so that peak demand periods for one product are the off-peak demand periods for another. Classic examples of such products are lawn mowers and snow blowers in the manufacturing sector, and ski resorts that become golf and tennis camps during the summer (service sector).

- **Reservation Systems** When the demand pattern cannot be stabilized, a firm might still be able to develop more cost-effective aggregate plans if it has more lead time to prepare for significant demand changes. A reservation system would allow a firm to make cost-effective capacity modifications well in advance. For example, a rental-car company could schedule extra employees or reposition its vehicles and other resources during unusual demand surges if it has sufficient notice, but it may not be able to do so (or do it cost-effectively) on shorter notice. Customers however, must be aware of the reservation system and have an incentive to use it. Incentives may include an iron-clad guarantee that the reservation will be honored at the time of service execution, and a price discount (made possible by more efficient scheduling).

Chapter 13

Inventory Management

Chapter 13 addresses traditional inventory control modeling which seeks a balance between inventory holding costs and the costs of potential lost sales.

In Chapter 11, the mechanics of just-in-time (JIT) manufacturing systems were discussed. It was noted that one of JIT's most significant advantages is the virtual elimination of all inventories, except for the few pre-made trays of parts and assemblies maintained at each workstation. Unfortunately, it is not always possible for a company to fax or telephone an order to an external supplier and expect to receive that order within a two-hour timeframe.

For those materials and parts that require long waits due to unavoidable time and distance factors, traditional inventory control models must still be used. Developed in 1912, these calculus-based models allow the firm to develop an inventory control "doctrine" for each material or component stocked. These doctrines answer two critical questions:

1. How much to buy (or produce in-house) each time a need arises.

2. When to buy (or produce in-house) each time a need arises.

The answer to the first question involves inventory cost tradeoffs, and the answer to the second question involves either a stockout cost or stockout/inventory cost tradeoff.

The purpose of this chapter is to introduce the basic building blocks of all inventory control models, the cost tradeoffs involved, and four (4) widely used applications.

Inventory Model Variables

Almost all types of business organizations, both manufacturing and service, have inventory which can assume the form of raw materials, work-in-process, or finished goods. Consequently, inventory control modeling is one of the most popular topics in operations management; and although the model variables number fewer than two (2) dozen, many have alternate symbols and/or different meanings within the manufacturing and service sectors.

Inventory Control Variable	Service Sector	Manufacturing Sector
Q* or EOQ (economic order quantity)	optimal purchase amount from outside vendor	optimal production run or lot size for each particular product or part
D or D_A	direct customer demand or external demand, on an annual basis	primarily internal demand from the production operation, or independent wholesaler demand on an annual basis
S or K or C_o	the administrative cost of ordering the Q*	the setup cost for Q* (the cost of changing over from one product to another on the same production line)
P or U	wholesale price per unit to the retailer	the manufacturing cost per unit (direct materials, direct labor, and applied overhead)
n	the number of times Q* is ordered per year	the number of production runs for a particular product or part each year
t	the length of the receipt time for purchased items	the length of the manufacturing period for the produced items
d	direct customer demand or external demand, on a daily, weekly, or monthly basis	internal demand from the production operation, or independent wholesaler demand on a daily, weekly, or monthly basis
p	the daily arrival rate of purchased items	the daily production rate of manufactured items
L	leadtime: the period between ordering and receiving purchased items	leadtime: the period between starting and finishing production of a certain item
I	the unit carry cost expressed as a percentage of the unit purchase price	the unit carry cost expressed as a percentage of the unit manufacturing cost
Q	non-optimal or any purchase amount from an outside vendor	non-optimal or any production run or lot size for each particular product or part

Inventory Model Variables Common to Both Manufacturing and Service Sectors

Variable	Definition
H or C_h or k_c	the carry, holding, or storage cost per unit per year. It is expressed as an *annual cost only*.
R or ROP	the reorder point—the level of stock which triggers a reorder of the Q or Q*. Its purpose is to reduce or eliminate the possibility of item stockouts during the reordering waiting period. It is *never* an optimal value.
SS or B	the safety stock or buffer stock—a level of stock maintained at all times as whole or partial protection against the possibilities of stockouts during the reordering period.
$Q*_B$	the optimal order quantity when backordering is allowed by company policy.
S*	the optimal size of a particular item's backorder.
Q* − S*	the amount of the optimal order quantity that goes into stock, after the order has arrived, and all existing backorders have been filled.
C_s	the stockout cost—lost profit from not having a particular item available, when demanded.
$Q*_P$	the optimal order quantity when purchased or manufactured items are received in partial shipments, by internal or external customers over an extended period of time.

Inventory Model Concepts

Service Sector	Manufacturing Sector

Annual Ordering Cost

$[D/Q] \times S$ or $n \times S$

Annual Production Set-up Cost

$[D/Q] \times S$ or $n \times S$

Annual Number of Orders Placed

$[D/Q] = n$

Annual Number of Production Runs

$[D/Q] = n$

Length of Order Receipt Period

$$\frac{Q_p^\star}{p} = t$$

Length of Production Run Period

$$\frac{Q_p^\star}{p} = t$$

Annual Purchase Cost

$P \times D$

Annual Manufacturing Cost

$P \times D$

Total Variable Cost (TVC)

[Annual Carry Costs + Annual Order Costs]

Total Variable Cost (TVC)

[Annual Carry Costs + Annual Setup Costs]

Annual Total Cost (TC)

$[TVC + (P \times D)]$

Annual Total Cost (TC)

$[TVC + (P \times D)]$

Annual Carry Costs

$[Q/2] \times H$

Annual Carry Costs

$[Q/2] \times H$

**Average Inventory Level
per cycle, and per year**

$Q/2$

**Average Inventory Level
per cycle, and per year**

$Q/2$

Reorder Point

ROP or $R = [d \times L]$

(where demand is known and constant,
  and where leadtime is known and
  and constant)

Reorder Point

ROP or $R = [d \times L]$

(where demand is known and constant,
  and where leadtime is known
  and constant)

Reorder Point

ROP or $R = [d \times L] + SS$ (or B)

(where demand and/or leadtime are
  uncertain and variable)

When to Produce Another Run

ROP or $R = [d \times L] + SS$ (or B)

(where demand and/or leadtime are
  uncertain and variable)

Final

Cost effective #

Final

Total Cost

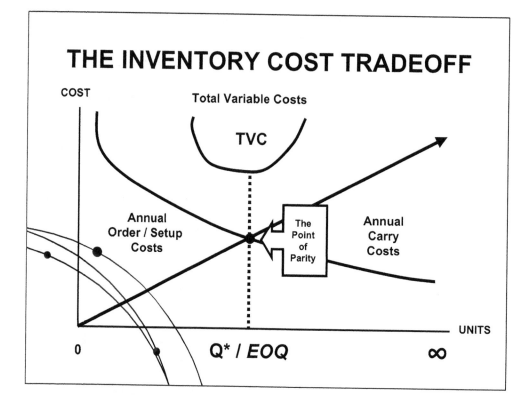

There is an inverse relationship between "H" and "S" costs as well as one between "S" and the number of units in "Q." Using an example from the service sector, as the order amount "Q" becomes larger, the number of orders that need to be placed per year decreases, which in turn, decreases annual order costs ("S").

Example

If Annual Demand Is:	If "Q" is:	Then "n" is	And Annual "S" is:
5,000 units	100 units	50/year	50 × $10* = $500
5,000 units	200 units	25/year	25 × $10* = $250

*(where "per order" costs = $10.00)

Optimal "Q" or "Q*" will always be found at the point where simultaneously "TVC" is minimized and at which annual "H" = annual "S" (the point of "parity" as it is called).

Knowing the values for the variables "H," "S," and "D" allows the firm to calculate its "Q*" for each stocked item, via the EOQ formula:

$$Q^\star = \sqrt{\frac{2\,D\,S}{H}}$$

(where "2" is a constant)

Example

A company forecasts the need for 5,000 units of a stocked item this year. The cost of ordering that item is $49.00, and the cost of holding that item in stock per year is $1.00.

What should be the firm's inventory control doctrine and associated costs for this item?

1. *optimal order quantity*

$$Q^\star = \sqrt{\frac{2\,(5000)(49.00)}{1.00}} = \sqrt{\frac{490,000}{1.00}} = \sqrt{490,000} = \underline{700} \text{ units}$$

2. *total variable costs associated with the above quantity:*

$$[Q/2 \times H] + [D/Q \times S] = TVC$$

$$\left[\frac{700}{2} \times 1.00\right] + \left[\frac{5,000}{700} \times 49.00\right] =$$

$$\left[\$350.00\right] + \left[\$350.00\right] = \underline{\$700.00}$$

3. and if the firm must expect to wait three (3) days for an order to arrive, during which time the daily average demand = 8 units, then:

$$ROP \text{ or } R = [d \times L] = [8 \times 3] = 24 \text{ units}$$

Therefore, the inventory doctrine for this particular stocked item is:

$$Q^\star = 700 \text{ units}$$

$$ROP \text{ or } R = 24 \text{ units}$$

That is, the firm should order 700 units at a time, whenever the unit's stockage level falls to 24 units. Total annual cost for this policy or doctrine (exclusive of annual purchase costs) is $700.00

NOTE: There is no relationship whatsoever between "Q" or "Q*" and "ROP." Moreover, "ROP" is never an optimal value.

The Inventory Order Cycle Chart

The basic $Q^\star$ or EOQ (Economic Order Quantity) model was used in the above example. It is the simplest form of the EOQ model and the basis on which all other model versions are built. It is essentially a single formula for determining the optimal order size that minimizes the sum of carry costs and ordering costs. The formula is derived under a set of restrictive assumptions:

1. daily, weekly, monthly, and annual demand are known with certainty, and relatively constant over time.

2. no inventory stockouts are allowed.

3. no backordering is allowed.

4. there are no physical limits on warehouse storage space.

5. the lead time for the receipt of orders is constant.

6. the order quantity is received all at once.

7. the unit price or manufacturing cost remains constant, i.e., no economies-of-scale or quantity discounts.

These assumptions are reflected below, in what is called a "picket-fence" inventory order cycle chart:

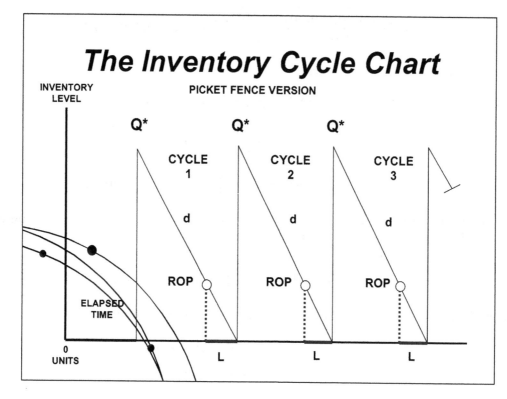

An order quantity, "Q" is received and is used up over time, at a constant rate. When the inventory level decreases to the reorder point, "R" or "ROP," a new order is placed, and a period of time, referred to as the lead time, "L," is required for delivery. The order is received all at once, just at the moment when demand depletes the entire stock of inventory (and the inventory level reaches zero), thus allowing no shortages (stockouts). This cycle is continuously repeated for the same order quantity, reorder point, and lead time.

Sensitivity Analysis

Definition: the process of determining how sensitive the optimal solution is to changes in the values used in the equation.

Examples

What effect would the following individual changes have on the value of Q?

1. *If ordering costs increase by a factor of "4" (i.e., 400%).* We can answer this question by inspecting the basic EOQ formula, and substituting "4" for "S":

$$Q^* = \sqrt{\frac{2DS}{H}} = 2 \cdot Q^* = \sqrt{\frac{2D(4)}{H}}$$

(the optimal Q^* will increase by a factor of "2" *only*)

2. *If carrying (holding) costs increase by a factor of "4" (i.e., 400%).*

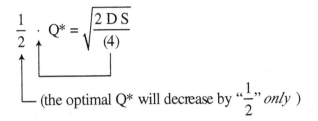

$$\frac{1}{2} \cdot Q^* = \sqrt{\frac{2\,D\,S}{(4)}}$$

(the optimal Q* will decrease by "$\frac{1}{2}$" *only*)

3. *If total Number of Units sold per year (i.e., annual demand) decreases by a factor of "9" (or 89%) (that is to 1/9 of what it was before).*

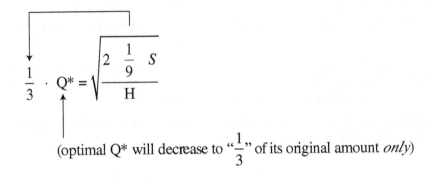

$$\frac{1}{3} \cdot Q^* = \sqrt{\frac{2\,\frac{1}{9}\,S}{H}}$$

(optimal Q* will decrease to "$\frac{1}{3}$" of its original amount *only*)

Sensitivity analysis has two purposes here:

1. it's a short-cut method for determining effects on the value of Q* without completely having to recalculate the Q*.

2. it demonstrates how even changes of "+" or "–" 25% or 30% in "H," "S," and "D" will have almost no effect on the value of Q*. Therefore, we can say that Q* is *robust*, (relatively insensitive to changes in its equation parameters). This is good to know since many firms cannot accurately determine their H, S, and D values, but even when they are rough estimates, Q* can be computed with confidence.

The Quantity Discount Model

- used whenever the firm is given the option of purchasing goods at several different unit prices.

- you would naturally obtain the lowest unit price by ordering the largest quantity. However, the largest quantity also incurs the highest average annual carry (holding) costs.

- a tradeoff must be effected between low material costs and high carry costs.

- three (3) cost elements, computed on an annual basis, must be considered; they comprise total annual inventory cost

$$TC \text{ or } T_c = H + S + [P \times D]$$

- in the above equation:

"H" (carry cost per unit) must be initially computed as "$I \times P$" (where "I" is the unit carry cost expressed as a percentage of the price "P").

"$P \times D$" (called the Material Cost, Fixed Cost, or Product Cost) is the unit price times the annual demand for the unit.

- To determine which order quantity will minimize T_c (total annual inventory cost), four (4) steps must be taken:

Step #1: compute $Q^\star$ at the lowest unit price obtainable from the vendor.
  compute $Q^\star$ at the second lowest unit price obtainable from the vendor.
  compute $Q^\star$ at the third lowest unit price obtainable from the vendor.
  compute $Q^\star$ at the fourth lowest unit price obtainable from the vendor.
    etc.

Step #2: If the vendor (by inspection of his price list) will not permit you to purchase a particular $Q^\star$ at that particular unit price, raise the $Q^\star$ to the minimum quantity you must order in order to qualify for that particular unit price.

Step #3: Compute the T_c (total annual inventory cost) for each of the order quantities (raised or not raised) in Step #2, using the equation:

$$T_c = D/Q \times S + Q/2 \times H + P \times D$$

Step #4: Select the order quantity (i.e., order strategy) with the lowest T_c.

- It is essential that the "H" be recomputed for each specific unit price in the above via "$I \times P$."

The reason why is because the carry costs per unit actually *do* change with the price per unit. If the unit price is less, then:

1. obsolescence costs are less.

2. spoilage costs are less.

3. the cost of capital by which to purchase the units is less.

4. inventory taxes are less.

However, materials-handling, heating, refrigeration, storage, security, and other similar costs would remain the same.

- There are no currently available optimization models to identify the appropriate order quantity; the QUANTITY DISCOUNT Model, with its laborious hand calculations, is the only available technique.

NOTE: an optimal Q ($Q^\star$) will not necessarily be selected. Whatever Q minimizes total annual inventory costs is selected.

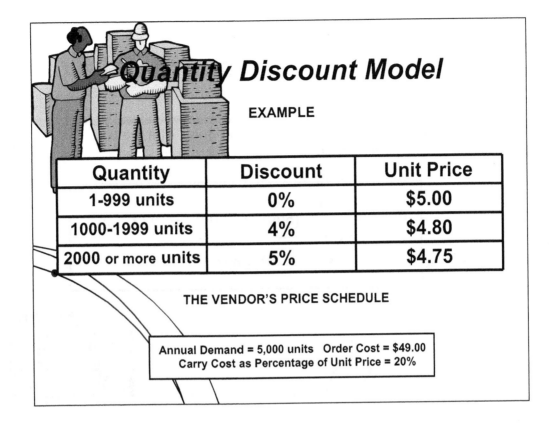

Quantity Discount Model

EXAMPLE

Quantity	Discount	Unit Price
1-999 units	0%	$5.00
1000-1999 units	4%	$4.80
2000 or more units	5%	$4.75

THE VENDOR'S PRICE SCHEDULE

Annual Demand = 5,000 units   Order Cost = $49.00
Carry Cost as Percentage of Unit Price = 20%

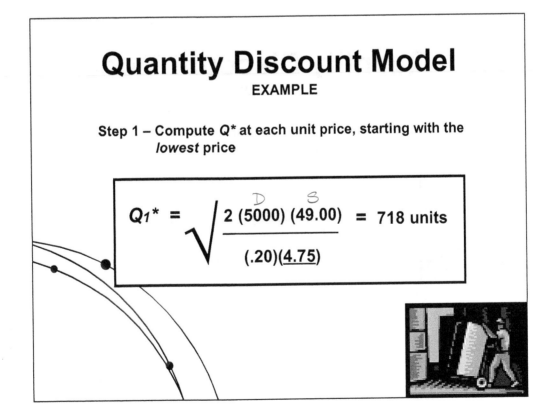

Quantity Discount Model
EXAMPLE

Step 1 – Compute Q^* at each unit price, starting with the *lowest* price

$$Q_1^* = \sqrt{\frac{2\,(5000)\,(49.00)}{(.20)(\underline{4.75})}} = 718 \text{ units}$$

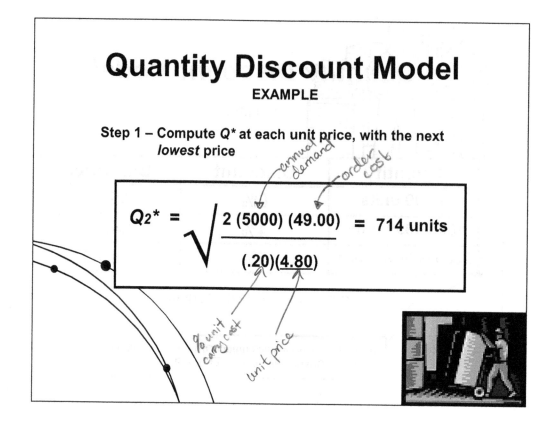

Quantity Discount Model
EXAMPLE

Step 1 – Compute Q^* at each unit price, with the next *lowest* price

$$Q_2^* = \sqrt{\frac{2\,(5000)\,(49.00)}{(.20)(4.80)}} = 714 \text{ units}$$

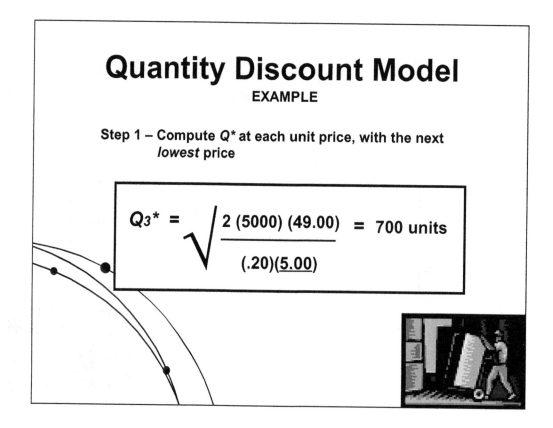

Quantity Discount Model
EXAMPLE

Step 1 – Compute Q^* at each unit price, with the next *lowest* price

$$Q_3^* = \sqrt{\frac{2\,(5000)\,(49.00)}{(.20)(5.00)}} = 700 \text{ units}$$

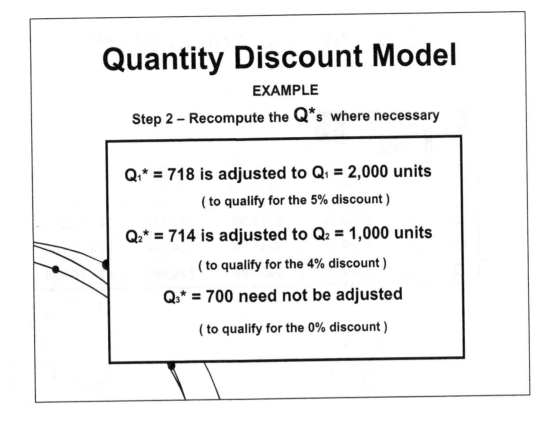

Quantity Discount Model

EXAMPLE

Step 2 – Recompute the Q^*s where necessary

$Q_1^* = 718$ is adjusted to $Q_1 = 2,000$ units

(to qualify for the 5% discount)

$Q_2^* = 714$ is adjusted to $Q_2 = 1,000$ units

(to qualify for the 4% discount)

$Q_3^* = 700$ need not be adjusted

(to qualify for the 0% discount)

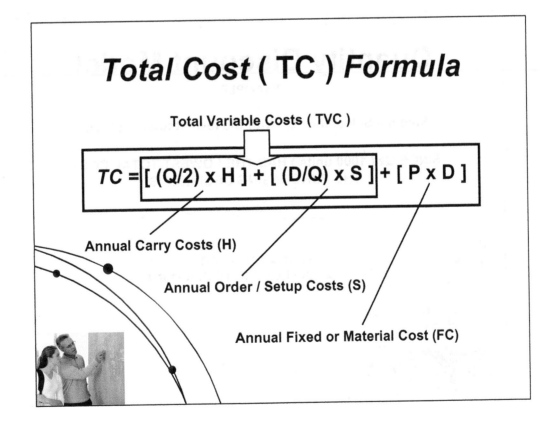

Total Cost (TC) Formula

Total Variable Costs (TVC)

$$TC = [(Q/2) \times H] + [(D/Q) \times S] + [P \times D]$$

Annual Carry Costs (H)

Annual Order / Setup Costs (S)

Annual Fixed or Material Cost (FC)

Quantity Discount Model

EXAMPLE

SUMMARY

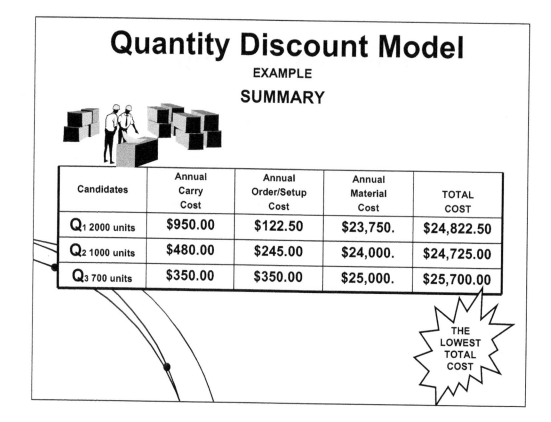

Candidates	Annual Carry Cost	Annual Order/Setup Cost	Annual Material Cost	TOTAL COST
Q_1 2000 units	$950.00	$122.50	$23,750.	$24,822.50
Q_2 1000 units	$480.00	$245.00	$24,000.	$24,725.00
Q_3 700 units	$350.00	$350.00	$25,000.	$25,700.00

THE LOWEST TOTAL COST

Quantity Discount Model

EXAMPLE

Step 4 – Select the "Q" with the lowest total cost (TC)

SINCE Q_2 (1000 units) HAS THE LOWEST TOTAL COST,
THE PURCHASING DECISION IS:

1. TAKE A DISCOUNT
2. SELECT THE 4% DISCOUNT

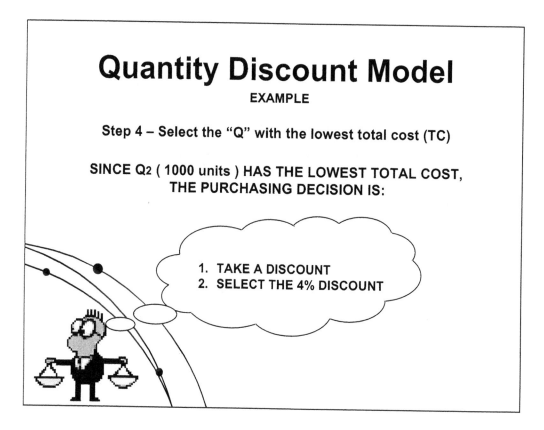

The detailed calculations:

$$\text{TC for } Q_3 = 700: \left[\frac{700}{2} \times (.20)(\$5.00)\right] + \left[\frac{5000}{700} \times \$49.\right] + \left[5.00 \times 5000\right]$$

$\underline{\$25,700} = \$350. + \$350. + \$25,000.$

$$\text{TC for } Q_2 = 1000: \left[\frac{1000}{2} \times (.20)(\$4.80)\right] + \left[\frac{5000}{1000} \times \$49.\right] + \left[\$4.80 \times 5000\right]$$

$\underline{\$24,725.} = \$480. + \$245. + \$24,000.$

$$\text{TC for } Q_1 = 2000: \left[\frac{2000}{2} \times (.20)(\$4.75)\right] + \left[\frac{5000}{2000} \times \$49.\right] + \left[\$4.75 \times 5000\right]$$

$\underline{\$24,822.50} = \$950. + \$122.50 + \$23,750.$

The Production Order Quantity Model

- alternate names: "Finite Correction Factor" model, "Production Run" model, "Serial-Rate Production" model.

- used when vendor cannot ship order all at once, or firm cannot produce order all at once (i.e., one day). That is, "instantaneous receipt" is no longer assumed.

- requires identification of a "P" or "p" (the replenishment rate or production rate) and a "D" or "d" (consumption rate or usage rate).

- model assumes that "P" is greater than "D" and that inventory levels continue to climb until the order is completed.

- all the other assumptions of the Basic EOQ model are the *same.*

- the inventory levels never reach the value of Q* or EOQ because the inventory is consumed as it actually arrives from the outside vendor or is shipped out to a customer as it is actually produced.

- the average inventory is no longer "Q/2" (as it is in the Basic EOQ model). It is *less.*

- the average inventory is equal to one-half of the "height of the triangle" or MAXIMUM INVENTORY LEVEL.

- originated in manufacturing, but easily used in the service sector for partial shipment situations.

These assumptions and operating characteristics are reflected below, in what is called a "sawtooth" inventory order cycle chart:

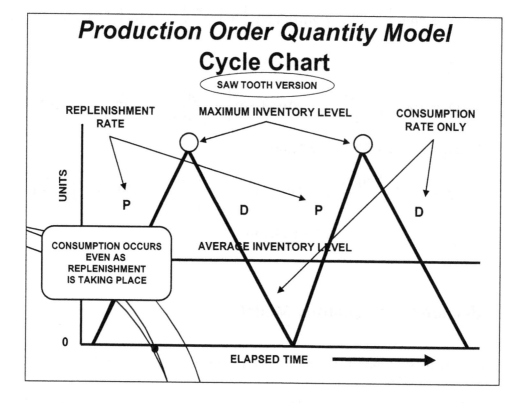

An order quantity, "Q" is received over several days, weeks, or months while simultaneously being consumed. Consequently, the maximum level of inventory will never reach the original value of "Q." After the maximum level of inventory is reached, consumption alone takes place, driving the inventory level down to zero in time. At that point, another order is placed, starting a new cycle.

- the optimal order quantity, $Q^\star$ or more properly $Q_p^\star$, becomes larger under the PRODUCTION ORDER QUANTITY model, as it must, since the $Q^\star$ is being drawn down even as it arrives on a piecemeal basis.

- the larger $Q_p^\star$ produces *no increase* in carry (holding) costs.

- annual carry (holding) costs are actually less than they would be under the Basic EOQ model!

- a larger $Q_p^\star$ means fewer orders need to be placed if the firm buys from an outside vendor, or that production runs will become larger (take place over more work days) if the firm is producing for customers.

- "P" and "D" can be expressed as daily, weekly, monthly, or annual figures without changing the value of the finite correction factor $(1 - D/P)$.

- the length of an order receipt cycle or the length of a production cycle is "t," computed as follows:

$$t = \frac{Q_p^\star}{p}$$

(if a customer requested an order for 400 units, and if the firm could only manufacture 8 units daily, then it would take 50 days, 400/8 = 50, to run the production cycle).

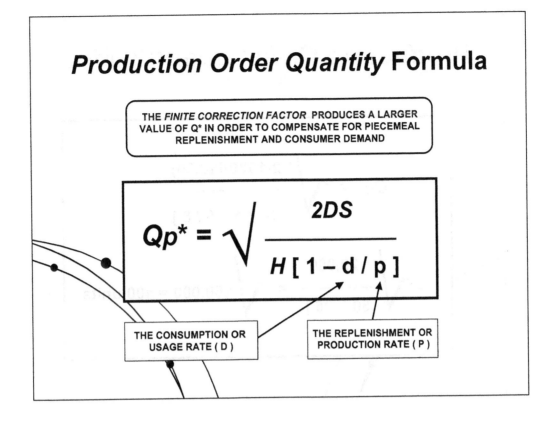

Production Order Quantity Formula

THE *FINITE CORRECTION FACTOR* PRODUCES A LARGER VALUE OF Q* IN ORDER TO COMPENSATE FOR PIECEMEAL REPLENISHMENT AND CONSUMER DEMAND

$$Qp^* = \sqrt{\frac{2DS}{H[1-d/p]}}$$

THE CONSUMPTION OR USAGE RATE (D)

THE REPLENISHMENT OR PRODUCTION RATE (P)

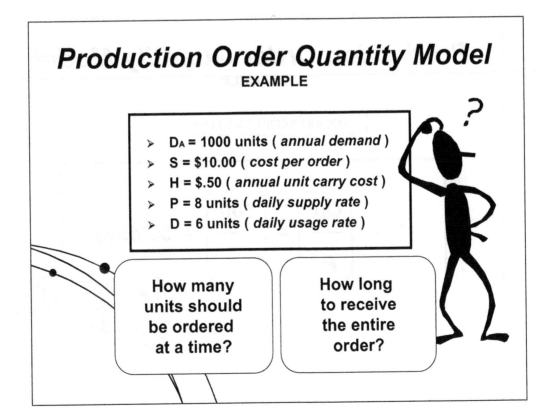

Production Order Quantity Model
EXAMPLE

➤ D_A = 1000 units (*annual demand*)
➤ S = $10.00 (*cost per order*)
➤ H = $.50 (*annual unit carry cost*)
➤ P = 8 units (*daily supply rate*)
➤ D = 6 units (*daily usage rate*)

How many units should be ordered at a time?

How long to receive the entire order?

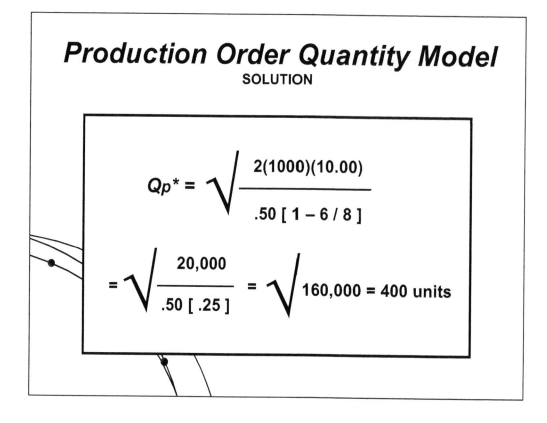

Production Order Quantity Model
SOLUTION

$$Qp^* = \sqrt{\frac{2(1000)(10.00)}{.50\,[\,1 - 6\,/\,8\,]}}$$

$$= \sqrt{\frac{20,000}{.50\,[\,.25\,]}} = \sqrt{160,000} = 400 \text{ units}$$

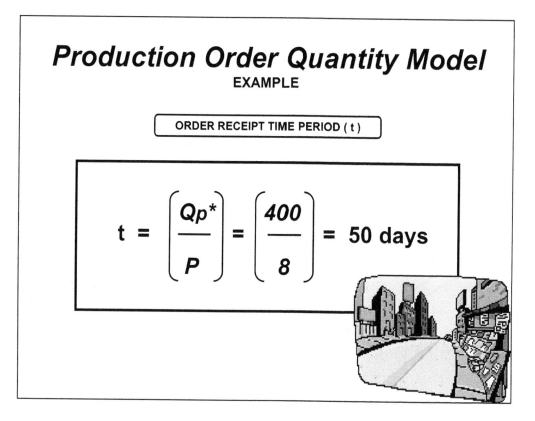

Production Order Quantity Model
EXAMPLE

ORDER RECEIPT TIME PERIOD (t)

$$t = \left(\frac{Qp^*}{P}\right) = \left(\frac{400}{8}\right) = 50 \text{ days}$$

Total variable costs (TVC) are:

$$TVC = \left[\frac{Q_P^\star}{2} \times \left(1 - \frac{D}{P}\right) \times H \right] + \left[\frac{D}{Q_P^\star} \times S \right]$$

$$= \left[\frac{400}{2} \times \left(1 - \frac{6}{8}\right) \times .50 \right] + \left[\frac{1,000}{400} \times 10.00 \right]$$

$$= [200 \times (.25)(.50)] + [2.5 \times \$10.00]$$

$$\underline{\underline{\$50.}} = [\$25] + [\$25]$$

The Backorder Inventory Model

- the tolerance of backorders is the only changed assumption from the Basic EOQ model. Backorders are an effective method of reducing inventory carry (holding) costs. The firm is asking customers to wait for their purchases over a period of time until a new Q is ordered and received. During the waiting period, the firm has no products in stock and therefore also has no carry costs!

- "B" is the symbol for backorder costs. These costs consist of lost productivity by the firm's employees as they are forced to stop what they are doing to handle customer questions about backordered products; the firm's costs of maintaining backorder records; and the estimated lost profits from not having the product available for immediate sale, since some customers will not wait (and go elsewhere).

- $Q_B^\star$ = the optimal order quantity in backordering-tolerated situations.

- $S^\star$ = the optimal number of backorders that should accumulate before a new $Q_B^\star$ is placed.

- as the number of backorders accumulate, average carry costs for the product in question fall. However, there's a limit as to how far backorders can mount before the customers start looking elsewhere. The expression:

$$\left(\frac{H}{H + B} \right)$$

puts limits on the number of backorders by balancing the costs of backorders against the carry costs.

- $Q_B^\star$ will be larger then the basic EOQ in order to compensate for the fact that the $Q_B^\star$ once it arrives in stock, must be reduced in order to fill the accumulated backorders.

- b or $(Q_B^\star - S^\star)$ = the remaining units of $Q^\star$ going into stock after the backorders have been filled.

- If backorder costs were to increase, the model would cause the number of backordered units to decrease, and vice-versa.

- The Backorder Model always yields lower overall system costs than does the simple EOQ model, due to lower annual "H" costs and lower annual "S" costs.

These assumptions and operating characteristics are reflected below in a "picket fence" inventory order cycle chart:

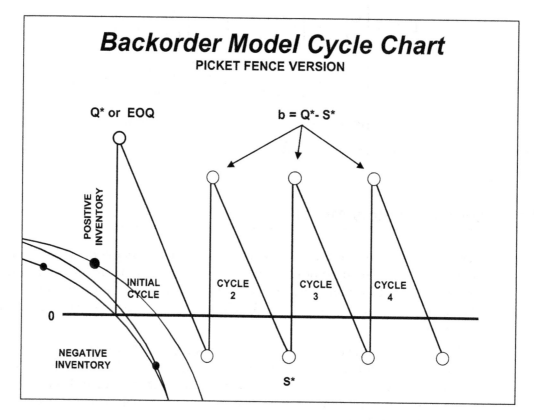

Backorder Inventory Model Example

Problem Statement

A tire dealer has very loyal customers who are content to wait until new shipments arrive. Brand "X" is not one of the dealer's most popular lines, but he does order on a regular basis.

- the annual demand for Brand "X" is 500 (five-hundred) units.
- the ordering cost is $4.00 each time an order is placed.
- the carry cost per unit per year is 50¢.
- the dealer estimates that the cost of placing a backorder for Brand "X" is $10.00 per unit

  1. How many tires of Brand "X" should the dealer order if he tolerates backordering?

  2. What is the amount backordered?

  3. Under a backordering policy, what are the TVC (total variable cost)?

  4. What would be the exact level of inventory at the moment a new shipment arrived and all existing backorders had been filled?

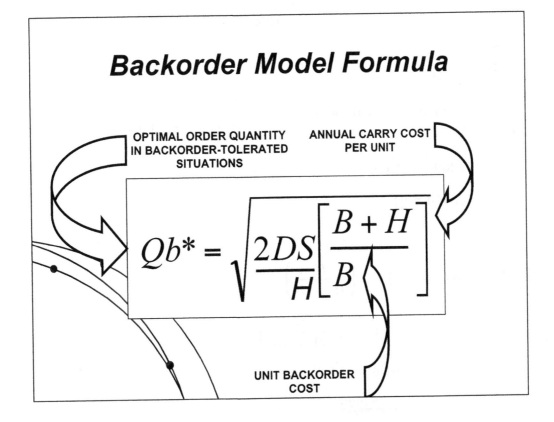

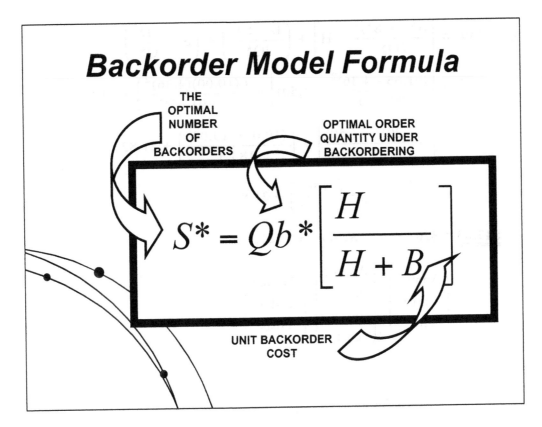

Solution

1. $Q_B^\star = \sqrt{\dfrac{2\,D\,S}{H} \cdot \left(\dfrac{B + H}{B}\right)}$

$\qquad = \sqrt{\dfrac{2(500)(4)}{.50} \cdot \left(\dfrac{10.00 + .50}{10.00}\right)}$ NOTE: $Q_B^\star$ must be computed before $S^\star$

$\qquad = \sqrt{8000 \cdot (1.05)}$

$\qquad = \sqrt{8400} = \underline{91.65}$ units

2. $S^\star$ or $(Q - b) = Q_B^\star \cdot \left(\dfrac{H}{H + B}\right)$

$\qquad = 91.65 \cdot \left(\dfrac{.50}{.50 + 10.}\right)$

$\qquad = 91.65 \cdot (.0476)$

$\qquad = \underline{4.36\ units}$

3. $\text{TVC} = \left[\dfrac{(Q_B^\star - S^\star)^2}{2Q_B^\star} \cdot H\right] + \left(\dfrac{B \cdot S^{\star 2}}{2Q_B^\star}\right) + \left(S \cdot \dfrac{D}{Q_B^\star}\right)$

$\qquad = \left[\dfrac{(91.65 - 4.36)^2}{2(91.65)} \cdot (.50)\right] + \left(\dfrac{(10.00)(4.36)^2}{2(91.65)}\right) + 21.82$

$\qquad = \left[\dfrac{(87.29)^2 \cdot (.50)}{183.3}\right] + \left(\dfrac{(10.00)\,(19.00)}{183.3}\right) + 21.82$

$\qquad = \left[\dfrac{3,809.77}{183.3}\right] + \left(\dfrac{190}{183.3}\right) + 21.82$

$\underline{\$43.63} = \$20.78 + \$1.03 + \$21.82$

$\qquad \begin{pmatrix} \text{Annual} \\ \text{carry} \\ \text{costs} \end{pmatrix} \begin{pmatrix} \text{Annual} \\ \text{back-} \\ \text{order} \\ \text{costs} \end{pmatrix} \begin{pmatrix} \text{Annual} \\ \text{order} \\ \text{costs} \end{pmatrix}$

4. $Q_B^\star - S^\star$ or $91.65 - 4.36 \cong \underline{87}$ units

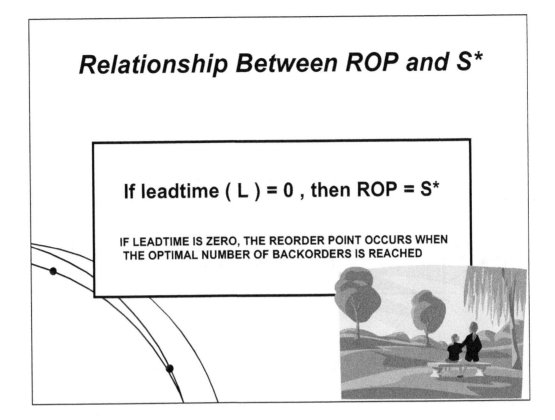

Relationship Between ROP and S*

If leadtime (L) = 0 , then ROP = S*

IF LEADTIME IS ZERO, THE REORDER POINT OCCURS WHEN
THE OPTIMAL NUMBER OF BACKORDERS IS REACHED

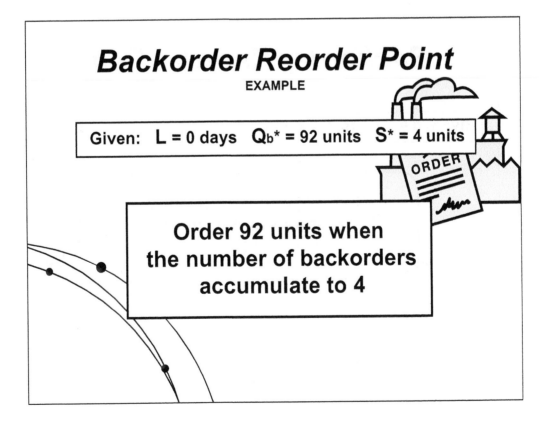

Backorder Reorder Point

EXAMPLE

Given: L = 0 days $Q_b^* = 92$ units   S* = 4 units

Order 92 units when
the number of backorders
accumulate to 4

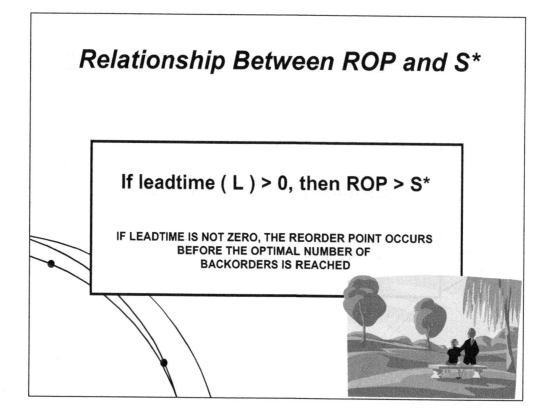

Relationship Between ROP and S*

If leadtime (L) > 0, then ROP > S*

IF LEADTIME IS NOT ZERO, THE REORDER POINT OCCURS
BEFORE THE OPTIMAL NUMBER OF
BACKORDERS IS REACHED

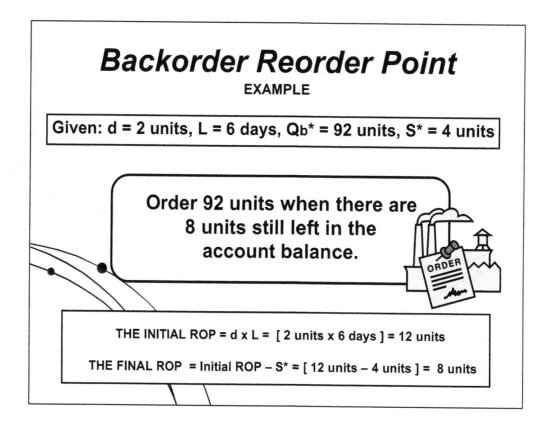

Backorder Reorder Point
EXAMPLE

Given: d = 2 units, L = 6 days, Q_b^* = 92 units, S* = 4 units

Order 92 units when there are
8 units still left in the
account balance.

THE INITIAL ROP = d x L = [2 units x 6 days] = 12 units

THE FINAL ROP = Initial ROP – S* = [12 units – 4 units] = 8 units

Markov Processes

Available on Student CD

Chapter 15

Short-Term Scheduling Tactics

Chapter 15 covers the five phases of planning scheduling, and controlling intermittent-flow ("job-shop") operations.

Perhaps the most complex planning, scheduling, and control responsibilities originate in intermittent-flow or "job shop" operations which were introduced in chapter seven. Here, manufacturing and service jobs of all description enter and leave the shop hourly and daily, with their needs accommodated by cross-trained, highly-skilled staff. Examples include custom furniture, automobile repairs, outpatient medical services, hairstyling, and college lectures. Despite their diversity, these and similar jobs have one element in common: they were all promised to their customers at a specific time, and it was the shop's responsibility to determine how it met those deadlines. It is interesting to note that estimated costs are only one of many criteria considered in job shop decision-making, and may even be assigned the lowest priority.

This chapter will examine the five (5) phases of the job-shop or short-term scheduling process as well as the assignment algorithm—a special version of linear programming widely used in job shop scheduling.

The Job Shop Scheduling Process

An Overview

Two Basic Issues or Goals:

1. How to assign the incoming jobs to the various work centers, departments, or stations within the job shop. Some jobs may only need to be assigned to one work center; others may need to be assigned to two or more before they are completed.

2. In what sequence or processing order should jobs assigned at each work center be placed? Many possible sequences and evaluation criteria exist.

The Steps:

1. *AGGREGATE PLANNING/SCHEDULING:* This function was described in chapter 12. Briefly, the job shop must formulate its own definition of a "quasi-unit" that best reflects its overall output of goods and services. It will then multiply the quasi-unit forecast by the quasi-unit resource consumption rate to arrive at its total human, equipment, and material resource requirement. The shop will then develop a plan that meets demand at lowest cost.

   Example:

   An automobile dealership forecasts "repairs" for 20,000 vehicles over the next calendar year. The number of service managers, mechanics, service bays, sets of diagnostic equipment, and inventoried parts will be predicated on what the average "repair" resource needs are, multiplied by the forecasted number of "repairs" for the year. A plan would then be developed to effect those repairs at lowest cost to the shop.

2. *LOADING:* (also known as "shop" or "machine" loading), is the assignment and commitment of incoming jobs to one or more specific work centers, for the day or week. At this point in time, only a generalized completion time can be estimated for the customer.

   Example:

   An automobile needing an oil and filter change and sheet metal repair would be "loaded" into two service departments: lubrication and body shop. The car could be promised to the owner at the end of two business days but the shop is not able to determine the exact hours of each day the car will be in either department, or exactly what hour of the second day it will be completed.

3. *SEQUENCING:* (also known as priority sequencing), establishes the order of processing for jobs in "queues" (waiting lines) at each work center. This task requires the adoption and implementation of a "priority sequence rule." The specific rule adopted will be the one that best meets management's chosen shop objectives.

   Example:

   Management may select the "SPT" or shortest-processing-time rule. This rule forces each work center to process its shortest-timed jobs first, which usually results in more jobs being processed than otherwise. The SPT rule would also meet the objectives of a job shop equally focused on efficiency and customer satisfaction, because SPT raises short-term productivity and also increases the probabilities of earlier completion times.

4. *DETAILED SCHEDULING:* (also known as supplementary scheduling), is performed only after the shop has estimated all job processing times, loaded the jobs into one or more work centers, and established those jobs' processing orders within each work center. It is here that specific processing start and completion times for each job at each work center are set, exercising caution to avoid the scheduling of the same job in two different centers at the same or partially-overlapping times.

   Example:

   On Monday, Job "A" will be scheduled in Center "#1" between 9:00 and 11:00 am; in Center "#5" between 12:00 and 2:00 pm; and in Center "#8" between 3:00 and 4:00 pm, with customer delivery by 4:30 pm.

5. *DISPATCHING:* is the physical releasing of a job or jobs from shop control to the first work center selected to process it.

   Example:

   The service manager of an automobile dealership releases the ignition keys and work order for a particular vehicle to a representative of the work center that will first be servicing it. The vehicle is then driven from the parking lot to the work center's open service bay.

The GANTT Chart for Shop Loading

Shows the cumulative work loads facing each work center or department per day, or per week.

Advantages:

1. graphically and instantly communicates the number of jobs committed to each work center for the day or the week, together with their estimated processing times at each work center, depicted as horizontal bars.

2. signals the need to reassign labor, equipment, and materials from the less-busy work centers to the busiest ones.

3. signals the need to enlist external labor, equipment, and materials when each and every work center in the job ship is equally busy.

4. serves as the foundation of the detailed shop schedule yet to come.

5. conveys the relative work loads at each work center.

Limitations:

1. must be updated to reflect new job arrivals, departures, and revised estimates for current jobs.

2. in especially dynamic job shops, updates may need to be done every few hours, at opening, lunchtime, and closing.

3. the estimated task times for loaded jobs may not accurately reflect variabilities in human or machine performance. For example, a particular job loaded into a work center may have its processing time underestimated by 20% due to inexperienced supervisors or recurring equipment malfunctions.

4. does not reflect the relative processing cost implications of loading an arriving job into each of several possible machines or workers in the same work center. This would suggest the use of the assignment algorithm rather than the gantt chart for loading purposes.

Priority Sequencing

Orders waiting to be processed build up in front of each work center or machine on the shop floor. Decisions must be made as to which job will be processed next. To accomplish this task, we need to establish a priority sequence rule, which, once chosen, is consistently used.

Several criteria (or yardsticks) can be used for measuring the relative effectiveness of various candidate priority sequence rules. There are literally dozens of potential priority sequence rules; however, we can only choose and employ one rule at a time in our job shop operations.

If you are primarily concerned with **Internal Facility Efficiency** you would screen potential sequence rules against the following criteria or performance parameters: 1) *set-up costs*, 2) *WIP* (work-in-process) *inventory costs*, and 3) *percentage of work station idle time*.

The GANTT Chart for Shop Loading

Weekly Schedule—Dept. 3985: Model Shop   **Schedule: 3/16—22**

Work Centers	Monday	Tuesday	Wednesday	Thursday	Friday	Saturday
1. Machining	D	E	F			
2. Fabrication	C	D	E	F		
3. Assembly	B	C	D	E		
4. Test	B	D				
5. Packaging	A	B	C			

If you are primarily concerned with **Customer Service** you would screen potential sequence rules against the following criteria or performance parameters: 1) *the percentage of jobs late,* 2) *average of lateness,* and 3) *the standard deviation of job lateness.*

If you are equally concerned about achieving both **Internal Shop Efficiency** and **Customer Service** you would screen potential sequence rules against the following criteria or performance parameters: 1) *the average number of jobs waiting to be processed,* 2) *the average job completion time,* and 3) *the standard deviation of job completion time.*

Additional criteria are introduced on the Student CD.

It is impossible to find a sequence rule that best satisfies all criteria simultaneously. The relative importance of the above performance criteria must be judged by the production manager and carefully considered.

Examples of some widely used priority sequencing rules:

FIFO *FCFS:* (First Come, First Served) all jobs are processed in the order of their arrival at the work center or machine.

LIFO *LCFS:* (Last Come, First Served) all jobs are processed in the reverse order of their arrival at the center/machine.

SPT: (Shortest Processing Time) waiting jobs with the shortest estimated processing times are processed next.

FISFS: (First in System, First Served) as jobs come into the shop, they are assigned a due date. Those jobs possessing early due dates are processed first when they arrive at a particular work center or machine.

SS: (Static Slack) *"static slack"* is the difference in time between the job's due date and its arrival time at the work center/machine. The job with the smallest static slack is done first.

SS/PT: (Static Slack divided by Remaining Processing Time for Each Job) as the SS/PT ratio gets smaller, the job gets higher priority for processing. (all times are expressed in "labor hours")

The "SPT" Rule has been found through empirical research, to be consistently superior to all other rules. It is in fact *optimal* for minimizing average job completion time, the average number of jobs in the total system, and the average job lateness.

The Truncated SPT Rule

The major drawback of the SPT rule however, is the much greater dispersion of "flow times" it causes by holding longer jobs in work center waiting lines over lengthy periods. Flow time is the total time that a job spends in the shop, both waiting and processing.

Example

If your shop had six (6) jobs (5 short and 1 long) waiting to be processed, then perhaps by mid-afternoon, the 5 shortest jobs would be processed and the 6th (and longest) job would just come to the head of the waiting line, when, suddenly, several new jobs arrive at the same center (requiring less processing time). As a result, the long job is pushed back to the rear of the waiting line. This situation could easily repeat itself several times before the long job finally got processed.

With "SPT" rule:

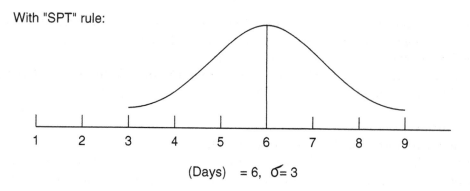

(Days) = 6, σ = 3

Average job flow time is 6 days; standard deviation of job flow time is 3 days.

With "truncated SPT" rule:

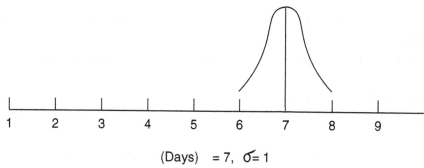

(Days) = 7, σ = 1

Average job flow time is 7 days; standard deviation or dispersion of job flow time is 1 day.

The modified or truncated SPT rule calls for management to put an absolute time limit on how long a job, regardless of processing time length, can be held back in the line before it must be processed. This results in a slight increase in average job flow time, but a significant decrease in the dispersion of job flow time.

The choice between SPT and Truncated SPT depends upon which is more important to you: AVERAGE FLOW TIME or STANDARD DEVIATION OF FLOW TIME, or to rephrase, which time estimate would most appeal to the customer?

6 days ± 3 days or between 3 to 9 days? Or 7 days ± 1 day or between 6 to 8 days?

Priority Sequencing Rules Example

Assume that it is the first day of the month, and that the job shop operates seven (7) days a week. This month's work consists of five (5) jobs, A, B, C, D, and E, with time estimates and deadlines as follows:

JOB	ESTIMATED TIMES (in days)	Deadline (day)
A	5	10th
B	10	15th
C	2	5th
D	8	12th
E	6	8th

The number of potential processing orders for the above five jobs is 5! (or $5 \times 4 \times 3 \times 2 \times 1 = 120$). For example:

A–B–C–D–E

E–D–C–B–A

B–A–D–C–E

D–E–B–C–A

A–E–D–B–C

C–B–D–E–A

etc.

It is neither cost nor time effective to evaluate all 120 possible processing sequences, and while the job shop's mission objectives of either 1. internal efficiency, 2. customer service, or 3. a combination of both efficiency and service will ultimately dictate the single priority sequence rule to be employed, the mechanics of five popular rules with their effects on each job's completion time and lateness are shown below:

Shortest Processing Time (SPT)

Processing Order	Processing Time	Completion Time	Deadline	Lateness
C	2	2nd	5th	0
A	5	7th	10th	0
E	6	13th	8th	5 days
D	8	21st	12th	9 days
B	10	31st	15th	16 days
Average		14.8		6 days

First-In, First-Out (FIFO) or First-Come, First-Served (FCFS)

Processing Order	Processing Time	Completion Time	Deadline	Lateness
A	5	5th	10th	0
B	10	15th	15th	0
C	2	17th	5th	12 days
D	8	25th	12th	13 days
E	6	31st	8th	23 days
Average		18.6		9.6 days

Static Slack (SS)

(each job's deadline date—current date—job's processing time; the job with the smallest static slack is done first). *See calculations below:

Processing Order	Processing Time	Completion Time	Deadline	Lateness
E	6	6th	8th	0
C	2	8th	5th	3 days
D	8	16th	12th	4 days
A	5	21st	10th	11 days
B	10	31st	15th	16 days
Average		16.4		6.8 days

*static slack computations:

Job A: 10th day – 1st day – 5 days = 4 days

    B: 15th day – 1st day – 10 days = 4 days

    C: 5th day – 1st day – 2 days = 2 days

    D: 12th day – 1st day – 8 days = 3 days

    E: 8th day – 1st day – 6 days = 1 day

CRITICAL RATIO (CR or SS/PT (Static Slack divided by Remaining Processing Time for Each Job). As the SS/PT ratio gets smaller, the job gets a higher priority for processing. Sequence jobs by smallest SS/PT ratio.

Processing Order	Processing Time	Completion Time	Deadline	Lateness
E	6	6th	8th	0
D	8	14th	12th	2 days
B	10	24th	15th	9 days
A	5	29th	10th	19 days
C	2	31st	5th	26 days
Average		20.8		11.2 days

CR(SS/PT) ratio computations:

$$CR\ (SS/PT) = \frac{\text{deadline date} - \text{current date}}{\text{remaining processing time}}$$

$$\text{Job A: } \frac{(10\text{th} - 1\text{st})}{5 \text{ days}} = 1.80$$

$$\text{Job B: } \frac{(15\text{th} - 1\text{st})}{10 \text{ days}} = 1.40$$

$$\text{Job C: } \frac{(5\text{th} - 1\text{st})}{2 \text{ days}} = 2.00$$

$$\text{Job D: } \frac{(12\text{th} - 1\text{st})}{8 \text{ days}} = 1.37$$

$$\text{Job E: } \frac{(8\text{th} - 1\text{st})}{6 \text{ days}} = 1.16$$

FISFS (First-in-System, First-Served) or DDATE (Due Date). As jobs come into the shop, they are assigned a due date. Those jobs possessing the earliest due dates are processed first.

Processing Order	Processing Time	Completion Time	Deadline	Lateness
C	2	2nd	5th	0
E	6	8th	8th	0
A	5	13th	10th	3 days
D	8	21st	12th	9 days
B	10	31st	15th	16 days
Average		15.0		5.6 days

Summary

Sequence Rule	Average Completion Time	Average Lateness	Number of Jobs Late	Maximum Lateness
SPT	14.8 days	6 days	3	16 days
FCFS	18.6 days	9.6 days	3	23 days
SS	16.4 days	6.8 days	4	16 days
CR (SS/PT)	20.8 days	11.2 days	4	26 days
FISFS (DDATE)	15.0 days	5.6 days	3	16 days

Conclusions

Performance Criterion	Priority Sequence Rule(s)
Best Average Completion Time	SPT
Best Average Job Lateness	FISFS
Best Number of Jobs Late	FISFS, SPT, FCFS
Best Maximum Lateness	FISFS, SPT, SS

—all rules completed the month's planned work.

—no rule completed all jobs in time.

—FISFS produced the lowest average lateness (5.6 days).

—SPT completed more jobs faster (14.8 days).

Empirical evidence suggests that:

- the SPT rule will always minimize average job completion time (or flowtime), and minimize the average number of jobs in the system.

- The FISFS (DDATE) rule will always minimize average job lateness and minimize job lateness.

- No definitive statements can be made about the other sequencing rules.

- There is no priority sequencing rule that optimizes both processing efficiency and deadline performance.

Guidelines for Selecting a Sequencing Rule

1. *SPT is most useful when the job shop is highly congested.*

   SPT tends to minimize mean flow time, mean number of jobs in the system (and thus work-in-process inventory), and percent of jobs tardy. By completing more jobs quickly, it theoretically satisfies a greater number of customers than the other rules.

2. *Use SLACK or S/OPN for periods of normal activity.*

   When capacity is not severely restrained, a SLACK-oriented rule that takes into account both due date and processing time will produce good results.

3. *Use DDATE when only small tardiness values can be tolerated.*

   DDATE tends to minimize mean tardiness and maximum tardiness. Although more jobs will be tardy under DDATE than SPT, the degree of tardiness will be much less.

4. *Use LPT if subcontracting is anticipated* so that larger jobs are completed in-house, and smaller jobs are sent out as their due date draws near.

5. *Use FCFS when operating at low-capacity levels.*

   FCFS allows the job shop to operate essentially without sequencing jobs. When the workload at a facility is light, any sequencing rule will do, and FCFS is certainly the easiest to apply.

6. *Do not use SPT to sequence jobs that have to be assembled with other jobs at a later date.* For assembly jobs, a sequencing rule that gives a common priority to the processing of different components in an assembly, such as assembly DDATE, produces a more effective schedule.

The Gantt Chart Used in Detailed (Supplementary) Scheduling

1. They continue to show the relative work loads at each work center.

2. Show the detailed scheduling for all jobs to include their start dates and completion dates (which are set at or before the customer promised date).

3. Allows management to monitor the progress of all jobs in the system (Gantt Chart shows in "real-time" which jobs are behind, ahead, or on schedule).

4. Provides the basis of the promised date of the job to the customer.

5. Will continue to indicate the need for shifting human and material resources from less-busy work centers to busy work centers.

6. Will continue to indicate the need for *additional* labor or equipment, if necessary (or the need for overtime labor pay).

7. Shows deliberately scheduled downtimes for machine maintenance or equipment replacements, or layout reworks.

8. Also allows management to reserve blocks of time for emergency purposes, i.e., extra time for variable jobs, or reservation of time for last-minute jobs.

9. Must be updated daily or weekly or bi-weekly.

10. Points out bottlenecks, i.e., work centers where jobs have a tendency to "pile-up."

11. One of the most important goals of the Gantt Chart in the detailed scheduling mode, is to insure that no job gets scheduled in more than one work center at the same time!

The Gantt Chart Used in Detailed (Supplementary) Scheduling

(Gantt Chart for Coordinating Work Centers' Schedules)

Weekly Schedule - Dept. 3985: Model Shop					Schedule 3/16 - 3/22	
Work Centers	Mon	Tues	Wed	Thurs	Fri	Sat
1. Machining	⊠ D	⊠	E ⊠		F	⊠
2. Fabrication	C	⊠	D ⊠	E ⊠		F
3. Assembly	B	C		D	⊠	E
4. Test	⊠	B ⊠			D	⊠
5. Packaging	A ⊠		B	⊠ C ⊠		

Legend:

☐	▬	Point in Real Time	⊠
Scheduled Job Time	Actual Job Progress		Nonproductive work, repairs, changeovers, etc.

Priority Sequence Rule Evaluation and Selection Via Simulation

Over the past decade, larger companies involved in job shop operations have been using simulation modeling as a vehicle for evaluating and selecting a priority sequence rule. Rather than physically adopting, implementing, and evaluating several rules, one at a time, over multi-year periods, a company can evaluate them in a matter of minutes.

Advantages:

1. simulation modeling creates a "clinical environment" wherein shop variables are held constant. These variables include:

   —labor force composition

   —equipment mix

   —labor force turnover

   —equipment efficiency

   —labor force training

   —equipment state-of-the-art

   —labor force skill levels

   —operating costs

   —pricing policies

   —the product mix

   —management style

   —operations policies

   —the aggregate plan that guides job shop operations

   —product revenues

   —tax laws/regulations

   —processing times per job

   —job arrival rates

   —job shop routings

2. the only differences in sequence rule performances under simulation are entirely attributable to the choice of sequence rule selected.

3. simulation can evaluate dozens of possible sequence rules within minutes, once a model has been developed. This advantage is called "time-compression."

Simulation Modeling in Intermittent Systems (Job Shop)

The following are the fundamental steps in building a computer-based simulation model and using it to test various sequencing rules:

1. **Shop Configuration:** The number of work centers in the shop must be specified in the model.

2. **Job Arrivals:** One segment of the model is needed to generate arrivals of new jobs entering the system. The pattern and timing of simulated arrivals can be based on historical patterns. The "Monte Carlo" technique can be used to select at random, the time of the next job arrival based on the data pattern supplied by the model designer.

3. **Job Classification:** Once a job arrives, its processing requirements (or routing) must be established. Again, historical data can reveal patterns of processing (routing) requirements that may be built into the model. When a new simulated job arrives, its routing is determined in the simulator, often using the "Monte Carlo" technique.

4. **Processing Times:** The "time" required to process a job at a work center can be determined based on historical service time patterns supplied by the model designer. Often, the service (processing) time is randomly selected from a service time distribution that is representative of that work center. The "Monte Carlo" technique is often used for this purpose.

5. **Specification of Shop Performance Parameters:** The designer must specify the shop performance characteristics of interest. These are the statistics that will be collected to evaluate subsequent alternatives. Such statistics might include percent of idle time at each center, length of job queues throughout the system, average waiting times for jobs, measures of job lateness and job flow times.

6. **Specification of Dispatching Rule:** The priority sequencing rule to be tested must be selected and built into the model.

7. **Simulation:** The simulation is conducted over time (this is called a simulation run). It is executed by generating new job arrival times, determining their routings, loading them to the appropriate work centers, sequencing them by use of the priority dispatching rule, and creating the representative service times for each job at each center. The simulation is done for a large number of job arrivals, say 10,000 or more. Typically, simulation is accomplished utilizing a digital computer, all of the above having been programmed in a general-purpose or special-purpose simulation language. When a job is finished at one center, it is placed in the waiting line at the next center in its routing to await processing there. When a work center finishes one job, it is free to begin servicing one of the jobs in its waiting line. The awaiting job with highest priority (based on the sequencing rule) is selected for processing next on the open work center.

8. **Recording Shop Performance Parameters:** After all jobs have been processed, the resulting shop performance statistics are recorded and saved for later evaluation and comparison. The simulation run has been completed.

9. **Replication:** At this point, the original dispatching (sequencing) rule can be replaced with an alternative rule in the model. Then, with all other model components unchanged, the simulation can be repeated. The shop performance characteristics from the second run can be compared with those of the first run to determine which of the two dispatching rules performs better. Systematic replications can be made for any number of different rules.

Example of Simulation Modeling

Evaluating Priority Sequence Rules at a Carpentry Shop

For generating job arrivals into the shop:

Type of Job Arrival	Probability	Cumulative Probability	Random No. Interval
Table	.35	.35	00 – 35
Chair	.30	.65	36 – 65
Bookcase	.35	1.00	66 – 99

Then, if the RN string were: 36, 84, 19, 49, 97, etc., the 1st simulated job would be a "Chair." For generating the particular chair model:

Type of Model	Probability	Cumulative Probability	Random No. Interval
Model "A"	.20	.20	00 – 20
Model "B"	.25	.45	21 – 45
Model "C"	.20	.65	46 – 65
Model "D"	.20	.85	66 – 85
Model "E"	.15	1.00	86 – 99

Then, if the RN string were: 42, 81, 27, 73, 08, etc., the type of chair to be produced would be "Model 'B'."

For generating the processing route for this job through the system:

Route	Probability	Cumulative Probability	Random No. Interval
1st	.50	.50	00 – 50
2nd	.25	.75	51 – 75
3rd	.25	1.00	76 – 99

Then, if the RN string were: 04, 73, 91, 46, 63, etc., our Model "B" chair would be taking route "no. 1" through the job shop.

For generating the processing time for this job through the system (or through the individual work center of the job shop):

Total Time (Flow Time)	Probability	Cumulative Probability	RN Interval
5 Hours	.25	.25	00 – 25
5.5 Hours	.30	.55	26 – 55
6 Hours	.25	.80	56 – 80
6.5 Hours	.20	1.00	81 – 99

Then, if the RN string were: 36, 66, 12, 79, 23, etc., our Model "B" chair would require "5.5" hours to travel along route "no. 1" in the job shop. Additional spreadsheets would tell us what the estimated processing times would be at each work center.

After simulating all jobs for the next several years, the simulation would be run for each of several priority sequence rules and operating statistics would be accumulated and summarized.

A decision would then be made to select one priority sequence rule that best supports the job shop's mission statement.

Service Sector Scheduling

Service system scheduling differs from manufacturing system scheduling in several ways:

- In manufacturing, scheduling emphasis is on materials, whereas in services, emphasis is on staffing levels.

- Service systems seldom store inventories.

- Services are labor-intensive and the demand for labor can be highly variable.

Service systems try to match fluctuating customer demand with the capability to meet that demand. In some businesses, such as physicians' and lawyers' offices, an appointment system is the schedule. In retail shops, a post office, or a fast-food restaurant, a first-come, first-served rule for serving customers may suffice. Scheduling in these businesses is handled by bringing in extra workers, often part-timers, to help during peak periods. Reservation systems work well in rental car agencies, symphony halls, hotels, and some restaurants as a means of minimizing customer waiting time and avoiding disappointment over unfilled service.

Hospitals

A hospital is an example of a service facility that may use a scheduling system as complex as one found in a job shop. Hospitals seldom use a machine shop priority system such as first-come, first-served for treating emergency patients. However, they do schedule products (such as surgeries) just like a factory, even though finished goods inventories cannot be kept, and capacities must meet wide variations in demand.

Banks

Cross training of the workforce in a bank allows loan officers and other managers to provide short-term help for tellers if there is a surge in demand. Banks also employ part-time personnel to provide a variable capacity.

Airlines

Airlines face two constraints in scheduling flight crews. First, a complex set of FAA work-time limitations, and second, union contracts that guarantee crew pay for some number of hours each day or each trip. Airline planners must build crew schedules that meet or exceed crews' pay guarantees. Planners must also make efficient use of their other huge resource: aircraft.

The Assignment Algorithm

1. a special version of linear programming (or resource allocation) model.

2. guarantees an optimal solution.

3. also called the "Hungarian Method," "Flood's Technique" and the "Reduced-Matrix Method."

4. an alternative method for performing the "loading" function in a job shop.

5. must be used whenever an arriving job can be loaded into one of several available machines or workers in the same work center.

6. determines the most efficient assignment of jobs to workers or machines, as well as workers to jobs.

7. examples include the assignment of teachers to courses, coast guard cutters to iceberg patrols, waiters and waitresses to tables, salespersons to territories, and projects to consultants.

8. can only be employed where all workers or machines are fully capable of processing all arriving jobs.

9. may employ one of several available performance criteria such as profit maximization, cost minimization, total job completion time minimization, and total job idle time minimization.

10. dictates that only one job can be assigned to each worker or machine, and vice-versa.

11. the total number of arriving jobs must equal the total number of workers or machines available.

12. if the number of arriving jobs is not equal to the number of available workers or machines, the model must, and can be modified through addition of fictitious jobs or facilities.

The Assignment Algorithm

Illustrated Example

The assignment algorithm reduces the problem to an opportunity cost matrix. An "opportunity" cost is the additional cost (or penalty) associated with assigning a job to any person or machine other than the most efficient one. An optimal solution will eventually be developed wherein all job assignments involve zero opportunity costs.

Problem

There are four (4) newly-arrived jobs in a work center, and four (4) workers are available to process them. The matrix below shows the estimated processing costs for each job under all four workers. The shop wants to assign each job to one worker in such a manner so as to minimize total processing costs.

Job \ Worker	1	2	3	4
A	$20.	25.	22.	28.
B	15.	18.	23.	17.
C	19.	17.	21.	24.
D	25.	23.	24.	24.

Step 1: ROW REDUCTION

Subtract the smallest number in each row from all other numbers in that row.

Job \ Worker	1	2	3	4
A	0	5	2	8
B	0	3	8	2
C	2	0	4	7
D	2	0	1	1

Step 2: COLUMN REDUCTION

Subtract the smallest number in each column from all other numbers in that column.

Worker Job	1	2	3	4
A	0	5	1	7
B	0	3	7	1
C	2	0	3	6
D	2	0	0	0

As a result of steps 1 and 2, an opportunity cost matrix (or reduced matrix) is created. Any cell containing a zero opportunity cost is a potential job assignment. For example Job "A" should be assigned to worker "1" because its opportunity cost is zero. To assign Job "A" to any other workers would incur penalty or opportunity costs of $5.00, $1.00, and $7.00 respectively. On the other hand, Job "D" may be assigned to either worker "2," "3," or "4" but only one of these workers can be assigned.

Step 3: ATTEMPT TO MAKE FOUR UNIQUE MINIMUM COST ASSIGNMENTS

Assign one job to one worker only, using only zero opportunity cost cells.

Worker Job	1	2	3	4
A	[0]	5	1	7
B	⊗	3	7	1
C	2	[0]	3	6
D	2	⊗	[0]	⊗

Make the assignments that must be made first. Job "A" must go to worker "1," and job "C" must go to worker "2." Job "D" can go to any of two workers, and worker "3" was arbitrarily chosen (assignments are denoted by squares).

Job "B" could not be assigned to worker "1" because that worker already had been assigned job "A." Job "D" could not be assigned to worker "2" because that worker had already been assigned job "C."

Step 4: THE "H" FACTOR TECHNIQUE

This technique is used whenever all required assignments cannot be made, which is usually the case. The purpose of the "h" factor technique is to create more zero cells in the matrix, so as to increase the chances of a complete assignment of jobs in the next attempt.

Procedure

1. Using a combination of vertical and/or horizontal lines, cover all the zeros in the matrix using the minimum number of lines. If the absolute minimum number of lines is not chosen, the optimal solution to the problem will be jeopardized.

2. Three categories of numbers will have been created as a result of step "1": uncovered numbers, single-line covered numbers, and crisscrossed numbers. Each category of numbers is handled differently.

   a. *uncovered numbers:* find the smallest of the uncovered numbers and subtract it from all the other uncovered numbers.

   b. *crisscrossed numbers:* add the smallest uncovered number to these. The smallest uncovered number is the "h" factor.

   c. *single-line covered numbers:* no action is taken.

Job \ Worker	1	2	3	4
A	0	5	1	7
B	0	3	7	1
C	2	0	3	6
D	2	0	0	0

The absolute minimum number of lines needed to cover all the zeros in the matrix was three (3). Row "D" was the first line. Column "1" was the second line. The zero in cell "C2" could have been covered by either a horizontal or vertical line. The horizontal line was arbitrarily chosen. The resulting matrix would then be:

Job \ Worker	1	2	3	4
A	0	4	0	6
B	0	2	6	0
C	3	0	3	6
D	3	0	0	0

Step 5: RE-ATTEMPT TO MAKE FOUR UNIQUE MINIMUM COST ASSIGNMENTS

Worker Job	1	2	3	4
A	[0]	4	✗	6
B	✗	2	6	[0]
C	3	[0]	3	6
D	3	✗	[0]	✗

This attempt proved to be successful. The solution is therefore:

Assign Job A to Worker 1, at a cost of $20.00

Assign Job B to Worker 4, at a cost of $17.00

Assign Job C to Worker 2, at a cost of $17.00

Assign Job D to Worker 3, at a cost of   <u>$24.00</u>

           Total Cost $78.00

In this problem, an alternate solution of the same cost could also be obtained as follows:

Worker Job	1	2	3	4
A	✗	4	[0]	6
B	[0]	2	6	✗
C	3	[0]	3	6
D	3	✗	✗	[0]

Assign Job A to Worker 3, at a cost of $22.00

Assign Job B to Worker 1, at a cost of $15.00

Assign Job C to Worker 2, at a cost of $17.00

Assign Job D to Worker 4, at a cost of   <u>$24.00</u>

           Total Cost $78.00

Special Situations

If there were five (5) jobs waiting to be processed, but only four (4) workers available, the matrix would need to be balanced via addition of a dummy fifth worker (dummy column) with zero processing costs.

The problem would then be solved in the same way as previously shown. In the optimal solution however, the particular job "assigned" to the fifth worker would in reality, be unassigned for the time being.

If there were four (4) jobs waiting to be processed, but five (5) workers available, the matrix would need to be balanced via addition of a dummy fifth job (dummy row) with zero processing costs.

In the optimal solution however, the particular worker "assigned" to the fifth job would in reality, be unassigned for the time being.

Maximization problems must be first converted into minimization problems before they may be solved.

If a realtor had five (5) potential buyers for five (5) sites, and wanted to know which site to offer each buyer at what price so as to maximize his total receipts, the initial matrix, representing profits would look like this:

Buyer \ Site	1	2	3	4	5
1	6	7	6	2	9
2	0	5	8	1	1
3	5	10	6	5	10
4	2	7	12	4	10
5	6	9	9	5	7

A conversion must be performed to reverse the magnitude. The largest entry is "12" (or $12,000 profit). The new cost matrix will have entries obtained from the original profit matrix by subtraction from "12," as follows:

Buyer \ Site	1	2	3	4	5
1	6	5	6	10	3
2	12	7	4	11	11
3	7	2	6	7	2
4	10	5	0	8	2
5	6	3	3	7	5

The problem would then be solved in the same way as previously shown.

16

Project Management

*C*hapter 16 *focuses on the planning, scheduling, and control of long-term, one-of-a-kind projects.*

Virtually every organization at one time or another is engaged in a special project far-removed from its normal operations. These projects are usually one-of-a-kind undertakings spanning months or years, involving personnel from every corner of the firm, and consuming significant amounts of capital, research, and development effort.

The managers of these projects confront a myriad of tasks that will severely test their management and technical skills, from beginning to end. If these managers are successful in realizing the project goals, their career prospects shine brighter and the organization is significantly stronger. If these managers fail, the long-term effects could linger for years, quite possibly destroying the organization in the process.

This chapter introduces PERT/CPM techniques as a tool for intelligently planning, scheduling, and controlling projects. These techniques were developed in the late 1950s as replacements for the inadequate gantt chart in the organized conduct of U.S. Government research and development of military weapons systems.

The chapter concludes with a discussion of several organizational structures to support project activity, and factors to be considered in making the selection.

PERT/CPM Project Management Techniques

PERT (Program Evaluation and Review Technique) and CPM (Critical Path Method) were developed independently during the late 1950s. Both possessed unique benefits and were eventually combined into a single technique known as PERT/CPM.

Examples of Projects Requiring PERT/CPM

- shopping centers
- bridges

- television specials and Broadway plays
- government missile system projects
- advertising and new product campaigns
- construction and expansion of transportation systems
- corporate restructuring programs
- new product development

Prerequisites for Use of PERT/CPM

- the project must have identifiable tasks or activities.
- all tasks or activities must have clear start and finish points.
- the project must be complex enough to possess many inter-related tasks.
- there are alternatives for the arrangement and sequence of tasks within the project.
- there are alternatives for task time durations within the project.

NOTE: Flexible time durations for the tasks within a project are important because:

  a. projects experience changing levels of funding as they proceed.

  b. projects also experience changing levels in the number and type of personnel.

  c. projects experience state-of-the-art technical problems.

  d. projects experience project progress problems such as distances between task groups, personnel conflicts, poor planning and management.

The Importance of PERT/CPM

- missed project completion dates result in:

  a. lost sales for new products

  b. contract penalties

  c. lack of repeat business from clients

  d. additional time and resources diverted from normal operations.

- project budget overruns.

PERT/CPM Conventions

It is possible to draw PERT/CPM networks differently. There are two conventions: activity-on-arc (AOA) and activity-on-node (AON).

In AOA networks, the arcs or arrows ($\rightarrow$) represent the tasks themselves, and the nodes ($\bigcirc$) represent the starting and ending points of those tasks. The AOA convention is the particular network shown in this chapter. It has been more common in the United States and thus more familiar to more managers.

In the AON networks, the arcs or arrows are only used to denote predecessor relationships among tasks, and the tasks themselves are denoted by nodes (see below).

The U.S. Government formally converted to the AON network in the fall of 2001. It is expected that the majority of U.S. firms will follow suit if they seek to compete for government contracts. An example and full discussion of the activity-on-node convention can be found on the student CD.

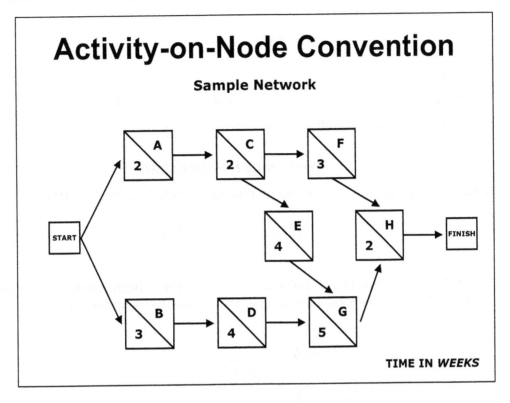

AON Advantages

- no dummy activities are required.
- the network is cleaner and uncluttered.
- it is natural to view nodes as tasks and to consider the network a depiction of natural work flow.
- it still shows ES, LS, S, and CP times.
- it still performs probabilistic PERT analysis and time/cost tradeoff analysis.
- commercial software programs are available for both AOA and AON.

Activity-on-Arc Building Blocks

The Arc/Arrow (→)

- rightward direction by convention.
- its length is immaterial.
- used to denote an activity or task, under the AOA (activity-on-arc) convention, commonly used in the United States.

- usually differentiated from other arcs via alphabetic characters shown just above the shaft (A, B, C, etc.). When there are more than 26 arcs in a network, the alphabetic characters carry subscripts (A_1, B_1, C_1). If there are more than 52 arcs in a network (A_2, B_2, C_2).

- its time duration may be stated in days, weeks, or months. It is shown just below the shaft.

Event or Node: (◯)

- a milestone in time.

- represents either the beginning or ending point in time for a task.

- usually numbered so as to differentiate it from other nodes.

Precedence Relationships

Precedence relationships among tasks are graphically depicted via PERT/CPM.

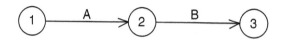

(denotes that task A must be completed before task B may begin; node 1 represents the start of task A; node 2 represents both the ending of task A and the beginning of task B)

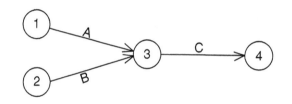

(denotes that task C cannot begin until both tasks A and B have first been completed)

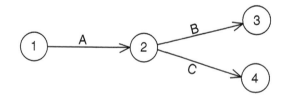

(denotes that tasks B and C cannot begin until task A has first been completed)

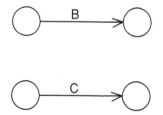

(denotes that tasks B and C are parallel activities, that is, independent but taking place simultaneously)

The Dummy Activity

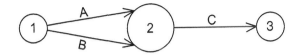

The network shown directly above is an incorrect one wherein it was intended to denote that task C cannot begin until tasks A and B have first been completed. Since each task must have a unique pair of numbered beginning and ending nodes, tasks A and B are in violation.

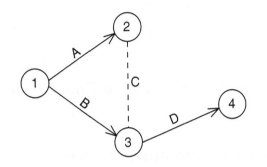

The network shown directly above is the correct one. Task A now has a unique pair of nodes (1-2) and task B does as well (1-3) A "dummy" task "C" made this possible. The original task C must be redesignated task D.

The Dummy Task

- distinguished from other tasks by dashed, wide, or colored lines.

- has a duration time of *zero* by definition.

- permits real tasks to have unique identities which avoids symbolic confusion in the assignment of budgets, responsibility, and control authority to the task groups involved.

- used to preserve the logic of the network.

- without dummy tasks, computer software packages (which only recognize tasks by their beginning and ending nodes) could not differentiate one task from another.

PERT/CPM Time Estimates

Time can be estimated in days, weeks, or months and should be done by experienced personnel.

Optimistic Time ("a"):

the fastest time in which an activity or task can be completed (no staff absences, good weather, dry ground, no equipment malfunctions, no technical problems, no group conflicts, no mistakes).

Pessimistic Time ("b"):

the slowest time in which a task can be completed (everything goes wrong at the same time!).

Most-Likely Time ("m"):

somewhere between optimistic and pessimistic time; not necessarily equi-distant between them.

Expected Time ("t_e"):

a weighted-average of optimistic, pessimistic, and most-likely times:

$$t_e = \frac{a + 4m + b}{6}$$

- places two-thirds of the weight on the most-likely time estimate.
- most widely-used time estimate in PERT/CPM.
- the weightings follow a "beta distribution" which, by tradition, is the accepted distribution of estimated time in project management.
- enables use of probabilistic PERT wherein a probability of project completion as of a specific date is given to the client.

Variance of Expected Time ("v" or "σ^2"):

a measure of dispersion of time above and below the expected time.

Standard Deviation of Expected Time ("σ"):

also a measure of dispersion of time above and below the expected time; it is the square root of the variance.

The following PERT/CPM network will serve to introduce the concepts of critical path (CP), early start (ES), late start (LS), and primary slack or float (S). The network comprises eleven (11) tasks (designated "A" through "K") with their estimated times in days, computed as t_es. No dummy tasks were required.

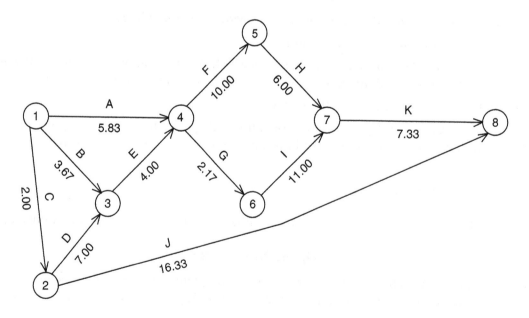

The Critical Path

The critical path is the "chain" of activities or tasks from the project's beginning to end that consumes the longest amount of estimated duration time. It is monitored closely because if any one of its tasks were to fall behind by even one day, the *entire* project would fall behind by one day as well. The critical path represents the project's expected (or mean, or average) completion time which is assumed to follow a normal probability distribution. Accordingly, there is a 50% probability that the project will be completed by the expected completion time, and a 100% probability that it will be completed sometime after the expected completion time.

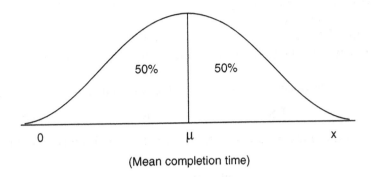

(Mean completion time)

Several CPs may exist within the network at any given time, and they may change or disappear as the project progresses.

At this point in the analysis, there is only one method by which to identify the CP. It is enumeration. In the example, there are seven (7) candidates for the CP:

Path (in alphabetic characters)	Path (in node numbers)	Total Time (in days)
A-F-H-K	1-4-5-7-8	29.16
B-E-F-H-K	1-3-4-5-7-8	31.00
C-J	1-2-8	18.33
B-E-G-I-K	1-3-4-6-7-8	28.17
C-D-E-G-I-K	1-2-3-4-6-7-8	33.5
C-D-E-F-H-K	1-2-3-4-5-7-8	36.33*
A-G-I-K	1-4-6-7-8	26.33

*(the critical path)

The tasks along the critical path are depicted in color, or heavily shaded-in on the PERT/CPM network:

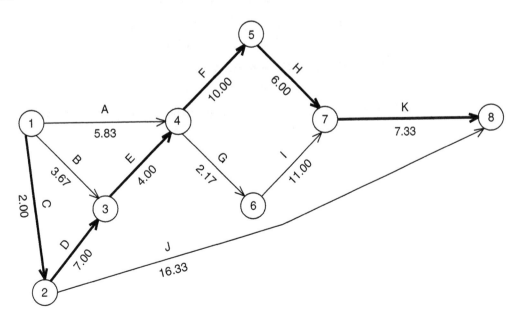

Early Start Time

As part of its scheduling responsibilities, management must also know the earliest point in time that each task can begin. Since most tasks have predecessors, they cannot begin until all predecessor tasks have first been completed. The longest of the predecessor tasks will of course dictate how early the follower task)s) can begin.

Early start time (ES) for all tasks in the PERT/CPM network is computed from left to right, that is, from the network's beginning to ending node. The formula is:

$$\text{Predecessor Task} + \text{Predecessor Task} = \text{Follower Task}$$
$$\text{ES} \qquad\qquad \text{te} \qquad\qquad \text{ES}$$

(if there are several candidates for ES, the highest value is selected)

The Computations

The ES for all initial project tasks is *zero* by definition. Therefore:

$$\text{ES (task A)} = 0,\ \text{ES (task B)} = 0,\ \text{ES (task C)} = 0$$

$$\text{ES (task C)} + \text{te (task C)} = \text{ES (task D)}$$
$$0 + 2.00 = 2.00$$

$$\text{ES (task C)} + \text{te (task C)} = \text{ES (task J)}$$
$$0 + 2.00 = 2.00$$

$$\text{ES (task D)} + \text{te (task D)} = \text{ES (task E)}$$
$$2.00 + 7.00 = 9.00$$

$$\text{ES (task E)} + \text{te (task E)} = \text{ES (task F)}$$
$$9.00 + 4.00 = 13.00$$

$$\text{ES (task E)} + \text{te (task E)} = \text{ES (task G)}$$
$$9.00 + 4.00 = 13.00$$

$$\text{ES (task F)} + \text{te (task F)} = \text{ES (task H)}$$
$$13.00 + 10.00 = 23.00$$

$$\text{ES (task G)} + \text{te (task G)} = \text{ES (task I)}$$
$$13.00 + 2.17 = 15.17$$

$$\text{ES (task H)} + \text{te (task H)} = \text{ES (task K)}$$
$$23.00 + 6.00 = 29.00$$

$$\text{ES (task K)} + \text{te (task K)} = \text{Early Project Completion Time}$$
$$29.00 + 7.33 = 36.33 \text{ days}$$

The early start (ES) times for all network tasks are shown below:

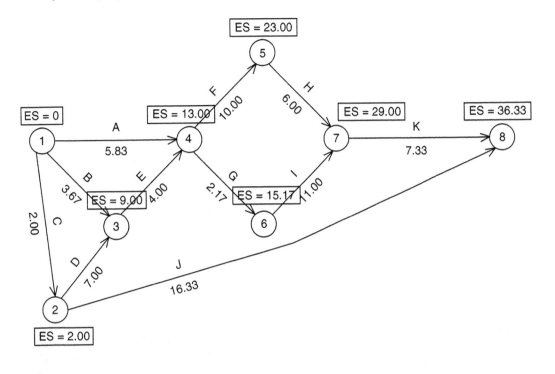

Late Finish Time

Management must also know the latest point in time that each task can finish, without jeopardizing the project's expected completion time. Late finish time (LF) for all tasks in the network is computed from right to left, that is, from the network's ending node to its beginning node. The formula is:

$$\text{Follower Task LF Time} - \text{Follower Task te} = \text{Predecessor Task LF Time}$$

(if there are several candidates, select the smallest LF)

The Computations

The late finish time of the last task(s) in the project is (are) equal to the *critical path time* by definition. Therefore:

$$LF \text{ (task K)} = 36.33$$

$$LF \text{ (task J)} = 36.33$$

then:

$$LF \text{ (task K)} - te \text{ (task K)} = LF \text{ (task H)}$$
$$36.33 - 7.33 = 29.00$$

$$LF \text{ (task K)} - te \text{ (task K)} = LF \text{ (task I)}$$
$$36.33 - 7.33 = 29.00$$

$$LF \text{ (task H)} - te \text{ (task H)} = LF \text{ (task F)}$$
$$29.00 - 6.00 = 23.00$$

$$LF \text{ (task I)} - te \text{ (task I)} = LF \text{ (task G)}$$
$$29.00 - 11.00 = 18.00$$

$$LF \text{ (task F)} - te \text{ (task F)} = LF \text{ (task E)}$$
$$23.00 - 10.00 = 13.00$$

$$LF \text{ (task E)} - te \text{ (task E)} = LF \text{ (task D)}$$
$$13.00 - 4.00 = 9.00$$

$$LF \text{ (task F)} - te \text{ (task F)} = LF \text{ (task A)}$$
$$23.00 - 10.00 = 13.00$$

$$LF \text{ (task E)} - te \text{ (task E)} = LF \text{ (task B)}$$
$$13.00 - 4.00 = 9.00$$

$$LF \text{ (task D)} - te \text{ (task D)} = LF \text{ (task C)}$$
$$9.00 - 7.00 = 2.00$$

The late finish (LF) times for all network tasks are shown below:

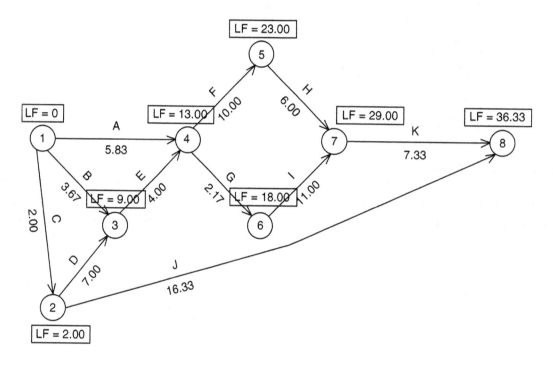

Late Start Time

Management must also know the latest point in time that each task can begin, without jeopardizing the project expected completion time. Late start time (LS) for all tasks in the network is computed from right to left, that is, from the network's ending to beginning node. The formula is:

$$\text{Task LF} - \text{Task te} = \text{Task LS}$$

(if there are several candidates for LS, the smallest value is selected)

The Computations

$$LF \text{ (task A)} - te \text{ (task A)} = LS \text{ (task A)}$$
$$13.00 - 5.83 = 7.17$$

$$LF \text{ (task B)} - te \text{ (task B)} = LS \text{ (task B)}$$
$$9.00 - 3.67 = 5.33$$

$$LF \text{ (task C)} - te \text{ (task C)} = LS \text{ (task C)}$$
$$2.00 - 2.00 = 0$$

$$LF \text{ (task D)} - te \text{ (task D)} = LS \text{ (task D)}$$
$$9.00 - 7.00 = 2.00$$

$$LF \text{ (task E)} - te \text{ (task E)} = LS \text{ (task E)}$$
$$13.00 - 4.00 = 9.00$$

$$LF \text{ (task F)} - te \text{ (task F)} = LS \text{ (task F)}$$
$$23.00 - 10.00 = 13.00$$

$$LF \text{ (task G)} - te \text{ (task G)} = LS \text{ (task G)}$$
$$18.00 - 2.17 = 15.83$$

$$LF \text{ (task H)} - te \text{ (task H)} = LS \text{ (task H)}$$
$$29.00 - 6.00 = 23.00$$

$$LF \text{ (task I)} - te \text{ (task I)} = LS \text{ (task I)}$$
$$29.00 - 11.00 = 18.00$$

$$LF \text{ (task J)} - te \text{ (task J)} = LS \text{ (task J)}$$
$$36.33 - 16.33 = 20.00$$

$$LF \text{ (task K)} - te \text{ (task K)} = LS \text{ (task K)}$$
$$36.33 - 7.33 = 29.00$$

Slack Time

Management can easily determine the number of days that each task in the network may be postponed before jeopardizing the project's expected completion time. This grace period is called slack time or float. It is the difference between each task's late start (LS) and early start (ES) times. The formula is:

$$S \text{ (any task)} = LS \text{ (for that task)} - ES \text{ (for that task)}$$

The Computations

1. $S(\text{Task A}) = LS(A) - ES(A) = 7.17 - 0.00 = 7.17$ days

2. $S(\text{Task B}) = LS(B) - ES(B) = 5.33 - 0.00 = 5.33$ days

3. $S(\text{Task C}) = LS(C) - ES(C) = 0.00 - 0.00 = 0.00$ days

4. $S(\text{Task D}) = LS(D) - ES(D) = 2.00 - 2.00 = 0.00$ days

5. $S(\text{Task E}) = LS(E) - ES(E) = 9.00 - 9.00 = 0.00$ days

6. $S(\text{Task F}) = LS(F) - ES(F) = 13.00 - 13.00 = 0.00$ days

7. $S(\text{Task G}) = LS(G) - ES(G) = 15.83 - 13.00 = 2.83$ days

8. $S(\text{Task H}) = LS(H) - ES(H) = 23.00 - 23.0 = 0.00$ days

9. $S(\text{Task I}) = LS(I) - ES(I) = 18.00 - 15.17 = 2.83$ days

10. $S(\text{Task J}) = LS(J) - ES(J) = 20.00 - 2.00 = 18.00$ days

11. $S(\text{Task K}) = LS(K) - ES(K) = 29.00 - 29.00 = 0.00$ days

The slack times (S) for all network tasks are shown below:

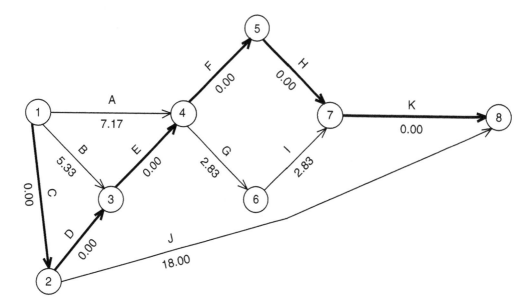

All tasks along the critical path (CP) have *zero* slack times by definition. This intuitively makes sense since none of the CP tasks can be postponed by even one day without jeopardizing the project's expected completion time. The critical path, as before, can be identified via zero slack tasks as C-D-E-F-H-K.

Probabilistic PERT

Management has the capability of generating various probabilities for completion of a project both before and after its expected deadline (average or mean time). The prerequisites are:

1. all task times must be expressed in t_es (expected time).

2. the expected time variances of all critical path (CP) tasks must be computed.

Example and Problem Statement

Given the identical project example used in this chapter to introduce the concepts of CP, ES, LS, and S, the firm wants to know the chances of finishing project:

1. in 30 days or less, and

2. in 40 days or less.

Step 1: Identify the project critical path and its expected completion time.

(C–D–E–F–H–K; 36.33 days)

Step 2: Compute the task time variance for each task on the critical path, using the formula:

$$v \text{ or } \sigma^2 = \left(\frac{b - a}{6}\right)^2$$

(where "a" = optimistic time; "b" = pessimistic time; "6" = a constant)

assume here that the variances are:

Task	Variance (in days)
C	.11
D	.11
E	.44
F	1.78
H	1.00
K	1.78

Total project completion = <u>5.22 days</u>
time variance $\left(\sigma_{CP}^2\right)$

Step 3: Calculate the standard deviation of project completion time.

$$\sigma_{CP} = \sqrt{\sigma_{CP}^2} = \sqrt{5.22} = \underline{2.28}\ days$$

Step 4: Since project completion time is normally distributed a curve can be drawn with its mean and standard deviation known:

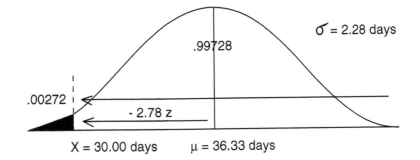

(a) find the number of standard deviates ("z," a measure of distance between 2 points) between the mean (μ) and the value of interest (X).

$$z = \left[\frac{X - \mu}{\sigma}\right] = \left[\frac{30.00 - 36.33}{2.28}\right] \cong \underline{-2.78}$$

The value of "30.00" is positioned 2.78 standard deviates to the left of the mean.

(b) find the area under the normal curve (the percentage) that 2.78 standard deviates represent. Use Appendix "A" (from page 273).

z	.08
2.7	.99728

(the percentage of the normal curve covered to a point that is 2.78 standard deviates to the left of the mean is 99.728%).

Therefore the probability of finishing the project in 30 days or less is:

$$P(t \leq 30) = 1.0000 - .99728$$

$$= .00272$$

$$\cong \underline{\underline{0\%}}$$

It could also be said that the probability of finishing the project in more than 30 days is:

$$P(t > 30) \cong \underline{\underline{100\%}}$$

Step 4—REPEATED (for 2nd Solution to the Problem):

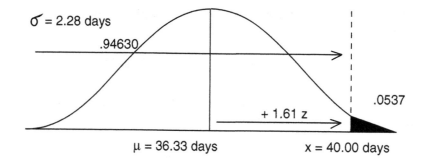

(a) find the number of standard deviates between the mean and the value of interest.

$$z = \left[\frac{X - \mu}{\sigma} \right] = \left[\frac{40.00 - 36.33}{2.28} \right] = \frac{3.67}{2.28}$$

$$= +\underline{\underline{1.61}}$$

(the value of "40.00" is positioned 1.61 standard deviates to the right of the mean.)

(b) find the area under the normal curve that 1.61 standard deviates represent. Use Appendix "A."

z	.01
1.6	.94630

(the percentage of the normal curve covered to a point that is 1.61 standard deviates to the right of the mean is 94.630%).

Therefore, the probability of finishing the project in 40 days or less is:

$$P(t \leq 40) \cong \underline{\underline{95\%}}$$

It could also be said that the probability of finishing the project in more than 40 days is only:

$$P(t > 40) \cong \underline{\underline{5\%}}$$

APPENDIX A: AREAS UNDER THE STANDARD NORMAL CURVE.

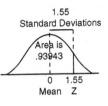

1.55
Standard Deviations

Area is
.93943

0   1.55
Mean   Z

To find the area under the normal curve, you must know how many standard deviations that point is to the right of the mean. Then, the area under the normal curve can be read directly from the normal table. For example, the total area under the normal curve for a point that is 1.55 standard deviations to the right of the mean is .93943.

	.00	.01	.02	.03	.04	.05	.06	.07	.08	.09
.0	.50000	.50399	.50798	.51197	.51595	.51994	.52392	.52790	.53188	.53586
.1	.53983	.54380	.54776	.55172	.55567	.55962	.56356	.56749	.57142	.57535
.2	.57926	.58317	.58706	.59095	.59483	.59871	.60257	.60642	.61026	.61409
.3	.61791	.62172	.62552	.62930	.63307	.63683	.64058	.64431	.64803	.65173
.4	.65542	.65910	.66276	.66640	.67003	.67364	.67724	.68082	.68439	.68793
.5	.69146	.69497	.69847	.70194	.70540	.70884	.71226	.71566	.71904	.72240
.6	.72575	.72907	.73237	.73536	.73891	.74215	.74537	.74857	.75175	.75490
.7	.75804	.76115	.76424	.76730	.77035	.77337	.77637	.77935	.78230	.78524
.8	.78814	.79103	.79389	.79673	.79955	.80234	.80511	.80785	.81057	.81327
.9	.81594	.81859	.82121	.82381	.82639	.82894	.83147	.83398	.83646	.83891
1.0	.84134	.84375	.84614	.84849	.85083	.85314	.85543	.85769	.85993	.86214
1.1	.86433	.86650	.86864	.87076	.87286	.87493	.87698	.87900	.88100	.88298
1.2	.88493	.88686	.88877	.89065	.89251	.89435	.89617	.89796	.89973	.90147
1.3	.90320	.90490	.90658	.90824	.90988	.91149	.91309	.91466	.91621	.91774
1.4	.91924	.92073	.92220	.92364	.92507	.92647	.92785	.92922	.93056	.93189
1.5	.93319	.93448	.93574	.93699	.93822	.93943	.94062	.94179	.94295	.94408
1.6	.94520	.94630	.94738	.94845	.94950	.95053	.95154	.95254	.95352	.95449
1.7	.95543	.95637	.95728	.95818	.95907	.95994	.96080	.96164	.96246	.96327
1.8	.96407	.96485	.96562	.96638	.96712	.96784	.96856	.96926	.96995	.97062
1.9	.97128	.97193	.97257	.97320	.97381	.97441	.97500	.97558	.97615	.97670
2.0	.97725	.97784	.97831	.97882	.97932	.97982	.98030	.98077	.98124	.98169
2.1	.98214	.98257	.98300	.98341	.98382	.98422	.98461	.98500	.98537	.98574
2.2	.98610	.98645	.98679	.98713	.98745	.98778	.98809	.98840	.98870	.98899
2.3	.98928	.98956	.98983	.99010	.99036	.99061	.99086	.99111	.99134	.99158
2.4	.99180	.99202	.99224	.99245	.99266	.99286	.99305	.99324	.99343	.99361
2.5	.99379	.99396	.99413	.99430	.99446	.99461	.99477	.99492	.99506	.99520
2.6	.99534	.99547	.99560	.99573	.99585	.99598	.99609	.99621	.99632	.99643
2.7	.99653	.99664	.99674	.99683	.99693	.99702	.99711	.99720	.99728	.99736
2.8	.99744	.99752	.99760	.99767	.99774	.99781	.99788	.99795	.99801	.99807
2.9	.99813	.99819	.99825	.99831	.99836	.99741	.99846	.99851	.99856	.99861
3.0	.99865	.99869	.99874	.99878	.99882	.99886	.99899	.99893	.99896	.99900
3.1	.99903	.99906	.99910	.99913	.99916	.99918	.99921	.99924	.99926	.99929
3.2	.99931	.99934	.99936	.99938	.99940	.99942	.99944	.99946	.99948	.99950
3.3	.99952	.99953	.99955	.99957	.99958	.99960	.99961	.99962	.99964	.99965
3.4	.99966	.99968	.99969	.99970	.99971	.99972	.99973	.99974	.99975	.99976
3.5	.99977	.99978	.99978	.99979	.99980	.99981	.99981	.99982	.99983	.99983
3.6	.99984	.99985	.99985	.99986	.99986	.99987	.99987	.99988	.99988	.99989
3.7	.99989	.99990	.99990	.99990	.99991	.99991	.99992	.99992	.99992	.99992
3.8	.99993	.99993	.99993	.99994	.99994	.99994	.99994	.99995	.99995	.99995
3.9	.99995	.99995	.99996	.99996	.99996	.99996	.99996	.99996	.99997	.99997

Source: from *Quantitative Approaches to Management*, 4th ed., by Richard I. Levin and Charles A. Kirkpatrick. Copyright © 1978, 1975, 1971, 1965 by McGraw-Hill, Inc. Used with permission of McGraw-Hill Book Company.

PERT/CPM Organizational Structures

1. Functional Areas Intact (Functional Approach)

- each functional department of the firm (i.e., Engineering, Marketing) gets a part of the project.
- An overall project coordinator is appointed to assign and monitor tasks but the coordinator has little or no formal authority.

Advantages:

-little disruption in the formal company organization.

-people always report to the same supervisors.

-specialists are grouped to share knowledge and report to supervisors who understand them.

-specialists are not worried about how the project affects their careers or what happens to them if the project fails or ends.

Disadvantages:

-difficulty to assign responsibility when problems arise; each group disclaims responsibility when tasks fall on organizational boundaries.

-lack of strong central authority complicates decision-making, extends leadtime, makes firms less responsive to changing conditions, and fosters competition among groups for assignments, praise, or blame.

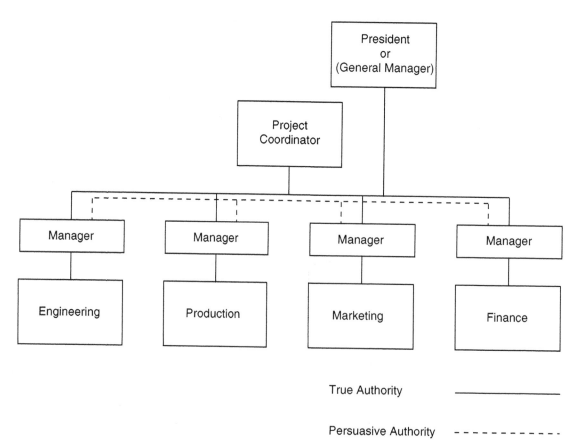

2. Formal Project Team (Project-Group Approach)

- a project manager is assigned complete responsibility for project completion.
- full-time team, reporting to the project manager for the duration.
- team consists of specialists from the various functional areas.
- the project manager and the project team are held totally responsible for budget, quality, and time.

Advantages:

–less opportunity for blaming another for problems and less occasion for politicking.

–the group is more oriented toward project goals.

–the team reacts more effectively to changing circumstances.

–no tasks fall between organizational cracks since the team has total responsibility.

–group morale and commitment increase as people identify more and more with the project and goals.

Disadvantages:

–less efficient use of specialists (at least in theory).

–specialists are uprooted from their "home" department and must get to know a new and temporary boss and coworkers.

–specialists perform jobs somewhat broader and less well-defined than they may be used to.

–uncertainty about project evaluation and the effect on their career progress.

–what happens when specialists are no longer needed? They might return to their "home" departments (if there are still "homes" to go to) but their "home" bosses and workloads may well have changed in the interim.

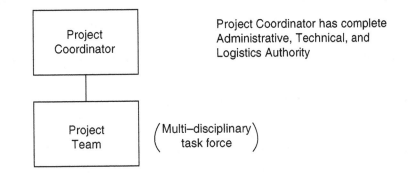

3. Matrix Approach (Matrix Organization)

- attempts to combine the best of No. 1 and No. 2.
- each project has a manager responsible for the project.
- specialists are assigned to the project but remain in their "home" departments.

- each functional specialist has two bosses: project manager and department head.
- Project manager is responsible for overall progress, whereas the department heads are responsible for technical excellence and technical evaluation.

Advantages:

–ideally, the advantages of the previous approaches and avoids their major disadvantages.

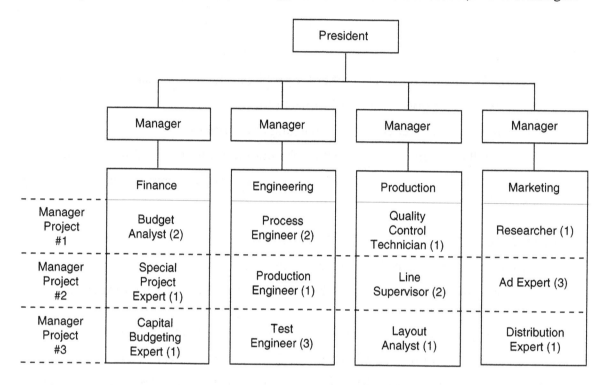

Shared Authority (Staff Reports to Two Supervisors)

A clear cost must be paid, however, for the MATRIX APPROACH:

1. increased administration and the burden of organizing and monitoring such a complex structure.
2. the confusion inherent in reporting to two supervisors.
3. the potential conflicts between project and functional lines.
4. in practice, there is even the possibility of realizing the major disadvantages of the No. 1 and No. 2 approaches while realizing none of their advantages.

Matrix Organization Ground Rules for Success

1. To ensure project loyalty, functional specialists must be assigned full-time to the project.
2. Participants must be able to make commitments to the project as well as to their functional specialties.

3. There must be an effective way to resolve conflicts.

4. There must be frequent communications between project and functional managers.

5. All managers must participate in the planning process.

6. Both project and functional managers must be willing to negotiate resource commitments.

7. The project manager must be given formal authority adequate to operate on at least a level equal to the functional managers.

Factors to Consider When Selecting an Approach

1. *Frequency of Projects:* A firm that continuously manages major engineering and construction projects can justify a more elaborate and sophisticated project management organization.

2. *Project Importance:* Large, important projects justify project group organizations; small less important projects justify functional organizational management.

3. *Internal Culture:* Firms with aggressive and competitive internal relations should choose techniques other than matrix organization, where cooperation and communication among many participants are essential.

4. *Management Preferences:* Good or ill will among managers contributes considerably toward success or failure, regardless of the method. In some cases, management is simply more comfortable with some approaches than with others.

Chapter 17

Statistical Quality Control

Available on Student CD

18

Chapter

Forecasting

Available on Student CD

Chapter
19

Linear Programming— Graph Method

Available on Student CD

Chapter 20

Linear Programming—Simplex Method

Available on Student CD

Linear Programming Applications

Available on Student CD

Available on Student CD

Goal Programming

Available on Student CD

Simple Regression Analysis

Available on Student CD

Chapter 25

Multiple Regression Analysis

Available on Student CD

Chapter 26

Advanced Multiple Regression Analysis

Available on Student CD

Minimal Spanning Trees

Available on Student CD

Chapter 28

Shortest Route Model

Available on Student CD